HINDU TEMPLES IN NORTH AMERICA

A Celebration of Life

MAHALINGUM KOLAPEN

Conventions

SANSKRIT: In cases where different variants of a Sanskrit term are used in the local vernaculars in different parts of India, the standard Sanskrit term is generally used in the current text; for example, *abhisheka*, not *abhishekam*; *darshana*, not *darshan*; *gopura*, not *gopuram*. The following conventions are followed in this text to transliterate Sanskrit devanagari script:

Phonetic sound	English equivalent	Depiction in text
long *a*	f*a*r	*a* (as in *sannyasa*)
long *i*	st*ee*r	*i* (as in *lila*)
long *u*	st*oo*l	*u* (as in *puja*)
two *sh* sounds	*sh*ove, bu*sh*el	*sh* (as in Shiva, Vishnu)
v / *w*	*v*ile / *w*ile	*v* in general Sanskrit terms
		v or *w* in proper nouns, depending on the most popular usage

We have standardized proper nouns as far as possible (e.g., Ganesha, Shiva, Vishnu, Venkateshwara), but have respected the specific spellings used in names of given institutions, thereby introducing some textual inconsistencies.

TEXTUAL STYLING: *Capitalization.* We acknowledge that many faiths conventionally use capital letters to designate divine names and divine manifestations. In the current text, we have adhered to the most recent English language publishing conventions, which keep capitalization to a minimum and use lowercase pronouns to refer to God (e.g., "God and his manifestations"). This use does not in any way indicate a lesser respect for a given faith's or temple's sacred personages or objects.

Spelling. American spelling is used throughout the text, except in specific proper nouns, such as names of institutions.

Italics. Italic type is used to highlight Sanskrit terminology; e.g., *puja* or *vastu*. However, Sanskrit-derived proper nouns are set in roman (not italic) type; e.g., Nandi, Mushika.

Font. The font used in the text is Giovanni.

HINDU TEMPLES IN NORTH AMERICA

A Celebration of Life

BY **MAHALINGUM KOLAPEN**

PHOTOGRAPHY BY **SAÑJAY KOLAPEN**

Published by

HINDU UNIVERSITY OF AMERICA
COUNCIL OF HINDU TEMPLES OF NORTH AMERICA
TITAN GRAPHICS AND PUBLICATIONS

HINDU TEMPLES
IN NORTH AMERICA

Hindu Temple of Atlanta, Atlanta, Georgia

Barsana Dham, Austin, Texas

Malibu Temple, Los Angeles, California

Palace of Gold, West Virginia

All religions are true and equal

I do not want my house to be walled in on all sides, and my windows to be stuffed. I want the culture of all lands to be blown about my house as freely as possible. But I refuse to be blown off my feet by any of them. Mine is not a religion of the prison house, it has room for the least of God's creations, but it is proof against insolent pride of race, religion or color....!

MAHATMA GANDHI

Dedicated to all those who so valiantly left the shores of India to start a new life in a land that was foreign to them. All these magnificent temples stand as a monument to them.

Contents

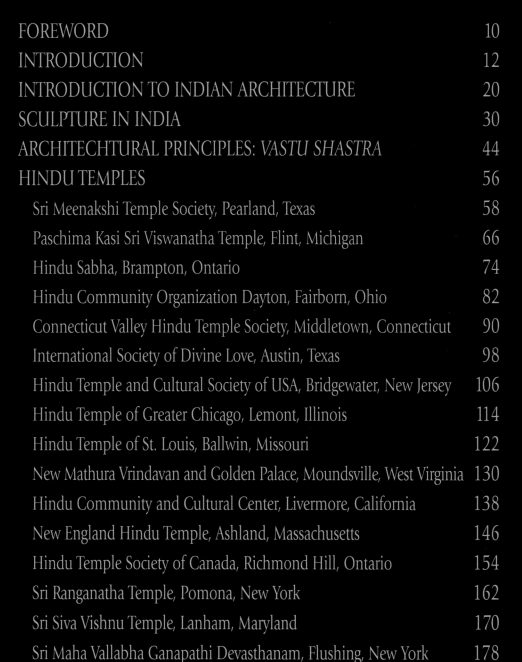

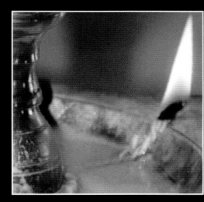

Foreword

"I am the Father of this world and the Mother,
the Supporter, and the Grandsire,
the one thing to be known, the Purifier,
the syllable Om,
and also the threefold Vedas.
I am the beginning and the end, the origin and
the dissolution . . ."
Bhagavadgita IX:17-18

The holy scriptures tell us that God is everywhere, in every part of his creation, whether moving or unmoving, yet many of us fail to see him there. We need a place where the Divine has been powerfully invoked—a house of God, a temple.

In India, for many centuries until this day, temple worship has been a natural part of life's daily rhythms. When immigrant Indians first arrived in North America, no temples were available in which to reestablish the habits of worship they had known in their homeland. Over time, however, temples began to emerge on both American and Canadian soil, and recent years have seen an overwhelming surge in temple-building in or near major metropolitan centers on the continent. *Hindu Temples in North America: A Celebration of Life* is a pioneer work celebrating this auspicious development in North America.

Although America is growing ever more diverse in its population and is learning daily about ways of worship that had been foreign to North America's predominately Judeo-Christian communities, recent surveys show that some seventy-five percent of Americans know little about Hinduism or the Hindu way of worship. This book not only opens the door to educating North America's Indian immigrants about the sacred art of temple architecture and the worship opportunities in their country of residence, but also provides a wealth of information for the non-Hindu population. The events of September 11, 2001, underscore ever more powerfully the need for all people in North America to understand the culture and religious beliefs of its diverse peoples.

As the face of America changes, immigrant populations are beginning to play an expanding role in community and national affairs. Mindful of this trend and the seminal role that education plays in this development, the Hindu University of America in Orlando, Florida, has co-published this book with Titan Graphics and Publications, also of Orlando, Florida, in association with the Hindu Temple Council of North America. Incorporated in 1992, Hindu University was authorized by the Florida Department of Education to offer Master's and Doctoral programs in seven fields of study (for additional details, see pages 312-313). Titan Graphics and Publications, which spearheaded the current publication, is the publisher of a number of richly illustrated editions relating to Hindu cultural and spiritual traditions, including *Glossary of Indian Dance* and *Chinmaya Mission: Transforming Lives*. The Council of Hindu Temples of North America, a nonprofit organization with head offices in New York, served as associate publisher and staunch supporter of the production of this volume, for which the co-publishers express their deep-felt thanks. But for their support, this book would not have been possible (for additional details on the Council, see page 314). The publishers would also like to thank Sañjay Kolapen, photographer, and Rudite Emir, editor, not only for lending their professional expertise in giving shape to this book, but also for their heartfelt support and personal guidance through the birthing process of the publication.

The publishers have selected thirty temples for inclusion in the volume, twenty-eight located in the Unites States and two in Canada. Acknowledging the diversity of religious traditions in India, the book presents temples not only from the Hindu tradition, but also offers representative samples of Jain, Sikh, and Buddhist temples. The book presents detailed depictions of the selected temple structures and their histories, as well as offering a brief yet comprehensive view into the tradition of Indian temple architecture, iconography, and the history of sacred architecture and sculpture. With 320 full-color pages of rare photographs and line drawings, the book offers relatively easy entry into the intricate world of sacred architecture of India—on North American soil.

In publishing this book, we are celebrating the need for more than one and a half million North Americans to preserve their cultural legacy. We invite the immigrant Indian reader to view these temples as a metaphor for the process by which new generations of Americans are making North America their home while preserving the roots from which they have risen. And to all those outside the Indian legacy, we offer an invitation to learn of the sacred traditions arising out of India's ancient spiritual heritage, a tradition that can but enhance the already rich texture of America's cultural and religious fabric.

Braham R. Aggarwal
Chairman
Hindu University of America

Introduction

A Hindu temple is believed to be the earthly seat of a deity and the place where the deity awaits his or her devotees. As such, temple structures are sacred spaces where gods partake of human offerings and in which the people can be in the presence of the Divine.

The Hindu temple is not just a congregational structure or prayer hall. It is the House of God, and the image inside is the soul. The *Agamas* and Upanishads make several references to the correspondence of the structure of the temple to the human body and soul. One saint has said: "Regard your body as the temple, your mind as the worshiper, and truth as the purity needed for worship—and perform worship of God." This attitude toward the House of God has influenced Hindu architecture and sacred sculpture.

Temples are normally dedicated to one primary deity (*pradhana devata*), with decorations specific to the deity being worshiped. Temples are often elaborately decorated on the outside, with stone or plaster carvings depicting religious stories. Mythological scenes are juxtaposed with scenes of everyday life and of important political events, such as royal coronations, conquests, and celebrations, or with portraits of royal and secular patrons.

PAGE 14: Statue of Swami Vivekananda of the Ramakrishna Mission, seen on the grounds of the Hindu Temple of Greater Chicago in Lemont, Illinios. In 1893, Vivekananda gave a memorable speech at the World Parliament of Religions in Chicago, opening up North America to Hindu thought and culture. This statue is the only life-size statue of Vivekananda outside India.

PAGE 15, BOTTOM LEFT and RIGHT: The first Hindu temple built in the United States, constructed in 1906 by the Vedanta Society, San Francisco.

SWAMI VIVEKANANDA
(1863 - 1902)

These images and mythological scenes on the outer walls of the temple help worshipers recall the sacred stories they have heard or read. The innermost sanctuary (*garbhagriha*) of the temple contains the principal image of the deity. The character of each shrine is determined by the deity being worshiped. Since Hindu religious tradition is rich in stories about gods and goddesses who manifest themselves or their powers in response to the supplications of their devotees, many temples include subsidiary shrines for attendants to the main deity.

Hindu Communities in North America

Hinduism has become increasingly established in the United States and in some parts of Canada through a series of encounters over the past 150 years. These encounters are emblematic of Americans' increasing familiarity with Indian and Asian traditions; of contact between Americans and Indian immigrants; and of relationships among cultural traditions in a society that is self-consciously pluralistic. Today, diverse cultural streams coexist in America, as they also do in India. The historical establishment of Hinduism in America reveals a distinctive pattern: For the first 100 years of Hinduism in the United States, its followers mainly practiced the self-help approach; during the past 30 years, building Hindu temples in the United States has become a dominant focus.

Hinduism first came to the United States in the form of the published word early in the nineteenth century. The two main figures in the Transcendentalist literary movement, Ralph Waldo Emerson (1803-82) and Henry David Thoreau (1817-62), were both influenced by translations of Hindu scriptures, especially the *Bhagavad Gita*. However, popular interest in Hinduism did not arise among Americans until the Parliament of Religions in 1893 in Chicago. A part of the Colombian Exposition, the Parliament convened in the building that was later to become the Art Institute of Chicago. Many representatives of Hinduism were invited to speak about their faith on an equal footing with representatives of other world religions. A charismatic young monk, Swami Vivekananda (1863-1902), captured the interest of the American press and inspired popular interest in Hinduism among the American people. For about 70 years after the Parliament, many swamis came from India and started enclaves of followers. In the late 1960s, due to changes in the immigration laws in 1965, large numbers of young professional Hindus started to immigrate to America and settle down with their families.

The Vedanta Society is credited with building the first Hindu temple in the United States, in San Francisco in 1906; others followed, such as the Hollywood Temple in 1938 and the Santa Barbara Temple in 1956. The phenomenon of building temples with a focus on the ritual worship of images of deities began in the 1970s and was directly related to the increasing number of Hindu immigrants in America. In order to provide an environment where they could freely practice their religion in their new homeland, various groups started to organize and build traditional Hindu temples. Now there are Hindu temples built on orthodox principles in practically every major city in the United States. Many cities have several temples, ministering to the diverse needs of the Hindu community.

Sikh, Jain, and Buddhist Traditions in North America

Part of the rich texture of religious traditions in India are those of the Sikhs, Jains, and Buddhists. Both the Jains and Sikhs have many parallels with Hinduism, but they also differ in key aspects. Buddhism had its roots in India, with Buddha having been born there as Siddhartha, a prince in a royal family. India is rich with monuments that mark some of the most sacred Buddhist places of worship. All three religious traditions have also found fertile soil on the North American continent.

The Sikh religion, founded by Guru Nanak (1469-1538), was originally intended to bring together the best of the Hindu and Islamic religions. Its basic tenets are similar to those of Hinduism, with the important modification that Sikhs are opposed to caste distinctions and to pilgrimages to rivers, though not to holy sites. They worship at temples called *gurudwaras*, emphasize faith in the guru, initiate their children when they are old enough to understand the religion, and cremate their dead. Their holy book is the *Guru Granth Sahib*, which contains the works of the ten Sikh gurus, together with Hindu and Islamic writings. United States and Canada now also have a large number of *gurudwaras* in which the Sikh communities worship.

Jains are known the world over as ardent proponents of nonviolence (*ahimsa*). The cardinal rule is nonviolence at all levels of human functioning—mental, verbal, and physical. For spiritual evolution, Jaina aspirants are required to observe vows of nonviolence, truthfulness, nonstealing, chastity, and nonpossessiveness. Monks and nuns observe these vows rigorously, while householders follow a less strict version of each vow. In practicing nonpossessiveness toward material things, a Jain aspirant practices self-control, abstinence from overindulgence, and voluntary curtailment of his personal needs. As a consequence, a sincere aspirant lessens the aggressive urge and develops deep compassion for all forms of life. Many Jain temples have been built in both the United States and Canada. There are more Jain temples and groups in the United States than in any other country outside India.

Buddhism has witnessed a great expansion in the West, drawing to it people from all walks of life and of many national origins. Many have found appeal in Buddhism's basic tenet of *dharma*, the law that accomplishes the greatest good of the greatest number. In the individual's life it becomes manifest as good and noble conduct. The four noble truths that Gautama Buddha expounded—now part and parcel of the religious history of the world—constitute the essence of *dharma* according to Buddhism. The last of these truths, the eight-fold path (*Arya Ashtangika Marga*) forms the spokes of the Wheel of Dharma. The Wheel cannot survive without the practice of these eight virtues, namely: right view, right resolution, right speech, right conduct, right means of livelihood, right effort, right mindfulness, and right concentration. Buddhist houses of worship can be found throughout North America, reflecting the broad diversity of Buddhist worshipers.

Surge in Temple-Building

Hindus of South Asian origin are an increasing presence in American society, now numbering approximately 1,800,000. Hindu communities have settled in most parts of the United States. To maintain religious traditions and celebrate their cultural heritage, they have dedicated some 450 temples in the United States over the past 30 years, with many becoming centers of pilgrimage. Along the way, many hurdles have been overcome to make the dream of establishing Hindu religious centers a reality. The hurdles can be broadly categorized as those issuing from within the Indian community and those initiated by local non-Indian neighbors.

When the Hindu communities first sought permission from a borough to build a new temple, the local non-Indian community frequently opposed it vigorously. Opposition arose largely out of fear of, and ignorance about, a foreign religion and unfamiliar religious practices. Some boroughs initially refused permission to build temples on health and other unrelated grounds. The Hindu community had to resort to using the legal system before such boroughs agreed to abide by the judge's verdict to allow temple-building. Such types of hindrances could be countered only by educating the neighbors, councilmen, and politicians in a calm, dignified, persistent manner and by showing up in large numbers at borough meetings.

Initially the new temples were opened only during weekends. On some occasions, during off-hours at the temple, neighborhood teenagers resorted to vandalism, spraying tar and breaking images of deities (*murtis*). The Hindu community often used such sad episodes to improve its legal standing by publicizing the event with the help of television and newspapers. In most cases, local Christian and Jewish religious leaders supported the cause by expressing a sense of outrage.

The earliest traditionally built temples in the United States, such as the renowned Sri Venkateswara Temple outside of Pittsburgh (consecrated in 1976) and the Temple of Sri Maha Vallabha Ganapati Devasthanam in Flushing, New York (consecrated in 1977) have followed the prescriptions of traditional Hindu texts on sacred architecture. Their exterior walls are adorned with detailed sculptures of deities and intricate bas-reliefs, as found on temples throughout India.

Only a few communities in larger metropolitan areas, however, can afford to build grandiose structures in traditional styles. Most temple exteriors in North America are not architecturally identifiable as Hindu. Smaller communities are opting for more modest buildings with a simplified exterior, saving traditional detailing of motifs and figures for the interior.

Temple Features

Two of the traditional features of Hindu temple architecture that are incorporated into American designs are the east-west orientation of the main sanctum and a circumambulatory path around that sanctum. Interior spaces of American Hindu temples are designed to be more communal as compared with the intimate spaces within traditional Hindu temples, reflecting changes in ritual practices among the diverse Hindu community in the United States, with added emphasis on communal gatherings.

In India, the architectural profile of many Hindu temples resembles a small mountain range. In classical northern temples, this effect is created by a series of pinnacles (*shikaras*), the tallest of which is centered over the main sanctum. In classical southern temples, an elaborately carved tower (*gopura*) depicting the feats of the gods rises above the main sanctuary, while smaller *gopuras* crown the gateways situated in the cardinal directions that open onto the courtyard that encompasses the temple complex.

The traditional Hindu temple is not designed for communal worship, though the outer courtyards or a separate assembly hall are often used for special events that draw large crowds during festivals. Entering a temple in India is like entering a mountain cavern: there is little natural light, and one progresses through a series of dark and damp antechambers until one reaches the innermost chamber, the sanctum sanctorum (*garbhagriha*) of the temple, wherein the main deity resides.

In India, where Hinduism in its many forms is the dominant religious tradition, one may find separate temples dedicated to popular deities such as Krishna, Shiva, and Mahadevi—all within one neighborhood or village. However, in North America, where Hindus are a minority, temples serve a wider range of Hindu denominations, and their worshiping communities incorporate a much wider diversity of regional and linguistic groups than do most temples in India.

American temples are typically built in stages, according to a master plan developed with an architect. Often a community hall for multiple purposes is erected first. Then sanctuaries are added to enshrine the deities. Plans often incorporate housing for the priest (*pujari*). Most communities arrange to have traditional temple architects (*sthapatis*) and stone carvers (*shilpis*) and other artisans to come from India to the United States to work on the Indian decor of the temple.

Interior ornamentation includes decorative painting and bas-reliefs, applied according to a master plan. The sculpting and placement of images of the deities (*murtis* or *vighrahas*) are regulated by religious tradition. These images are made in India by sculptors knowledgeable about traditional iconography, and then shipped to the American temples that have commissioned them. The installation and consecration of these images signify that the temple can officially open to the numerous devotees who come to worship (participate in *pujas* conducted by the priest) and behold the images of the consecrated deities (have *darshana* of them).

Following tradition, each temple deity is worshiped every day. In addition, there are weekly and monthly litanies, as well as yearly festivals. Priests perform the services on behalf of the worshipers because the rituals are often complicated and require specialized training, including memorization of vast amounts of Sanskrit text. Many of the priests are trained from boyhood in the performance of their duties. They may marry and raise families, but they remain the primary ritual specialists.

In a temple, Hindus may worship the Supreme Being in a number of ways. Some individuals or families sponsor special ritual services that are performed with the help of priests. Many worshipers show their subservience and devotion to the Supreme Being by bowing down in various ways before an icon. Some circumambulate the shrines. Almost everyone stands before the shrines and, with folded hands, has *darshana* of the icons. While looking at an icon, the worshiper feels that he or she is looking directly at the Supreme Being, with all of the flowers, ornaments, and symbols serving to bring to mind the power, glory, and beauty of the Divine. Worshipers reverently honor articles like flowers, water, and lamps that have been used in the worship of the deity. In addition to these individual ways of worship, temples have a liturgical calendar with many festivals that allow believers to worship as a congregation.

Whereas in India it is typical for temple patrons to stop by throughout the day for *darshana* and *puja* at the temple, in the United States such regular activity is less feasible, especially since temples are few and far between. These factors have led to the development of communal worship on weekends, which can draw anywhere from 30 to 2,000 worshipers. Such gatherings require large and flexible spaces.

Most Hindu temples in the United States also serve as cultural centers for families of South Asian background, and the diverse cultural and religious needs of these communities are often taken into consideration in the design and layout of American temples. However, the architects of American Hindu temples have followed the age-old guidelines for sacred architecture. Ancient Hindu temples were built by

anonymous sculptor-architects who practiced an inherited profession and were members of a guild. Apprentices in the field had to take training from a master. These artists worked in accordance with the rules expounded in texts called the *Vastu Shastras* and *Shilpa Shastras*. The rules in these texts determined the form and proportion as well as techniques for the construction of a building, an image in stone or metal, or a painting. Although the ancient texts prescribed a framework for the artist to create an object of art, they gave enough room for the talented artist to infuse his work with personal interpretation.

The two source scriptures for both temple architecture and sculpture are the *Vastu Shastra* and *Shilpa Shastra*. In the strict sense, the two terms are synonymous because the significance of *vastu tattva* and that of *shilpa tattva* are one and the same. They have a common root with a unique science of energy and matter, time and space, and rhythm and form. The common name for the two branches is *Sthapatya Veda*. The *shastras* were authored by *Shilpi Rishis* (temple artisan-seers), and from time immemorial they have been consulted by *sthapatis* for designing architectural as well as sculptural forms.

Vastu plays a prominent role in the design and execution of architectural structures, providing a grammar book of visual forms, whether for the construction of temples or other buildings, and also extending to town and village planning. *Shilpa* refers to the vision or form that appears in the inner space of the sculptor, complete with all the features and measures that go into the composition of a sculptural form—virtually, a visual poem. The trained *shilpi* sculpts exactly what he experiences as this internal image. The inner vision is called *shilpa*, and its external, material expression is known as *pratima*. In one *Vastu-sutro-upanishad* this process is defined as *shilpa pratimaha jayante*, which means "from *shilpa* the *pratimas* are born." The word *pratima* means "measured form," the term deriving from *prati*, meaning "a copy" or "replica," and *ma*, meaning "measure." These measures are provided by the *Shilpi Rishis* in the *Shilpa Shastra*, and are known as *Pratima Lakshana*.

The *pratimas* so sculpted, with all the measures as given in the *Pratima Lakshana*, have the quality of becoming divine and vibrant. This is a scientific process as stated by an Upanishad called *Shilpa Vidya Rahasyopanishad*: "*vijnanam shilpa kaushalyam, jagat sarvam shilpameva bhavati,*" meaning that the *shilpa's* greatness lies in

its being scientific.

In the making of worshipable images, these *shastric* measures have to be strictly followed with all aesthetic attributes related to the conceptual form. The attributes determine the meaning of the form so rendered by the *shilpi*. These aspects are taken into consideration by the *sthapati* for form figuration and passed on to the *shilpis* at the craft level.

This is the process involved in the making of worshipable images in the temple. Arbitrary measures and imagined forms, however beautiful they may be, are not accepted by the *Agama* for worship. However, according to one *Makutagam* (*Agamic*) text, if the measures "as given in the *shastras*," are strictly applied, then "the divinity gets expressed in the image."

Hindu temples built in North America are truly a meeting of East and West. The layout, proportions, decorations, and architecture are all based on detailed specifications contained in the *Vastu Shastra* and *Shilpa Shastra*. In addition, Hindu temples constructed in North America have heating, cooling, and public facilities not usually found in temples in India.

Looking to the Future

A question frequently asked about the many temples springing up in North America is: "We have built these temples at great expense, and have spent a lot of time and energy. Will the temples survive after this generation is gone?" To quote Omar Khayyam, "How many kings, emperors have come and gone! Yet, not for a moment does the wheel of the universe stand still; when one is removed, another steps into the breach." That is Nature's law. Only the omnipotent Master of the Universe knows what the future will bring. His is the divine, eternal dance called *lila*!

Temples are not just places of worship for the local Hindu community. They are also to be admired as works of art. Exquisite structures and images abound: a rich array of sculpted figures on the temple walls, including dancers, musicians, kings, mythological figures, elephants, monkeys, and horses; elaborately designed towers (*gopuras*) crowning the temple entrances; and intricately fashioned sanctuaries (*garha-grihas*) that house the presiding deity.

Captured in stone with sublime craftsmanship and artistry, a Hindu temple is, indeed, *"a celebration of life."*

Introduction to Indian Architecture

One of the most enduring achievements of Indian civilization is undoubtedly its architecture. The artistic and architectural heritage of India is almost five millennia old. The Indus Valley sites of Harappa, Mohenjodaro, and Lothal provide substantial evidence of extensive town planning. However, the beginnings of Indian architecture are traced to the reign of Ashoka (circa 270-232 B.C.) during the Mauryan empire, when the construction of Buddhist monasteries and shrines (*stupas*) began. Buddhist architecture remained predominant for several centuries and left a legacy of stupendous architectural marvels still standing today, such as the Great Stupa at Sanchi and the rock-cut caves at Ajanta.

The Guptas, Chandellas, Solankis, and Gangas, representing dynasties spanning twelve centuries (320 A.D. to 1586 A.D.), were great patrons of art and architecture. The Gupta period (320-600 A.D.) can be described as the zenith of Indian architecture. By the eighth century, the southern Hindu school of architecture began to flourish. The Pallavas, Cholas, Hoysalas, and the rulers of the Vijayanagara empire contributed a great deal to the advancement of architecture in South India.

The rock-cut temples of Mahabalipuram, the temples of Kanchipuram, the Hoysala temples at Belur and Halebid, and the Meenakshi temple in Madurai are some of the excellent examples of South Indian architecture.

The advent of Muslim rulers toward the end of the twelfth century brought in new elements of architectural finesse such as floral motifs, domes, and beautiful calligraphy. Islamic architecture reached its acme in the fifteenth to the sixteenth centuries under the Moguls, who constructed many forts, palaces, mosques, and gardens. The Red Fort and Jama Masjid in Delhi; the Taj Mahal, Agra Fort, and Fatehpur Sikhri in Agra; the Badshahi Gardens at Lahore; and the Shalimar Gardens at Kashmir are fine specimens of Mogul architecture.

New elements of Gothic, Imperial, Christian, and Victorian architectural styles were introduced into Indian architecture during the Colonial Period. The British constructed a number of important buildings in different parts of the country, including St. Martin's Garrison Church in New Delhi, the Presidency College in Madras, the Gateway of India in Mumbai, and the Rashtrapati Bhawan in New Delhi. The departure of the British following Indian independence created a temporary vacuum in the building activities in the country. Gradually, under the inspiration of leading foreign architects like Le Corbusier, several indigenous architects like Balakrishna Doshi and Charles Correa came on the scene and provided much-needed dynamics to the dormant architectural scene in India.

The Indus Valley, or Harappan, civilization, which flourished during the Bronze Age (2500-2000 B.C.), is ranked among the four widely known civilizations of the ancient world. Extensive excavation work that has been done since independence has so far identified more than 100 sites belonging to this civilization. A few prominent ones among them are Dholavira (Gujarat), Kalibangan (Rajasthan), Lothal (Gujarat), Sarkotada (Gujarat), Diamabad (Maharashtra), Alamgirpur (Uttar Pradesh), Bhagwanpura (Haryana), Banawali (Haryana), Kuntasi (Gujarat), Padri (Gujarat), and Mauda (Jammu).

Extensive town planning was the characteristic of this civilization, which is evident from the gridiron pattern for the layout of cities, some with fortifications and elaborate drainage and water management systems. The houses were built of baked bricks, a rare practice in contemporary civilizations in Mesopotamia and Egypt. Bricks of fixed size, as well as stone and wood, were also used for building. The most imposing of the buildings is the Great Bath of Mohenjodaro. It is 54.86 meters long and 32.91 meters wide, with 2.43-meter thick outer walls. The bath had galleries and rooms on all sides. Another important structure was the granary complex comprised of blocks with an overall area of 55 by 43 meters. The granaries had air ducts and platforms divided into units.

The Mauryan Dynasty

If the remnants of the Indus culture are excluded, the earliest surviving architectural heritage in India is that of the Mauryans (322-185 B.C.). The Mauryan period was a great landmark in the history of Indian art. Some of the monuments and pillars belonging to this period are considered as the finest specimens of Indian art. Mauryan structures were constructed of timber, for rocks and stones were not as freely in use then. The art of polishing wood reached such perfection during the Mauryan period that master craftsmen could make wood glisten like a mirror. Chandragupta Maurya, founder of the Mauryan dynasty, built many buildings, palaces, and monuments with wood, most of which perished with time. In 300 B.C., Chandragupta Maurya constructed a wooden fort 14.48 km. long and 2.41km. wide, along the Ganges in Bihar. However, only a couple of teak beams have survived from this fort today.

Ashoka was the first Mauryan emperor who began to "think in stone." The stonework of the Ashokan Period (third century B.C.) was of a highly diversified order and was comprised of lofty free-

standing pillars, railings of the *stupas*, lion thrones, and other colossal figures. The use of stone had reached such great perfection during this time that even small fragments of stone art were given a high lustrous polish resembling fine enamel. While most of the shapes and decorative forms employed were indigenous in origin, some exotic forms show the influence of Greek, Persian, and Egyptian cultures.

The Ashokan period marked the beginning of the Buddhist School of Architecture in India. It witnessed the construction of many rock-cut caves, pillars, *stupas*, and palaces. A number of cave-shrines belonging to this period have been excavated in the Barabar and Nagarjuni hills and in Sitamarhi in the state of Bihar. These rock-cut sanctuaries, quarried from large masses of rock called *gneisses*, are simple in plan and are devoid of all interior decorative carvings. The caves served as the residences of monks. Several inscriptions indicate that these rock-cut sanctuaries were constructed by Emperor Ashoka for the monks of the Ajivika sect, who were more closely related to Jains than to Buddhists.

The Ashokan rock-cut sculpture at Dhauli, near Bhubaneshwar, is considered to be the earliest such sculpture in India. It has a sculpted elephant on the top, which signifies the emperor's conversion to Buddhism after his Kalinga victory. The monolithic Ashokan pillars are marvels of architecture and sculpture—lofty free-standing monolithic columns erected on sacred sites. Originally there were about thirty pillars, but now only ten are in existence, of which only two with lion capitals stand in situ in good condition, one each at Kolhua and Laurya Nandangarh. Each pillar was about 15.24 meters high, weighed about 50 tons, and was made out of fine sandstone. Each pillar consisted of three parts—the prop, the shaft, and the capital. The capital consisted of fine polished stone containing one or more animal figures in the round. Made of bricks, the pillars carried declarations from the king regarding Buddhism and other topics. The pillars did not stand in isolation, but were usually found near *stupas* in a spot either unknowingly marked by the Buddha himself or along the royal route to Magadha, the capital. The Sarnath pillar is one of the finest pieces of sculpture of the Ashokan period. The Ashokan pillars also throw light on the contacts India had with Persia and other countries. Two of the Ashokan pillars have also been found at Laghman, near Jalalabad in modern Afghanistan.

Ashoka was responsible for the construction of a number of *stupas*, large halls capped with domes and bearing symbols of the Buddha. The most important ones are located at Bharhut, Bodhgaya, Sanchi, Amravati, and Nagarjunakonda. Buddhist shrines and monasteries were built in somewhat irregular design following the Gandhara style of architecture. Built on the pattern of a fort and defended by a stone wall, the monasteries evolved from sites of ancient *stupas*. The principal buildings were housed within a rectangular courtyard with a *stupa* at the south and the monastery at the north.

Ashoka also built palaces, but most of them have perished. Ashoka's palace near Patna was a masterpiece. Enclosed by a high brick wall, the highlight of the palace was an immense 76.2-meter-high pillared hall three stories high. The Chinese traveler Fahien was so impressed by this palace that he stated that "it was made by spirits" and that its carvings were so elegantly executed that "no human hands of this world could accomplish" such a feat. Made mostly of wood, the palace seems to have been destroyed by fire. Its existence was pointed out during the excavations at Kumrahar, near Patna, where its ashes have been found preserved for several thousand years.

SANCHI STUPAS: The early *stupas* were hemispherical in shape with a low base, the hemispherical shape symbolizing the cosmic mountain. Later *stupas* assumed an increasingly cylindrical form. The early *stupas* were known for their simplicity. Apart from the ruins of the *stupa* at Piprahwa (Nepal), the core of the first *stupa* at Sanchi can be considered as the oldest of the *stupas*. Originally built by Ashoka, it was enlarged in subsequent centuries. An inscription by the ivory carvers of Vidisha

at the southern gateway throws light on the transference of building material from perishable wood and ivory to the more durable stone.

AMRAVATI STUPA: The Amravati *stupa*, built in the second or first century B.C., was probably like the one at Sanchi, but in later centuries it was transformed from a Hinayana shrine to a Mahayana shrine. The diameter of the dome of the *stupa* at ground level was about 48.76 meters and its height was about 30 meters. The Amravati *stupa* is different from the Bharhut and Sanchi *stupas*. It had free-standing columns surmounted by lions near the gateways. The dome was covered with sculptured panels. The *stupa* had an upper circumambulatory path on the drum as at Sanchi. This path had two intricately carved railings. The stone is greenish-white limestone found in the region.

NAGARJUNAKONDA STUPAS: This Gandhara-style *stupa* is a further development of *stupas* at Sanchi and Bharhut. In Gandhara *stupas* the base, dome, and the hemisphere dome are sculpted. The *stupa* tapers upward to form a towerlike structure. The *stupas* of Nagarjunakonda in Krishna Valley were very large. At the base were brick walls forming a wheel with spokes, which were filled with earth. The Maha Chaitya of Nagarjunakonda has a base in the form of swastika, which is a sun symbol.

The Sunga, Kushan, and Satavahana Dynasties

The Mauryan dynasty crumbled after Ashoka's death in 232 B.C. In its wake came the Sungas and Kushans in the north and the Satavahanas in the south. The period between the second century B.C. and the third century A.D. marked the beginning of the sculptural idiom in Indian art where the elements of physical form were evolving into a more refined, realistic, and expressive style. The sculptors strived at mastering their art, especially of the human body, which was carved in high relief and bore heaviness and vigor. These dynasties made advances in art and architecture in such areas as stone construction, stone carving, symbolism, and the beginning of temple, or prayer hall (*chaitya* hall), and monastery (*vihara*) construction.

Under these dynasties the Ashokan *stupas* were enlarged, and the earlier brickwork and woodwork were replaced with stonework. For instance, the Sanchi *stupa* was enlarged to nearly twice its size in 150 B.C., and elaborate gateways were added later. The Sungas also reconstructed the railings around the Bharhut *stupa* and built gateways (*toranas*) to the *stupas*. An inscription at the Bharhut *stupa* indicates that the *torana* was built during the reign of Sungas, that is, 184-72 B.C. These *toranas* indicate the influence of Hellenistic and other foreign schools on Sunga architecture.

The Satavahanas constructed a large number of *stupas* at Goli, Jaggiahpeta, Bhattiprolu, Gantasala, Nagarjunakonda, and Amravati. During the Kushan period (first to third centuries A.D.), the Buddha was represented in human form instead of with symbols. Buddha's image in endless

forms and replicas became the principal element in Buddhist sculpture during the Kushan period. Another feature of this period was that the emperor himself was shown as a divine person. The Kushans were the pioneers of the Gandhara School of Art; a large number of monasteries, *stupas*, and statues were constructed during the reign of Kanishka.

Schools of Art

THE GANDHARA SCHOOL OF ART (50 B.C. TO 500 A.D.): The Gandhara region, extending from Punjab to the borders of Afghanistan, was an important center of Mahayana Buddhism up to the fifth century A.D. The region became famous throughout the world since a new school of Indian sculpture known as the Gandhara School developed during that period. Owing to its strategic location, the Gandhara School imbibed all kinds of foreign influences like Persian, Greek, Roman, Saka, and Kushan. The origin of Gandhara art can be traced to the Greek rulers of Bactria and northwestern India. But it was during the reign of Kanishka that the art received great patronage.

The Gandhara School of Art is also known as the Graeco-Buddhist School of Art since Greek techniques of art were applied to Buddhist subjects. The most important contribution of the Gandhara School of Art was the evolution of beautiful images of the Buddha and *bodhisattvas* (evolved souls who postpone full enlightenment to help humankind), which were executed in black stone and modeled on identical characters of the Graeco-Roman pantheon. Hence it is said, "The Gandhara artist had the hand of a Greek but the heart of an Indian." The most characteristic trait of Gandhara sculpture is the depiction of Lord Buddha in the standing or seated position. The seated Buddha is always shown cross-legged in the traditional Indian way. Another typical feature of Gandhara art is the rich carving, elaborate ornamentation, and complex symbolism. The best specimens of Gandhara art are from Jaulian and Dharmarajika *stupas* at Taxila and from Hadda near Jalalabad in modern-day Afghanistan. The tallest rock-cut statue of Lord Buddha was also located in modern-day Afghanistan (at Bamiyan, with the sculpture dating back to the third and fourth centuries A.D.), before it was destroyed by the Taliban regime in March 2001.

THE MATHURA SCHOOL OF ART: The Mathura School of Art flourished at the holy city of Mathura, with its zenith between the first and third centuries A.D. It established the tradition of transforming Buddhist symbols into human form. Buddha's first image can be traced to emperor Kanishka's reign (about 78 A.D.). Buddha's images were depicted with a powerfully built body, with the right hand raised in protection and the left hand at the waist. The figures produced by this school of art, now seen in the museum of Mathura, do not have moustaches and beards as in Gandhara art. The standing Buddha figures resemble *yaksha* figures (nature spirits) and indicate Kushan influence. The seated figures are in cross-legged

(*padmasana*) posture. The Mathura School not only produced beautiful images of Buddha but also of the Jain *Tirthankaras* (seers) and gods and goddesses of the Hindu pantheon. Many scholars believe that the Mathura School of Art, although of indigenous origin, was greatly influenced by the Gandhara School of Art. The Guptas adopted the Mathura School of Art and further improvised and perfected it.

THE AMRAVATI SCHOOL OF ART: This school of art developed at Amravati, on the banks of the Krishna River in modern Andhra Pradesh. It is the site of the largest Buddhist *stupa* of South India. Its construction began in 200 B.C. and was completed in 200 A.D. The diameter of the *stupa* at the base was 51 meters. The height of the dome was 31 meters and its outer railing was 5 meters wide. This stupendous *stupa* could not withstand the ravages of time; its ruins are preserved in the London Museum.

Temple Architecture of India

Despite the vastness of the land, Indian temple architecture is remarkably uniform. It is, however, often divided into two chief styles, each having numerous substyles. The Northern, or Indo-Aryan, style is marked by a tower with a rounded top and curvilinear outline while the Southern, or Dravidian, style has the tower usually in the shape of a rectangular truncated pyramid.

The standard type of Hindu temple has remained fundamentally the same from the sixth century A.D. to the present day. The construction of temples—whether in the north or in the south—essentially followed a similar pattern. There is the sanctuary (*vimana*), of which the upper and outer pyramidal and tapering portion is called the *shikhara*, or pinnacle. The *vimana* is a rather dark place that houses the deity. The small area within the *vimana* where the deity resides is called *garbhagriha*, literally meaning "womb house." The entrance is through a doorway, normally from the eastern side. The doorway is reached through a pillared hall (*mandapa*), where devotees congregate for prayers. However, earlier temples may have had the *mandapa* at a little distance from the main temple (for instance, at the Shore Temple in Mamallapuram near Chennai, circa 700 A.D.), although this practice was disbanded in later

constructions. Later it became necessary to unite both buildings, making way for the *antarala*, or intermediate vestibule. A porch or a smaller room (*arthamandapa*) leads up to a hall (*mandapa*), which in turn goes into a large hall (*mahamandapa*). A tower (*gopura*) generally surmounts the shrine-room while smaller towers rise from other parts of the building. The whole conception is set in a rectangular courtyard, which sometimes contains lesser shrines and is often placed on a raised platform. The most perfect examples of temples of this type are the Khajuraho temples. Here, each chamber has its own separate pyramidal roof rising in gradual steps so that the final sanctum's roof towers up, surrounded by smaller spires, finally forming a graceful, rising stepped pyramid.

In some parts of India, the ascending pyramid roof format was not followed. The roof in such temples was still pyramidal, but was formed of layers that gradually became narrower as they rose. A courtyard was built around the temple, and sometimes a wall was constructed to ensure seclusion. The outer walls were carved in orderly groupings of repetitive miniatures. The *shikhara* was specifically based on this design, which may have originated from the domed huts of central and eastern India.

THE PRATIHARAS: The Pratiharas, who ruled over an extensive empire from Ujjain during the eighth and ninth centuries, were among the significant successors of the Guptas. The Pratihara temples of central India have their own unique designs and decorative schemes. The important temples of Ujjain include the Mahakaleshwar temple, which has one of the twelve *jyotirlingas* (rare types of Shiva images called *lingas*) of India, Kal Bhairava temple, which finds mention in the *Skanda Purana*, and Mangalnath temple, which is regarded as the birthplace of Mars, according to the *Matsya Purana*.

THE PALAS: The Pala School of Architecture (eighth through thirteenth centuries A.D.) flourished in Bengal and Bihar under the Pala and the Sena rulers. Nalanda was its most active center, whose influence was spread to Nepal, Myanmar, and even Indonesia. Stone sculptures of this period are found at Nalanda, Rajagriha, Bodh Gaya, Rajashahi, and other places. The Pala School of art is seen at its best at Nalanda and several sculptures belonging to this period have been unearthed in excavations.

THE CHANDELLAS: The Chandellas of Jijihoti or Bundelkhand were known as great builders during the tenth and eleventh centuries. It is they who built the temples at Khajuraho justly famous for their graceful contours and erotic sculptures. These 22 temples (out of the original 85) are regarded as among the world's greatest artistic wonders. The Khajuraho temples do not illustrate a development over a long period of time but were built within a short period of a hundred years from 950 to 1050 A.D. The Khajuraho temples have highly individualistic architectural character and are generally small in size. Each temple is divided into three main compartments—a sanctum (*garbhagriha*), a *mandapa*, and an entrance portico (*arthamandapa*). Some temples also contain a vestibule (*antarala*) between the sanctum and the *mahamandapa*. The Kendriya Mahadev temple is the largest and most beautiful of the Khajuraho Temples. The Shiva Temple at Visvanath and the Vishnu Temple at Chaturbhanj are other important temples at Khajuraho.

Cave Architecture

The earliest manmade caves date back to the second century B.C. while the latest date to the seventh century A.D. The splendid sculpture and lovely frescoes adorning these caves mark them as some of the most glorious monuments of India's past.

AJANTA CAVES: The Buddhist cave temples of Ajanta, situated north of Aurangabad, were first mentioned in the writings of the Chinese pilgrim Huen Tsang, who visited India between 629 A.D. and 645 A.D. The caves were discovered by British officers in 1819 A.D. The thirty temples at Ajanta are set into the rocky sides of a crescent-shaped gorge in the Inhyadri hills of the Sahyadri ranges. At the head of the gorge is a natural pool fed by a waterfall. The excavations spanned a period of about six centuries. The earlier monuments, dating from the second to first centuries B.C., included both *chaitya* halls and monasteries. After a period of more than six centuries, excavations once again revived during the reign of the Vakataka ruler Harishena. The sculptures contain an impressive array of votive figures, accessory figures, depictions of narrative episodes, and decorative motifs. The series of paintings is unparalleled in the history of Indian art, both for the wide range of subjects and the medium. The caves depict a large number of incidents from the life of the Buddha (*Jataka Tales*). The figures reveal harmonious blending of perspective and color and exquisite artistry in the sinuous line work. However, the identities of the artists responsible for the execution of the Ajanta caves are unknown.

BHIMBETAKA CAVES: The Bhimbetaka caves are located in the Raisen District of Madhya Pradesh about 45 km. southeast of Bhopal near a hill village called Bhiyanpur. Bhimbetaka, discovered in 1958 by V. S. Wakanker, is the biggest prehistoric art depository in India. Atop the hill, a large number of rock-shelters have been discovered, of which more than 130 contain paintings. Excavations in some of the rock-shelters revealed history of continuous habitation from the early Stone Age (about 10,000 years ago) to the end of the Stone Age, as seen from artificially made stone tools and implements.

ELEPHANTA CAVES: The sixth-century Shiva temple in the Elephanta caves on an island off the coast of Mumbai is one of the most exquisitely carved temples in India. The central attraction is a 20-ft.-high bust of the deity in three-headed form known as Maheshamurti. The idol is built deep into a recess and looms up from the darkness to fill the full height of the cave. This image symbolizes the fierce, feminine, and meditative aspects of the great ascetic and the three heads represent Lord Shiva as Aghori, Ardhanarishwara, and Mahayogi. Aghori is the aggressive form of Shiva, in which he is intent on destruction. Ardhanarishwara represents Lord Shiva in half-male and half-female form. This divine union of Shiva and Parvati represents the unified existence of word (*vak*) and form (*artha*), wherein *word* indicates light energy and *form* indicates sound energy. The Ardhanarishwara form of Lord Shiva is an anthropomorphic expression of the unified existence of light and sound energies in space. The Mahayogi posture symbolizes the meditative aspect of the Divine, with Lord Shiva being shown in his most serene form. Other sculptures in these caves depict Shiva's cosmic dance of primordial creation and destruction and his marriage to Parvati.

MAHAKALI CAVES: These are rock-cut Buddhist caves situated in the Udayagiri hills, about 6.5 km. from Mumbai. These were excavated from 200 B.C. to 600 A.D. and are now in ruins. They are comprised of four caves on the southeastern face and fifteen caves on the northwestern face. Cave 9 is the chief cave and is the oldest, consisting of a *stupa* and figures of Buddha.

JOGESHWAR AND KANHERI CAVES: Located in the western suburbs of Mumbai, Jogeshwar

is the second largest known cave after the Kailasa cave in Ellora and houses a Brahmanical temple dating back to the sixth century A.D.

Excavated between the first and second centuries, Kanheri is a 109-cave complex located near Borivili National Park in Mumbai. The Kanheri caves contain illustrations from Hinayana and Mahayana Buddhism and show carvings dating back to 200 B.C.

KARLA AND BHAJA CAVES: About 50 to 60 km. from Pune, these rock-cut Buddhist caves date back to the first and second centuries B.C. The caves consist of several *viharas* and *chaitya* halls.

Jain Architecture

The contribution of Jain art to mainstream art in India has been considerable. Every phase of Indian art is represented by a Jain version, and each phase is worthy of meticulous study and understanding, even though Jain architecture cannot be credited with a style of its own, for it was largely an offshoot of Hindu and Buddhist styles. In the initial years, many Jain temples were made adjoining Buddhist temples and followed the Buddhist rock-cut style. Initially these temples were mainly carved out of rock faces, and the use of bricks was almost negligible. However, in later years Jains started building temple-cities on hills based on the concept of "mountains of immortality."

Compared to the number of Hindu temples in India, Jain temples are few and spaced out across the country. Surrounded by embattled walls, the temples are divided into wards, guarded by massive bastions at their ends, with fortified gateways as the main entrances. These temple-cities were not built on a specific plan but were the result of sporadic construction. Natural levels of the hill on which the "city" was built accommodated various levels so that the grandeur of the architecture increased with each successive level. The only variation in these temples was in the form of four-faced temples (*chamukhs*). In these temples, the image of a Jain seer (*Tirthankara*) faces the four sides, or four *Tirthankaras* are placed back to back to face four cardinal points. Entry into this temple is also from four doors. The *chamukh* temple of Adinath (1618 A.D.) is a characteristic example of the four-door temple.

The great Jain temples and sculptured monuments of Karnataka, Maharashtra,

and Rajasthan are world-renowned. The most spectacular of all Jain temples are found at Ranakpur and Mount Abu in Rajasthan. Deogarh (Madhya Pradesh), Lalitpur (Uttar Pradesh), Ellora (Maharashtra), Badami (Karnataka), and Aihole (Karnataka) also have some important specimens of Jain art.

Indo-Islamic Architecture

Indian architecture took new shape with the advent of Islamic rule in India toward the end of the twelfth century A.D. New elements were introduced into the Indian architecture that include: use of shapes (instead of natural forms); inscriptional art using decorative lettering or calligraphy; inlay decoration; and use of colored marble, painted plaster, and brilliantly glazed tiles. In contrast to indigenous Indian architecture, which was of the *trabeate* order, that is, all spaces were spanned by means of horizontal beams, Islamic architecture was *arcuate*, that is, an arch or dome was adopted as a method of bridging a space. The concept of arch or dome was not invented by the Muslims but was, in fact, borrowed by them from the architectural styles of the post-Roman period and then further perfected by Muslim architects. Muslims used a cementing agent in the form of mortar for the first time in the construction of buildings in India. They further applied certain scientific and mechanical formulas (derived from the experience of other civilizations) in their constructions in India. Such use of scientific principles helped not only in obtaining greater strength and stability of the construction materials, but also provided greater flexibility to the architects and builders.

An important fact to note is that Islamic elements of architecture had already passed through different experimental phases in other countries such as Egypt, Iran, and Iraq before these were introduced in India. Unlike most Islamic monuments of these countries, which were largely constructed in brick, plaster, and rubble, the Indo-Islamic monuments were typical mortar-masonry works formed of dressed stones. It must be emphasized that the development of Indo-Islamic architecture was greatly facilitated by the knowledge and skill possessed by Indian craftsmen, who had mastered the art of stonework for centuries and used their experience while constructing Islamic monuments in India.

In simple terms the Islamic architecture in

India can be divided into religious and secular. Mosques and tombs represent religious architecture, while palaces and forts are examples of secular Islamic architecture.

Sikh Architecture

Sikh shrines, or *gurudwaras*, are basically simple in their structure, the main requirement being that of a room in which the sacred text, the *Sri Guru Granth Sahib*, can be placed and the congregation can be seated. Most of the historical *gurudwaras* were built toward the end of the eighteenth century and in the nineteenth century, when the Sikhs had gained political power in Punjab. Today, *gurudwaras* can be found in all parts of the world.

Among the Sikh temples, the Golden Temple of Amritsar is the only one that rises like an island in the middle of a large pool. However, the structure of this temple has provided a model and an inspiration to builders of many other shrines. Most *gurudwaras* are two-storied. The first floor has a gallery in the middle, overlooking the hall below and is supported by four or more columns and the outer walls. On the ground floor, in the space thus marked out by the four columns, or approximately in the center, the *Sri Guru Granth Sahib* is enshrined on a platform or a movable palanquin with a canopy above it.

A dome tops the building, especially in the case of older shrines. The dome is usually white, and sometimes gilded, as in the Golden Temple of Amritsar, Tarn Taran, and Sis Ganj in Delhi. Apart from the big central dome, there are often four other smaller cupolas, one on each corner. Several turrets decorate the parapet. The big domes are fluted and usually have an inverted lotus symbol fashioned at the top. The bottom of the dome is often decorated with floral or other designs. Starting with a wide base, the dome reaches its maximum circumference less than half of the way up. On the pinnacle is a *kalas*, a short, straight, cylindrical construction, often with a very small canopy at the top and pendants hanging at the outer rim.

The temples have entrances from all sides, signifying that they are open to all without any distinction whatsoever, and that God is omnipresent. Where space shortage makes it impossible to provide entrances from all four sides, as in Sis Ganj in Delhi, the style has been varied. Generally, windows bulge out on all sides from the first floor, supported on brackets, with shallow elliptical cornices on top.

Many temples have a *deorhi* through which one has to pass before reaching the shrine proper. They are often impressive structures with a high gate and sometimes accommodation for an office or other use. From the *deorhi* one gets the first glimpse of the sanctum sanctorum.

In their architecture, the *gurudwaras* owe much to the Mogul style, as the artisans of the day in Punjab were trained in that style. However, in the course of time, they developed certain prominent characteristics, such as use of *chhatris* (domes supported by pillars) and ornamenting of parapets, corners, angles, and other permanent projections. Over the doorways, florid ornamentation is sometimes found.

In some of the temples, especially in the Golden Temple, Akal Takht and Baba Atal at Amritsar, the shrine at Tarn Taran, and Baoli Sahib at Goindwal, artists have provided decorative embellishment through various disciplines, including *jaralkari*, or inlay work of precious and colored stones in marble slabs. Much of the artistic execution is in the *naqqash* style of mural decoration—intricate floral patterns interspersed with animal motifs, with *gach*, a sort of gypsum. Beautiful designs are made on the walls with *gach* and then covered over with gold leaves.

Some of the shrines have frescoes, generally depicting episodes from the lives of the gurus. Vines, plants, flowers, birds, and animals also figure therein. The largest number of such frescoes can be seen on the first floor of Baba Atal. In a staircase in the Golden Temple is a fine painting of Guru Gobind Singh, riding a horse and accompanied by some of his followers.

The holiest room in a *gurudwara* is the *sachkhand*, where the holy scriptures are housed during the night. The *sachkhand* is normally situated at the highest point in the *gurudwara*, most often it is a separate room within the *darbar*, the main hall. All ceremonies are performed in the *darbar*, which holds a stage or platform on which the *Guru Granth Sahib* is placed. There is normally another platform, placed lower than the *Guru Granth Sahib*, where all speeches, narrations, and *kirtan* are performed. An additional hall in the *gurudwara* is the *langar*, where food is distributed.

Sculpture in India

The origins of Indian sculpture go back to the Stone Age. The Megalithic people buried their dead and constructed monuments of stone over them and worshiped the departed. The transition from worshiping ancestral spirits to revering a personal God was marked by the creation of icons of deities with specific attributes. Tiny terra-cotta seals discovered in the Indus Valley reveal carvings of pipal (peepul) leaves, deities, and animals. Also the tradition of bronze casting goes back to the Indus Valley civilization (2500-1500 B.C.). The earliest find is the bronze figure of the dancing girl of Mohenjodaro, a figure fashioned with tremendous sophistication and artistry.

The earliest archeological evidence of sculpture work in metal, terra-cotta, wood, and stone on the Indian subcontinent is provided by the remains found at the pre-Harappan sites of Baluchistan, the Makran areas of Pakistan, and Kalibangan in Rajasthan, dating back to 3000 B.C. Literary evidence from the *Rigveda* reveals that copper- and bronzework was a specialized science and that craftsmen were held in high esteem. Whether working in wood, stone, or ivory, the Indian carver-craftsmen have, over the centuries, been extremely versatile in applying their techniques and designs to various media. Carved wooden facades and fixtures of dwellings; domestic shrines; temples; churches and palaces in Rajasthan, Gujarat, Kashmir, and Kulu in Himachal Pradesh are marked by their intricate designs.

Sculpted stone started appearing in India in the third century B.C., with the stone pillars of Ashoka; the Buddhist shrines (*stupas*) and gateways (*toranas*) of Sanchi, Bharhut, and Amravati; and the rock-cut monasteries (*viharas*) of Barabar, Bhaja, Pitalkhoda, Karle, Bedsa, Ajanta, and others. These early examples of sculpture continued to be created until the twelfth century A.D. During the reign of the Mauryan emperor Ashoka, nearly 85,000 *stupas* were constructed. Many awe-inspiring statues exhibiting a serene Buddha, with a glowing face, were crafted in large numbers. Although Buddhism deplored idol worship, the human form of Lord Buddha began to be depicted with various features such as a halo around his head and the *dharmachakra* (the "wheel of law") engraved upon his palms and soles of his feet. A lion throne for his seat represented his royal ancestry.

Stone Sculpture

The centuries from fourth to the sixth A.D. marked the age when the statues found in temples indicated the various dimensions of early Hindu art and sculpture. The period, marked by the emergence of innumerable images of Hindu gods and goddesses, also saw a tremendous resurgence of Hinduism. It became an official religion of the Guptas. Images of Vishnu, Shiva, Krishna, the Sun-God, and Durga evolved during this period. The Udaigiri caves in Madhya Pradesh house a colossal image of Vishnu, represented as the great savior who rescued Mother Earth from the depths of the ocean, in his incarnation as a boar (*varha*).

The temples of Khajuraho in the central state of Madhya Pradesh are world-renowned for their erotic sculptures. Besides sculptures of couples in erotic poses, the temples include statues of gods and goddesses, warriors, celestial dancers, and animals. The Hindu concepts of *yoga* (union with the Divine) and *bhoga* (worldly pleasures) seem to be the underlying theme of these sculptures. All life was seen as an expression of divinity, including human love. The other sculptures in these temples depict the daily lives of people during the tenth and eleventh centuries.

Home to significant artistic movements, Mathura occupies a prominent place on the art map of India. The sculptural marvels excavated here provide an insight into Indian art from early times to the medieval period. However, the golden period of its art was from the first to the fifth century A.D., when the Kushan and Gupta kings were in power.

The Kushans, who were great patrons of art, ruled over a large empire in North India from 1 to 175 A.D. Two schools of sculptural art developed during this period: Gandhara and Mathura. Although it portrayed Indian themes, the Gandhara School was based on Graeco-Roman norms, encapsulating foreign techniques and an alien spirit. On the other hand, the Mathura school was completely Indian.

The Mathura School of Art, noted for its vitality and assimilative character, was a result of the religious zeal of Brahmanism, Jainism, and Buddhism. Although it was inspired by the early Indian art of Bharhut and Sanchi, the influence of Gandhara art was also manifested in its sculptures. Further, it amalgamated the features of old folk cults like *yaksha* worship with contemporary cults, creating a style rich in aesthetic appeal.

There are few creations in the whole range of Indian art that can vie in elegance, delicacy, and charm with the lovely feminine figures created by Mathura artists. The innocent but seductive damsels of the Mathura School display highly alluring sexual grace and charm. A *yakshi* is usually portrayed nude with globular breasts, invariably covered, smooth thighs, and the lower garments either shown as transparent or suggestively parted. Her physical charms, combined with soft and pleasant facial expressions, make her extremely enticing.

The sculptures of the Buddha, on the other hand, radiate the religious feelings of gentleness and compassion. In fact, it was during the Kushan period that the Buddha was conceived in human form and sculpted in

PAGE 32: Nataraja, Lord of Dance. One of the most well-known bronze sculptures in the world. *Photograph courtesy of India Archives, New Delhi, India.*

PAGE 33: Line drawing of Lord Nataraja with his consort Shivakami. *Line drawing courtesy of V. Ganapati Sthapati & Associates, Chennai, India.*

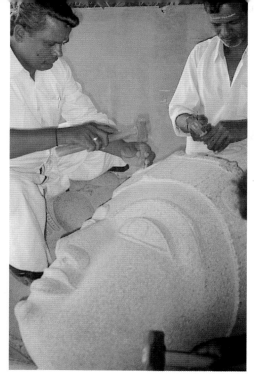

PAGES 34 and 35, TOP: Sculpting at the V. Ganapati Sthapati Works in Mahabalipuram, South India. An 18-ft. statue of Sri Ranganatha being worked on for a temple in Sri Lanka. This is just one part of a three-part statue, the other two parts being the base (Adisesha, the serpent bed) and the hood of Adisesha.

PAGE 34, BOTTOM LEFT: Dr. V. Ganapati Sthapati examining the work being carried out while the sculptors, *shilpis,* look on.

PAGES 34 and 35, BOTTOM CENTER: *Shilpi* working on a pillar that will eventually be assembled at the Iraivan Temple, Hawaii.

PAGE 35, TOP: S. Perumal Sthapati, the *sthapati* (master architect) at the V. Ganapati Sthapati Works who is in charge of the sculpting of this enormous idol of Sri Perumal (Vishnu).

PAGE 35, CENTER: *Shilpi* working on the base of a pillar that will eventually be assembled at the Iraivan Temple, Hawaii.

PAGE 35, BOTTOM: Detail of the Sri Perumal (Vishnu) idol.

PAGE 36, RIGHT: Sita, Sri Rama's consort, seen here wearing sumptuous traditional jewelry and hair adornments. Sita, the heroine of the *Ramayana,* is the embodiment of the perfect wife. This tenth century Chola bronze exemplifies the feminine ideal of Dravidian India.
Photograph courtesy of India Archives, New Delhi, India.

PAGE 36, LEFT: Line drawing of a typical female form of South Indian art.
Line drawing courtesy of V. Ganapati Sthapati & Associates, Chennai, India.

PAGE 37, BOTTOM LEFT: Line drawing of a design showing how a linear male form is transformed into an ornate, aesthetic form.
Line drawing courtesy of V. Ganapati Sthapati & Associates, Chennai, India.

PAGE 37, BOTTOM RIGHT: Line drawing of a female figure showing how the initial measurements are transformed into a graceful form.
Line drawing courtesy of V. Ganapati Sthapati & Associates, Chennai, India.

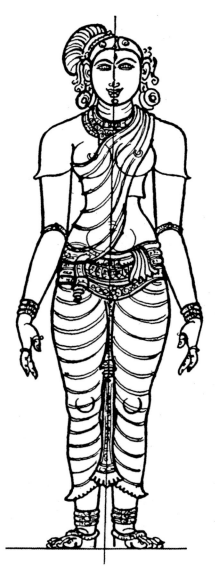

stone. Carved in bold relief, the features were given a three-dimensional effect, a concept that was probably borrowed from the West.

Established in 1874, the Mathura Museum holds an enviable position among the museums in India. Exhibiting a rich and variegated collection of sculptures belonging to the Mathura School, it has earned worldwide acclaim. Its sculptures of great beauty, some dating back to the second century B.C., include graceful statues of Buddha and exquisitely carved female figures in addition to images of deities. Perhaps the most impressive work of art displayed here is the headless life-size statue of Kanishka. One of the masterpieces of the Mathura Museum, this huge statue makes its presence felt as one enters the museum. It is the only statue of Kanishka in the world.

Bronze Sculpture

The Pallava and Chola dynasties witnessed the flowering of the bronze casting technique that was extant from the time of the Indus Valley civilization. The Chola bronzes (850-1275 A.D.) are unparalleled in their depiction of facile expression, the suppleness of the human form, and flowing movement. The images of Shiva Nataraja, Parvati, Kodanda Rama, and Navanita Krishna have perennially delighted devotees and aroused their religious fervor. Besides being votive images, the Chola bronzes mark a phase in the development of Indian sculpture that is simply magnificent in form and style.

The distinctive Chola style emerged during the reign of Aditya Chola (870-906 A.D.). The bronzes of this period are characterized by a supple body with flowing contours and an oval face. The world-renowned bronze images of Nataraja, the dancing form of Lord Shiva, appeared for the first time during the reign of Parantaka I, Aditya Chola's son. Shiva as Nataraja, the King of Dance, assumed such breathtaking perfection that the image danced its way into the hearts of devotees then, and even of Western connoisseurs such as French sculptor Rodin 1000 years later. Representing cosmic energy, encapsulating the motion, rest, and rhythm of the universe, stamping out the evil demon of ignorance, matted locks flying, foot upraised and arm flung out, the image of Nataraja embodies the consummate skill of the master iconographer (*sthapati*). Millennia later, it is still the favorite form of the craftsmen of India's sacred art. Lord Shiva inspired a myriad of forms, each of which the *sthapati* imprinted with his own consciousness.

After 975 A.D., the Chola bronzes are divided into two groups: the Sembiyan Mahadev School and Rajaraja School, each having its own characteristics but both developing simultaneously. The bronzes of the Sembiyan School are slender and tall and the figures are adorned by intricate ornamentation. The Konerirjapuram Temple at Thanjavur (Tamil Nadu) contains several bronzes of this school. The bronzes of the Rajaraja School are more masculine and majestic and radiate a sense of power and strength, both physical and spiritual.

The antiquity of the art of bronze casting can be traced back to the epic called the *Matsya Purana*. Later, among the findings in the ruins of Mohenjodara, came the discovery of the figure of the dancing girl, further reemphasizing the fact that sculpture along with the use of metal alloys was well known to people even then. Of course, all along sculptors were equipped with a detailed treatise on iconography—the *Shilpa Shastra*. All this adds to the exciting mystique of traditions when one finds there is no definite answer to the question of when experimentation with this form of artistic expression actually began.

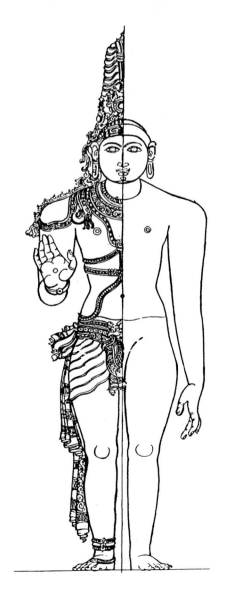

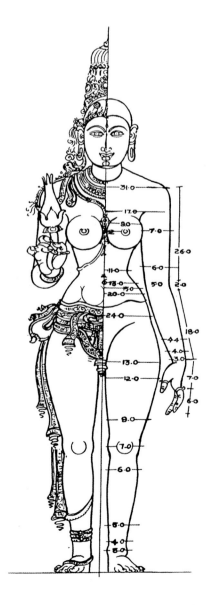

The art of bronze sculpting is poignantly related in a story about a king called Vajra. He was a pious and devout man. One day he found himself standing at the feet of sage Markandeya with a request. "Oh! Great sir, grant me but one wish," begged the king. "Teach me the art of iconography so that I may make my own idol for worship, using devotion as yet another input." Though the sage appreciated King Vajra's sentiment, he was forced to ask him a few questions before handing him the first piece of metal. "Do you know how to paint?" asked the sage. The king did not know painting, but requested that he be taught the art if it was a prerequisite to learning sculpture. "But for that you need to know how to dance," insisted the sage. To learn dancing the king was required to have rudimentary knowledge of instrumental music, which required, in turn, a foundation in vocal music. So the king had to begin with the octaves to be able to pour his sensibilities into any other material and make a form! It is no surprise, there-

fore, that the beauty of Indian bronzes lies in their efficient capturing of all these artistic forms within the sculpted figure. So close is the association that the different disciplines also share certain common terminology, for example, the word *tala*. To a sculptor *tala* means "one measure." To a musician or a dancer it refers to "one beat."

This unified aspect of art forms is more than evident when one sees the fluidity of movement in static pieces of sculpture. Symbolizing the cosmic forces of Nature, Shiva Nataraja becomes the epitome of life's rhythmic motion. The master iconographer seeks to capture this motion in bronze. The contours of the legs, the arms, and the whole body of an erect figure have so much resemblance to reality that one can perceive not only the previous stance but also the subsequent one: a fractional movement captured from the fluid transition of one pose to another, seemingly with a lens set at an exposure of one five hundredth of a second!

The highly evolved techniques and the materials used contributed in no small measure to the magnificence of the end product in these bronze figurines. The conventions, rituals, and instructions on measurements used today are the same traditional ones that have come down through the ages.

While bronze iconography is age-old, it was only around the tenth century A.D. that there was a large-scale revival in the practice of this art form. Subsequently, within a few centuries, it reached its zenith. At this time, there was strong religious fervor in the southern Indian states following the waning of the influence of Buddhism and Jainism. Generally, deities were made from bronze, the favorite ones being Lord Shiva; Ganesha, the elephant-faced god; Lord Rama, the incarnation of Vishnu; and Parvati, Lord Shiva's consort. However, there are innumerable variations upon the same theme that capture every myth that is associated with the deities.

In their chiseled splendor and symmetrical form, the bronzes of Tamil Nadu testify to the grandeur of an art form that reached the peak of perfection a thousand years ago. Acclaimed as among the finest achievements of metal sculpture in the world, the Chola and Pallava bronzes embody grace and precision that bring together in one composite whole the artist's imagination, the poet's sensibility, and the craftsman's skill. Through the finely proportioned torsos, the slim waists, and the exquisitely molded limbs, the *sthapatis* imbued the images with beauty so perfect that the human form was transcended to suggest the Divine, invoking a sense of wonder in the devotee.

South India, especially Tamil Nadu, has been the home of the art of creating bronze idols. Although the art of making bronze images dates back to antiquity and was known in many centers on the subcontinent, Tamil Nadu holds pride of place. Even in a country where continuity is a distinctive feature of life, the icon makers of Swamimalai, some 10 km. from Kumbakonam, principal town in Thanjavur district, are an outstanding example of an unbroken tradition. For even today in this village on the banks of the Cauvery, a hereditary craft is pursued by the descendants of those *sthapatis* whose creative spirit and religious fervor saw idols of surpassing beauty adorn hundreds of temples, big and small.

After the Cholas, the degree of finesse seemed to fade away and was never carried into subsequent generations; however,

39

newer styles evolved, almost as beautiful. The tradition remained unbroken and just as cherished, invoking wonder at the fascinating degree of perfection that is associated with the universal definition of beauty.

The bronzes of India defy age, looking as fresh today as they would have been just out of the sculptor's mold many centuries ago. Indian bronzes speak volumes about the expertise of an art form that was born very long ago but even today maintains threads of continuity woven into the story of Indian sacred sculpture.

The Tradition of Sacred Art and Architecture

The artisans, craftsmen, and masters of sacred Indian art and architecture, the *sthapatis*, belong to the Vishwakarma community and claim descent from the celestial architect Vishwakarma, who is said to be the builder of the palaces of the gods. In the past, these craftsmen were greatly respected since they performed such an exalted function in society. Even to this day, the traditional art of the *sthapatis* has been preserved and, in recent years, revived.

The processes and guidelines for practicing the art—the rules on iconometry and iconography—have been precisely defined in the *Shilpa Shastras* and the *Agamas*. An entire corpus of literature—the Vedas, the Upanishads, and the *shastras* specific to sacred art and architecture—guides the *sthapati* in the making of icons. The ancient texts, codified between the fourth and sixth centuries A.D., are followed to this day in varying degrees. In the past, each step of the artisan's task was approached with great devotion. Fire rituals (*homas*) had to be performed and other rituals observed from the moment of obtaining the wax for the model until the grand culmination, when the eyes of the idol would be "opened," proclaiming readiness for worship (*puja*).

Buddhism and Jainism were the dominant religions in Tamil Nadu until the *bhakti* movement (devotional worship of God) swept across the land. The appearance of the great Shaivite saints—Sundarar, Sambandar, Thirunavukkarasar, and Manikavasagar—and the Alwars, who propagated Vaishnavism, made inroads into Buddhism and Jainism. The Pallavas gave vent from the seventh to the ninth century to their religious ardor through rock-cut marvels and bronzes.

Under the Cholas, who were ardent Shaivites, magnificent temples arose, adorned with images of great beauty. The presiding deity was constructed in granite and fixed permanently in the sanctum. But there was also a need for idols that could be carried around the village or town on festive occasions. These figures were called *utsavamurtis*. The images that were permanently in the sanctum and in the subsidiary shrines were called *achala bimba*, or "immovable reflections of divinity." The transportable idols for worship were called *chala bimbas*, or "moveable reflections of divinity," used in daily festivities, and weekly, monthly, or annual processions.

Since granite was too heavy for this purpose, an alloy of five metals symbolizing the five elements was created. The metals were copper, brass, and lead with a little bit of gold and silver added. So effectively was this combination of metals chosen that they seemed to imbue the icons with life-like vitality. The vibrancy and elan of the *utsavamurtis* marked the apex of form and inspiration of the *sthapati* tradition.

The ancient *Agamas* include instructions for establishing deities and worshiping them, describing every possible detail of handling icons and maintaining them. These books are also the source of the *Vastu Shastra*, the science of sacred architecture that has gained immense popularity today.

Bronze and other metal icons of Tamil Nadu mostly belong to the Pallava and Chola eras of history between the sixth and eleventh centuries A.D. The Pallava Dynasty built temples across the landscape of Tamil Nadu. Their temples were small, with spires rising to heights of 20 to 60 feet. Thus, their bronzes of Shiva, Vishnu, Parvati, Lakshmi, Karttikeya, and Ganesha

were also small, in consonance with the rules of the *Agamas*.

The Cholas, who were true empire builders, built huge temple complexes, and their icons were also proportionately larger and more perfectly designed than those of the Pallavas. Bronzes and other metal icons of the Chola era were either cast hollow or solid. The greatest temple builder of the Chola dynasty was Rajaraja, "The Great King." He built the Brihadeeshwara temple in Thanjavur, which is 200 ft. tall.

Rajaraja called this temple the Dakshina-meru, or "the golden mountain of the south," and covered the entire spire of the temple in gold. For centuries, bronze iconography flourished in and around this temple. It is known from the records and inscriptions in the temple that a total of 85 idols of Shiva Nataraja, Tripurantaka, and Kalyansundara, as well as some icons of Vishnu were housed in this temple. However, there are only a few extant today. Sembian Mahadevi, a Chola queen who

ruled this territory, was also a great promoter of the iconography of Shiva and Vishnu, and many exquisite and classic bronzes came to be made during her rule. The facial expressions, the ornamentation, the grace of posture, and the proportions of limbs of these bronzes are incomparable.

Rajendra, the great conqueror of the Chola dynasty, expanded his empire to Bengal and built the Gangai Cholapuram temple, based on the laws of the *Agamas*, to celebrate his victory over the Gangetic plain. His queen Lokdevi also built her own temple 11 km. away. It is recorded that the workers, managers, and administrators in this temple were all women. Women, judging from the records the queen has left behind, were given high positions and equal status in the Chola era.

Many icons lie buried, according to the rites prescribed in the *Agamas* for times of war. Such rites were followed when the invading Muslim armies came from the north. The icons were hidden in secret vaults under sand brought from rivers for conservation. Since it was customary to bury them during floods, famines, enemy attacks, and scourges, it is possible that even today there are treasures of bronzes lying underground, waiting to be discovered and given the glorious place they deserve in our lives.

Lord Shiva as the dancing Nataraja; Vishnu, the Preserver, in his various incarnations; the auspicious Vinayaka; the beauteous Lakshmi; the graceful Shivakami; the rare Sarasvati; serene saints and reverential kings—the *sthapati* fashioned them all with verve and vitality. Working within the strict canons of the scriptures, he still was able to impart his own glowing spark of individuality to the images he fashioned through the Pallava and Chola reigns. The long faces had given way to the round, the rather flat features to the sharp, the austere ornamentation to the elaborate. An entire gallery of icons had taken shape.

Decline and Revival of Sacred Art

However, along the way, the finely achieved balance was lost. In the Vijayanagar period, the decline slowly set

in. Excessive ornamentation and highly rigid and conventionalized forms spoke of the flame dying out. But it continued to flicker, as it still does today, in the images fashioned in Swamimalai, Tamil Nadu.

The advent of the British spelled a death-knell to royal patronage of the arts, but the traditional art and craft of the *sthapatis* did not die out. Once thriving around the temple towns of Thanjavur, Madurai, and Chidambaram, *sthapatis* drifted toward Swamimalai and were discovered there by those who wanted to revive the art. In 1957, these descendents of the ancient artisans received a fresh lease on artistic life.

The Tamil Nadu Handicrafts Development Corporation was set up in Swamimalai in the 1950s to train artisans and to foster the art. It had just seven families as members then. Now there are 200 *sthapatis* in the town, belonging to 50 families. Although most of them are from the Vishwakarma community, agricultural workers, masons, and carpenters with a yen for the art are fresh entrants into the field.

The village is an unusual one, the long narrow lanes opening into small houses and cluttered, slushy courtyards resounding to the rhythmic tap of chisel on metal. Stepping into the training center is like stepping back in time. Huge framed photographs of classic Chola and Pallava bronzes—Vrishabhavahanavar, Kalyana Sundara, Ardhanarishwara—line the walls. The restrained expressions and sharp features are captured with varying degrees of success. Idols in unfinished states stand in a corner, casting aureoles of golden radiance and speaking eloquently of the enduring art of India's master craftsmen.

In today's India, modern sculpture, like other art media, has experienced a revival. While the traditionalists continue to follow the rhythmic, decorative tradition of the earlier periods, there is a growing breed of modern sculptors who are endeavoring to simplify the art form and to bring contemporary elements and social awareness into their art. Sculptors of this group freely assimilate art forms from Europe and other places to evolve their own individualistic styles.

Architectural Principles: *Vastu Shastra*

Until recent years, modern society has viewed much of the world's ancient architecture as simply decorative or else as a tribute to God, not considering that it might have any practical function in helping us to understand the nature of the world we live in. However, recent studies in the field of sacred architecture (*Vastu Shastra*) by scholars like Keith Critchlow of the Royal College of Art in London have uncovered hidden dimensions revealing a far-reaching connection between architecture and the nature of existence. Critchlow, perhaps the best-known advocate of the theory of sacred architecture, believes that basic architectural principles on the physical level are integral with structures at the metaphysical level.

Most sacred architects maintain that an ultimate reality exists beyond the mundane plane of temporary forms. Although infinite in nature, that Higher Reality can make itself known to the finite living entities in this world. It does so through revealed forms that, while seemingly limited and temporary, provide a bridge between the finite and the infinite.

Some regard the ideal forms of sacred *Vastu* architecture as metaphors, while others prefer to see them as fixed, eternal truths. In any case, it is a fact that sacred architectural forms (as presented in the *Vastu Shastra*) have the ability to uplift human consciousness from mundane reality to the supernatural.

Sacred Calling

The world over, we find examples of sacred architecture that evoke in us feelings of profound sacredness. William Irwin Thompson of the Lindisfarne Mountain Retreat in Colorado says about his chapel, "Anyone entering our chapel, no matter what their religion, would feel the sacred calling of the place and wish to sit in silence." Architect Michael Baron reports that people sometimes cry the first time they enter the Lindisfarne Chapel. He explains, "They find it touches something very familiar inside them. Others don't say a word; they sense the sacredness of the place. They may not be sure what's going on, but they are affected by it."

Although the world has many such sacred spaces, it's hard to find a place where sacred architecture is as developed a science as the one in India. India's ancient temples and palaces are certainly among the finest ever built. From the Sri Venkateswara Temple in Tirupati to the Pagodas of Tamil Nadu, from the Himalayan hill shrines to the great temple at Jagannatha Puri, India is a veritable treasure house of sacred architecture. In fact there are more existing examples of sacred architecture in India than in all other countries of the world combined.

Knowledge of sacred architecture in India has existed in the oral tradition since before the Vedic Age, some five thousand years ago. From the oral tradition it was later recorded in Sanskrit mantras and compiled under the title *Vastu Shastra*. According to Indian authorities, the *Vastu Shastra* is possibly the oldest known architectural treatise in the world.

The word *shastra* means "literature" or more accurately, "enlightened literature." The word *vastu*, meaning "the manifest," comes from the word *vustu*, meaning "the unmanifest." The philosophical purport of the words *vustu* and *vastu* form the basic concepts of India's sacred architecture and define an important aspect of the first lessons taught to the students of the *Vastu Shastra*. That which is manifest in this world, *vastu*, it is said, has its original existence on the plane of the transcendental and unmanifest, *vustu*.

The science of the *Vastu Shastra* is traceable to at least the year 3000 B.C., if not before. The earliest known master of the *Vastu Shastra* was Maya Danava, recognized as the founder of the tradition of India's sacred architecture. Today, *Vastu Shastra* still exists as a living tradition in India and is in no danger of becoming extinct.

Preparatory Steps

Of all types of structures in the field of sacred architecture, the building of a temple requires the utmost degree of knowledge and training. Those building a house, a school, or even an office building take into consideration the basic knowledge of sacred architecture for successful execution; but the temple, being the very abode of divinity, requires the greatest skills and is the most painstaking in its execution. In the development of a temple project all phases of construction from beginning to

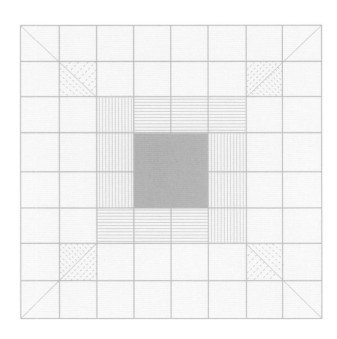

PAPARAKSASI			PILIPINJA						CARAKI
ROGA	AHI	MUKHYA	BHALLATA	SOMA	BHUJAGA	ADITI	DITI	AGNI	
PAPAYAK-SMAN	RUDRA						APA	PARJANYA	
SOSA		RAJAYAK-SMAN	PRTNIVIDHARA			APA-VATSA		JAYANTA	
ASURA								INDRA	
VARUNA		MITRA	BRAHMASTHANA			ARYAMAN		SURYA	SARVA-SKANDA
KUSUMA-DANTA								SATYA	
SUGRIVA		INDRA	VIVASAYAN			SAVITR		BHRSA	
DU-VARIKA	JAYA						SAVITR	ANTA-RIKSA	
PITARAH	MRGA	BHRN-GARAJA	GAN-DHARVA	YAMA	BRHAT-KSATA	VITATHA	PUSAN	ANILA	
PUTANA			ARYAMAN					VIDARI	

JAMBHAKA (left side)

end are thought out and executed according to the directions in the *Vastu Shastra*.

First of all, it is necessary to select a suitable place for building the temple. The suitable choices are indicated in the *Vastu Shastra*. The best location to build a temple is at a holy place (*tirtha*). A *tirtha* is a ford or crossing place from this world to the world above—a point of marriage between the transcendent and the mundane. A *tirtha* provides a crossing place for the upward journey of the soul and a place for the downward crossing of higher entities, who sometimes descend to this world for the good of humankind.

If construction of the temple at a *tirtha* is not possible, then another appropriate location should be found. The *Vastu Shastra* then says that the temple of the Godhead should be situated in a beautiful place where rivers flow, on the banks of a lake, or by the seashore; on hilltops, mountain slopes, or in a hidden valley. The site of the temple may be selected in a forest, a grove, or in a beautiful garden. Temples should also be built in villages, towns, and cities or on an island, surrounded by water.

Next, a construction plan is required, and here begins the highly technical aspect of sacred architecture—to bring about the descent or manifestation of the unmanifest and unseen. The architect (*sthapati*) begins by drafting a square. The square is literally the fundamental form of sacred architecture in India. It is considered the essential and perfect form. It presupposes the circle and results from it: expanding energy shapes the circle from the center; it is established in the shape of the square. The circle and curved lines suggest life in its growth and movement, whereas the

square is the mark of order, the finality to the expanding life, life's form, and the perfection beyond life and death. From the square all requisite forms can be derived: the triangle, hexagon, octagon, circle, and so on. The architect calls this square the *vastu-purusha-mandala*—*vastu*, the manifest; *purusha*, the Cosmic Being; and *mandala*, in this case, the polygon.

When completed, the *vastu-purusha-mandala* will represent the manifest form of the Cosmic Being, upon which the temple is built and in whom the temple rests. The temple is situated in that Being, comes from him, and is a manifestation of him. The *vastu-purusha-mandala* is a mystical diagram. It is both the body of the Cosmic Being and a physical device by which those who have the requisite knowledge attain the best results in temple building.

The concept of the Cosmic Being as a person has held a prominent place in Indian theistic thought since time immemorial. There is an interesting quotation in ancient Sanskrit literature that illustrates the personal features of the Cosmic Being: "The planetary systems in space from the highest down to the lowest represent the head, neck, chest, thighs, legs, and feet, respectively, of the Great Universal Being. His arms are the divine entities headed by Indra, the ten directional sides are his ears, and physical sound is his sense of hearing. His mouth is blazing fire. The sphere of outer space constitutes his eye sockets, and the eyeball is the sun—the power of seeing. The rivers are his veins, the trees are the hair of his body, and the omnipotent air is his breath. The passing ages are his movements." The perception of the Cosmic Being is considered to be the preliminary stage of God-realization and thereby a qualified form of pantheism,

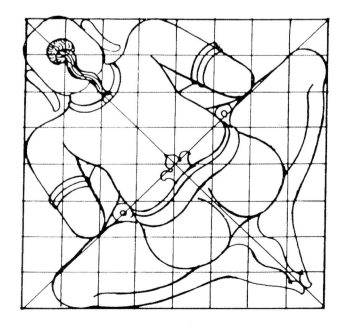

PAGE 48: Line drawing of a sequence from a cubic micro energy particle to a full-fledged *garbhagriha*. *Line drawing courtesy of V. Ganapati Sthapati & Associates, Chennai, India.*

PAGE 49: Line drawing showing the uniformity of temple concept and form across various regions of India, as well as the relationship of a temple structure to the human form. *Line drawing courtesy of V. Ganapati Sthapati & Associates, Chennai, India.*

which gradually leads one to understand the personal features of the transcendent Godhead.

The concept of spirituality in the system of sacred architecture in India is something that goes beyond mere static relations between inert objects and space as found in other architectural traditions. The relationship of objects with one another and space in India's sacred architecture extends to include higher entities said to be in charge of various aspects of universal affairs, all of whom carry out their work in accordance with the will of God.

In order to establish the *vastu-purusha-mandala* at the construction site, it is first drafted on planning sheets and later drawn upon the earth at the actual building site. The knowledge of its meaning and execution is the first discipline that the architect must master, and it requires in-depth understanding of astrology. The drawing of the *mandala* upon the earth at the commencement of construction is a sacred rite in itself. The rites and execution of the *vastu-purusha-mandala*, for which a priest will also be summoned later on, are not accessory, nor are they a mere accompaniment to the temple. They sustain the temple in their own sphere of effectiveness to the same extent that the actual foundation supports its weight.

Based on astrological calculations, the border of the *vastu-purusha-mandala* is subdivided into 32 smaller squares called *nakshatras*. These *nakshatras* correspond to the constellations or lunar mansions through which the moon passes in its monthly course. The number 32 geometrically results from a repeated division of the border of the single square. It denotes four times the eight positions in space: north, east, south, west, and their intermediate

points. The closed polygon of thirty-two squares is now symbolical of the recurrent cycles of time as calculated by the movements of the moon. Each of the *nakshatras* is ruled over by a divine entity, called a *deva*, which extends its influence to the *mandala*. Outside the *mandala* lie the four directions, symbolic of the meeting of Heaven and Earth and also representing the ecliptic of the sun—east to west—and its rotation to the northern and southern hemispheres.

The center of the *mandala* is called the station of Brahma (*Brahmasthana*), Brahma being the first of all beings and the engineer of universal order. Surrounding Brahma are the places of twelve other entities known as the sons of Aditi, who assist in the affairs of universal management. The remaining empty squares represent pure space (*akasha*). The *vastu-purusha-mandala* is now complete, forming a sort of map or diagram of astrological influences that constitute the order of the universe and the destinies of human lives. When placed on the building site, the *vastu-purusha-mandala* determines the time for beginning construction. Only by the combination of the *vastu-purusha-mandala* and astrological calculations can this factor be ascertained.

The temple itself should always face east, as that is considered the most auspicious direction—the place of origin of the sun. From the east appears the rising sun, the destroyer of darkness and the giver of life. It brings joy and happiness and is the watchful eye of the Cosmic Being. The *Vastu Shastra* states that a building with improper proportions and wrong orientation will create an environment that is conducive to disturbances like disease, death, and destruction, and may be inhabited by subtle entities with envious and deceitful natures.

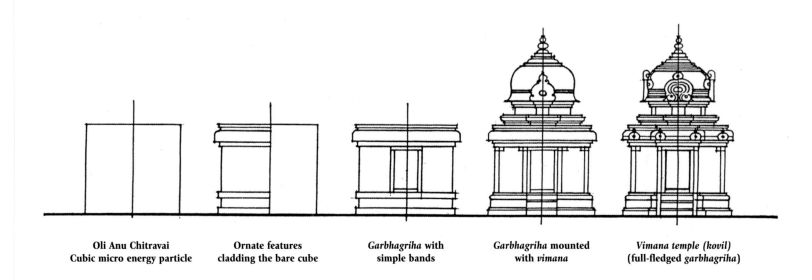

Oli Anu Chitravai **Cubic micro energy particle**	**Ornate features** **cladding the bare cube**	**Garbhagriha with** **simple bands**	**Garbhagriha mounted** **with vimana**	**Vimana temple (kovil)** **(full-fledged garbhagriha)**

Through the science of sacred architecture it becomes apparent that the construction of a domestic building or of a temple is something like the birth of a human being, who according to the time and place of his birth will come under certain astrological influences throughout life. The time of construction and the place and position of a structure are all important factors for the future of the building. Therefore, according to the *Vastu Shastra*, all structures should be erected according to auspicious astrological calculations to assure successful execution, longevity, and lasting prosperity.

From the diagram of the *vastu-purusha-mandala* the architect next proceeds to develop the vertical and horizontal dimensions of the temple. Here too a wide range of factors must be taken into consideration. To guide the sacred architect of today a long and rich tradition of already existing temples and sacred buildings in India serves as a great inspiration for his work. The architect's creative intelligence is an all-important ingredient in the final design, while the *mandala* and the *Vastu Shastra* continue to be the tools of his execution.

The size of the structure will determine the various kinds of building materials to be used at different stages of the construction. Building materials such as stone, marble, brick, plaster, and wood are selected for the main body of the temple, whereas elements like gold and silver are used for final ornamentation. Only organic materials are used in sacred architecture. Manmade materials like simulated marble, plastic, and asbestos are not acceptable building materials, the reason being that inorganic materials are not considered adequate conductors of cosmic energies.

The plotting graphs of the temple are divided into two main sections—the ground plan and the vertical alignment. The square, the rectangle, the octagon, and the pentagon are fundamental patterns in the horizontal, or ground, plan. In the vertical alignment, the pyramid, the circle, and the curve are most prominent. The subdivisions of the ground plan include the main shrine (*Brahmasthana*) and smaller chapels, and the balconies, assembly halls, and auditoriums (*mandapas*). The vertical plan consists of drawings for the entranceway towers (*gopuras*), the structure above the main shrine or chapel (*vimana*), and the walls (*prakaras*).

The *Brahmasthana* is said to be the principal location in a temple since it is here that the seat of Godhead will eventually be placed. At the base of the foundation of the *Brahmasthana*, located at the station of Brahma on the *vastu-purusha-mandala*, a ritual is performed called *garbhadhana*, the ritual that invites the soul of the temple to enter within the building's confines. As part of this ritual, the priest places a golden box in the earth during the ground-breaking ceremonies. The interior of the

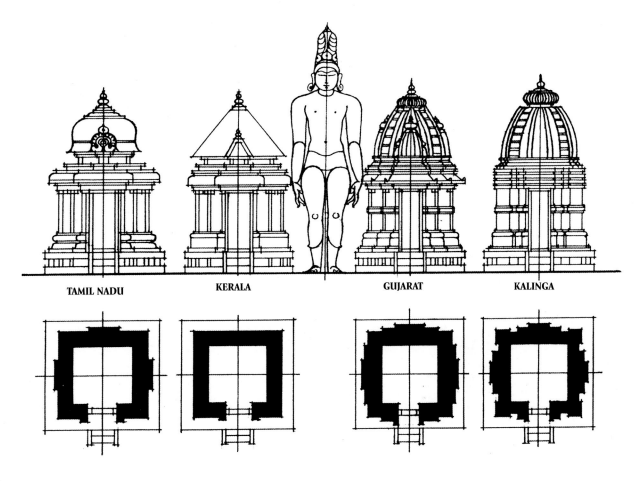

TAMIL NADU   KERALA   GUJARAT   KALINGA

PAGE 50, BOTTOM LEFT: M. Muthiah Sthapathi doing a detailed drawing of a temple on site. *Photograph courtesy of M. Muthiah Sthapathi.*

PAGE 50, BOTTOM CENTER: Line drawing representing one-fourth of an actual *hasta* measure. *Line drawing courtesy of V. Ganapati Sthapati & Associates, Chennai, India.*

PAGE 50, BOTTOM RIGHT: Line drawing of a design set against the measures of the Indian musical scale. *Line drawing courtesy of V. Ganapati Sthapati & Associates, Chennai, India.*

PAGE 51: Line drawing of a temple as human form. *Line drawing courtesy of V. Ganapati Sthapati & Associates, Chennai, India.*

PAGES 52 and 53: Line drawing of a complete temple. *Line drawing courtesy of V. Ganapati Sthapati & Associates, Chennai, India.*

box is divided into smaller units exactly resembling the *vastu-purusha-mandala*. All the units of the gold box are first partially filled with dirt. In the thirty-two units representing the *nakshatras*, the units of Brahma, and the twelve sons of Aditi, the priest places an appropriate mantra in written form to invoke the presence of the corresponding divinity.

The Sanskrit mantras chanted by the priest are in no way less important than the *mandala* itself. Whereas the *mandala* sets up an archetypal diagram of universal order, the mantras infuse the *mandala* with spiritual powers. The mantras chanted by the priest are distinct from ordinary mundane sounds. Mantras, composed of "atomic" monosyllabic sounds derived from the Sanskrit alphabet, are said to be nondifferent from the very substance that they invoke. The mantras are the subtle form of the *mandala* and are inseparable from it. As the architect must have undergone extensive training in the field of sacred architecture and astrology to construct the *mandala*, similarly the priest who chants the mantras

must also have requisite knowledge of the science of sacred sound vibrations.

In the unit of Brahma, a golden serpent with many raised hoods is placed. The serpent form is then surrounded with nine precious jewels (*navaratna*). The serpent represents the energy that supports the very existence of the universe. The universe rests in space, and that space is the energy of Godhead appearing as a serpent. The nine jewels—diamonds, emeralds, rubies, pearls, yellow sapphire, blue sapphire, red coral, cat's-eye, and jade—invoke the astrological influence of the nine planets.

A gold lid with the seven continents of the earth engraved on it is placed on top of the box. When this is done, the priest performs the ritual fire sacrifice, or sanctification ceremony called *agnihotra*. During the *agnihotra*, the priest offers clarified butter, the symbol of religious principles, into the fire, which represents the mouth of the Cosmic Being. Along with the offering of clarified butter, five types of grains—rice, wheat, barley, rye, and dal, all produced of the

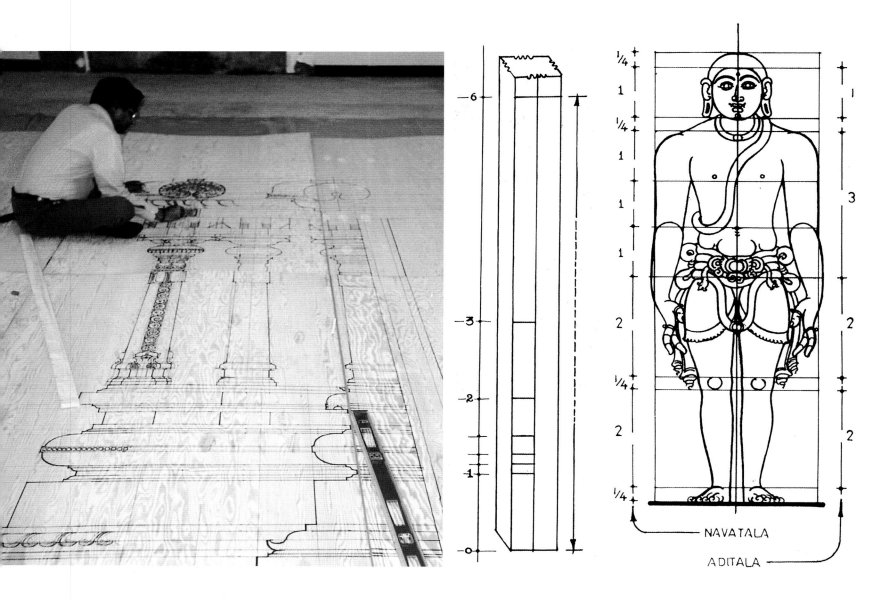

NAVATALA

ADITALA

earth—are also offered in the fire. This too is performed with the chanting of mantras.

Construction

Once the *garbhadhana* and *agnihotra* ceremonies are completed, the actual construction of the temple takes place according to the previous preparations. When the foundation is finished, the vertical structure is raised and the body of the Cosmic Being becomes visible to the naked eye. The external features of the temple are brought to life through finely sculpted figures and paintings. The art and sculpture frequently portray the forms of divine entities and the different stages of consciousness in the gradual evolution of life throughout the universe. This is no less exacting a science than that of the architect or of the priest. It is often the work of the master artisan (*shilpi*) through painting and sculpture that most enables one to perceive the sacredness of the temple.

The *prakaras* that fortify the temple may vary in size and number according to the dimensions of the temple. Larger temples are sometimes surrounded by up to seven concentric walls that represent the seven layers of matter—earth, water, fire, air, space, mind, and intelligence—that cover the original consciousness of the living entities in the material world. The gateways through the *prakaras* are symbolic of being liberated from the bondage of matter as one enters the temple and proceeds toward the central shrine.

The grand entrance tower of the temple is called *rajagopura*, its very name, *raja*, "royal," implying its high significance. Depending on its size, a temple can have one or more towers representing different entrances of the temple; however, the *rajagopura* is the main entrance. It is in line with the main sanctum, flagpole (*dhvajastambha*), and the offering pedestal (*balipitha*). Normally, the *rajagopura* will be the largest in size of all the *gopuras* in the temple. When the images of the deities are taken out of the temple, they leave and reenter the temple by way of the *rajagopura*.

The *rajagopura* is a fine representation of Hindu temple architecture. It has many sculptures and decorations placed in it, meeting the requirements of a solid structure. If the temple structure can be compared to a human body, the main sanctum is the head, the large hall called the *mahamandapa* is the central portion of the body, and the *rajagopura* symbolizes the feet. It is believed that just having a glimpse of the *rajagopura*, even from a distance, is equivalent to coming to the temple and offering prayers to the deities in the temple.

The *dhvajastambha* is placed between the *rajagopura* and the main sanctum, and the *balipitha*, between the *dhvajastambha* and the *rajagopura*. Final services are conducted at this site after the completion of the daily *puja* for all the deities in the temple.

The *vimana* is raised to its final height above the sanctum as the last stones are put into place. Resembling a great mountain, the *vimana* is crowned with a golden spire called *kailasa*, "the heavenly abode." At the sides of the *vimana* are fixed the fierce faces of Yali, the protector of the temple. The temple is now ready for the ceremony known as *Pratishthana*, the installation of the deity. The sacred altar in the central shrine (*Brahmasthana*) is located directly above the gold box, placed in the earth during the *garbhadhana* ceremony. Here on the sacred altar representing the heart of the Cosmic Being, the deity of Godhead called the *archa-vigraha*, the manifest form of total divinity, is installed. The *mandala*, the mantra, and above all the sincerity and faith of the participants combine together to invoke the appearance of the Godhead. The universe is the manifestation of the divine form of Godhead in the world of mundane existence. The body of the temple is the representation of that cosmic form, whereas the *archa-vigraha* is the manifestation of the transcendental form of the Godhead descending from beyond the mundane. The ceremony for installing the deity is performed with great pomp, and upon its completion the temple is complete.

There are altogether 45 basic varieties of temples mentioned in the *Vastu Shastra*. These too have their many variations, and

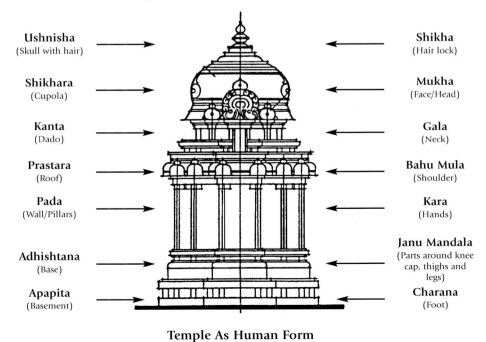

Ushnisha (Skull with hair)	**Shikha** (Hair lock)
Shikhara (Cupola)	**Mukha** (Face/Head)
Kanta (Dado)	**Gala** (Neck)
Prastara (Roof)	**Bahu Mula** (Shoulder)
Pada (Wall/Pillars)	**Kara** (Hands)
	Janu Mandala (Parts around knee cap, thighs and legs)
Adhishtana (Base)	
Apapita (Basement)	**Charana** (Foot)

Temple As Human Form

thus the styles of sacred temple architecture in India are as unlimited and diverse as the very nature of the infinite being they represent.

From the drawing table to the finished product of a magnificent temple, sacred architecture in India is a science and a work of art. Moreover, it is an attempt to raise human consciousness to the stage of God-realization where one ultimately sees the Godhead everywhere, in all things, and at all times.

Consecration of Images

A Hindu temple complex is a miniature cosmos. In addition to the five elements that are present in appropriate forms, the central figure is the presiding deity of the temple. The God-figure is not just a statue, but a concretized form of all that is good and godly in the universe. As gifted leader Rajaji says, "God in his stone image is present for all times, captured within the majestic figure, radiating love and grace for the benefit of his devotees." The worship of divine images (*vigraha*) is mentioned in the *Upanishads*, which talk about the following

abodes of God: Vaikuntha/Kailasa in the heavens (*para*), the ocean (*vyuha*), the heart of every human being (*antaryami*), and the figurines made of molten metals or of stone. According to the *Pancharatra Agama Shastra*, God has declared that he assumes whatever form his devotees give him either ethereal or physical. When a devotee gives God a physical form, he does so by pouring into the figure all his devotion, love, skill, and every good thought. Thus, the *vigraha* is the final outcome of a concentrated, dedicated effort in which all good feelings and noble actions are combined together to form a formidable force, keeping out all that is bad. No wonder, therefore, that a properly made *vigraha*, consecrated and installed according to established norms by people who are steeped in devotion to God, is a venerable representative of the One.

Only highly evolved beings like saints and sages can visualize God as a formless, all-pervasive force that, in spite of its boundless power, can be encased within the confines of a human heart. Common people need a physical form that they can see with their eyes and worship, as they do not possess the inward sight to look within themselves.

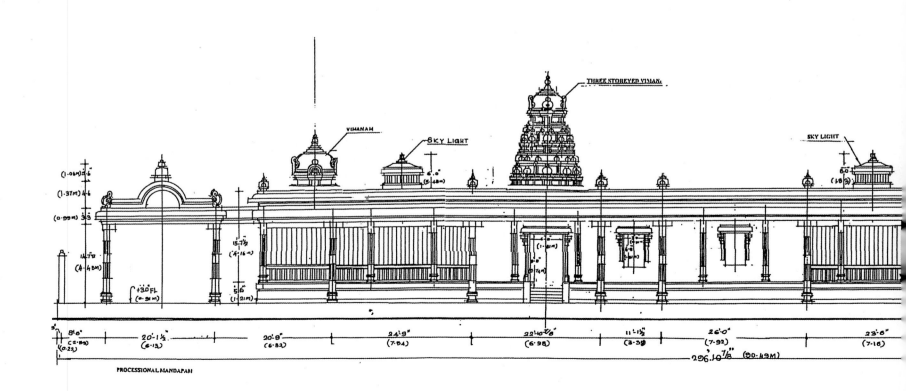

That is why the Vedas have sanctioned *vigraha* worship as one of the approaches to God.

Any *vigraha* cannot become a true house of God. The *shastras* have laid down rules regarding how a *vigraha* has to be cast, consecrated, and installed with Vedic rites before it can become a divine form. The metals used for casting the images (*utsava-murtis*, the images that can be transported during religious festivals) are carefully chosen and purified. Similarly, the stone used for carving the main deity is obtained from mountainsides known for the purity of their location. By the sound that a rock emits when struck, an expert sculptor can differentiate between a "male" and a "female" rock. The artisans who sculpture the stone into a *vigraha* are skilled workers who are well versed in the art of transforming a stone into a divine figure. The external beauty and perfection of form of the sculptured *vigraha* contribute to the godliness of the figure.

Vedic rites accompany the consecration and installation of the *vigraha* in the *garbhagriha*. The purpose of these ceremonies is to purify the *vigraha* and to confer divinity upon it. The power and vibrations of the Vedic mantras recited clearly and loudly have their echoes captured within the divine image for all time to come. During the consecration, the *vigraha* is given a ceremonial bath (*abhisheka*). The water used for this purpose is kept in a *kumbha*, a receptacle with a narrow mouth and a wide middle portion. Water for the Kumbhabhisheka is collected from holy rivers or from a *pushkarni* (holy tank that gets its water from springs located in the bed) situated within or near the precincts of the temple. Before major festivals the old water is drained out, and the openings of the springs are cleaned so that fresh ground water can seep in to fill up the tank. Ground water can be called water from the heavens, as it is formed from captured rainwater.

The *kumbha* (ceremonial vessel) symbolizes the body. The water kept inside it with its dissolved air is life-giving and life-sustaining matter in fluid form. To it are added flavoring agents such as cardamom, saffron, camphor, nutmeg, mace, and sandalwood (*sugandha dravyas*). The vessel is

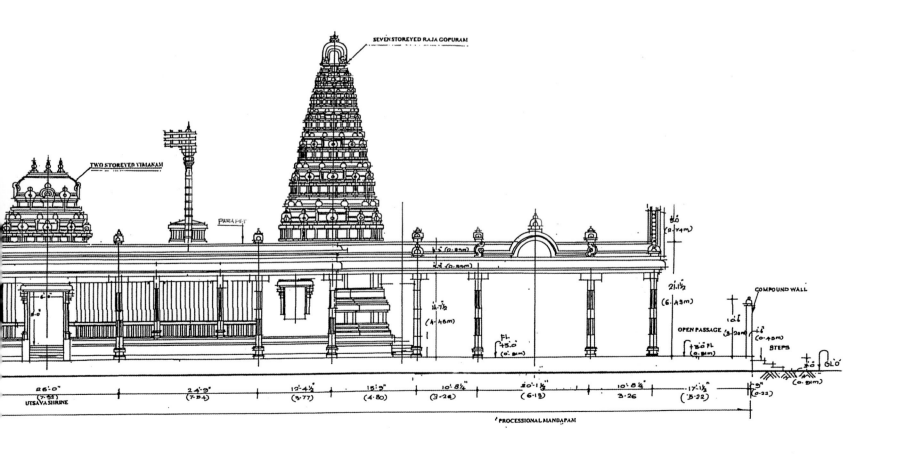

PAGE 54: Line drawing of different elevations of a *rajagopura*.
Line drawing courtesy of V. Ganapati Sthapati & Associates, Chennai, India.

PAGE 55, LEFT: Line drawing of *dhvajastambha*.
Line drawing courtesy of V. Ganapati Sthapati & Associates, Chennai, India.

PAGE 55, RIGHT: Line drawing of a *balipitha*.
Line drawing courtesy of V. Ganapati Sthapati & Associates, Chennai, India.

surrounded by a ceremonial thread that is wound around it in a crisscross pattern, symbolizing a cloth covering for the body. The mouth of the vessel is covered by a bunch of mango leaves that represent the head. A bundle made up of sixteen special grass (*kusa* grass) blades known as *dharba* is used as a conductor for transmitting the power of the Vedic mantras and the ceremonial fire (*agni kunda*) to the *kumbha* through the performing priests. The *darbha*, which is held in one hand while performing oblations to the holy fire, can be compared to a blood vessel or an artery through which flows the life principle. The *kumbha*, properly prepared as described

earlier, is installed in the *yajnashala*, the place where oblations to the holy fire (*homa*) are performed. One end of the *darbha* is placed on the *kumbha*, which thus absorbs the power and divinity of the fire and the Vedic mantras. The water, thus consecrated and purified, is used for bathing the *vigrahas* and is also sprinkled over the precincts of the temple.

A *Kumbhabhisheka* is usually held for three to five days in a row. The minor ritualistic details vary depending upon such factors as the occasion (such as the first installation of the *vigraha* or the consecration of the *rajagopura*) as well as upon the local

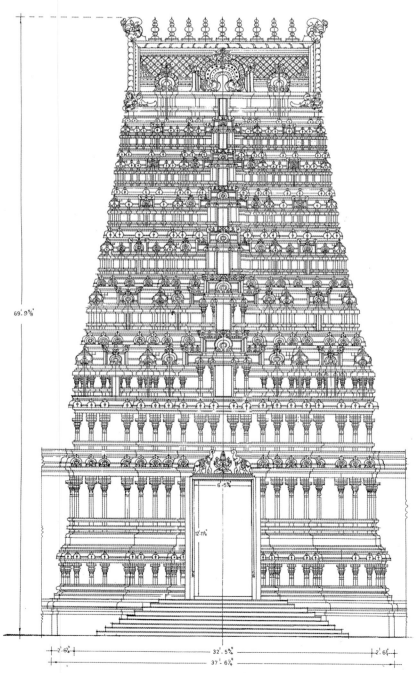

FRONT ELEVATION OF RAJAGOPURAM

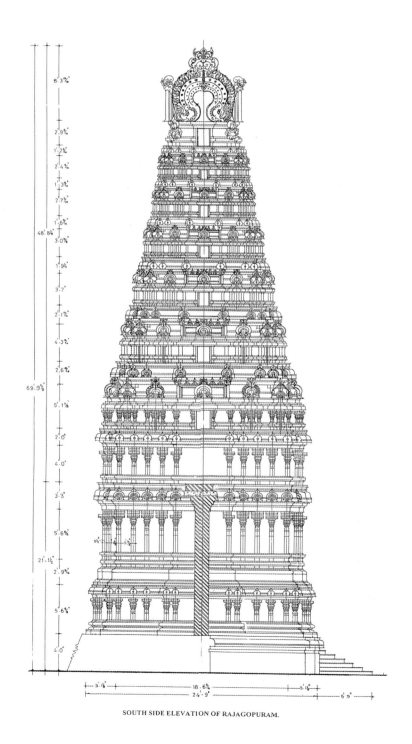

SOUTH SIDE ELEVATION OF RAJAGOPURAM.

traditions of the temple. In the case of the consecration of the *rajagopura* itself, the *kalashas* atop the *gopura* are washed with the water from the *kumbha*. When a temple is newly constructed, the *Kumbhabhisheka* performed thereafter is called *avartha*; when additions are made to the existing temple complex, one speaks of a *punaravartha*, whereas an *anthanitha* is performed after a natural catastrophe has damaged the temple.

Kumbhabhisheka, being a purifying as well as a rejuvenating ceremony, is also held periodically over several years depending upon the developmental activities in the temple. Any new erection like a tower, or the installation of a new *vigraha*, or any new structural addition to the temple complex is consecrated with a *Kumbhabhisheka*. A comprehensive ritual of this kind—which incorporates the daily form of worship into a larger framework, invoking the powers of the elements, the divine force of the Vedas, and the benefits accruing from propitiating the different gods—strengthen and consolidate the inherent divinity residing in the *vigraha*. Frequent ceremonies of this type and annual religious festivals add luster to the temple and enhance its inner spirit, as well as provide opportunities for bonding among the devotees.

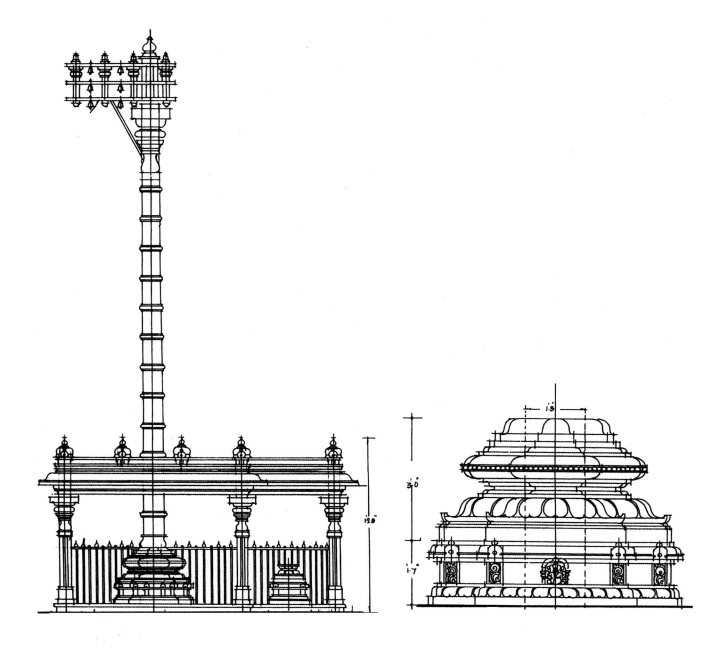

HINDU TEMPLES

Venkateswara Temple, Pittsburgh, Pennsylvania

Meenakshi Temple, Houston, Texas

Ranganatha Temple, Pomona, New York

Rama Temple, Chicago, Illinois

Sri Meenakshi Temple Society

Pearland, Texas

The Sri Meenakshi Temple is considered to be one of the finest Hindu temples outside of India. It is the first traditional temple in North America devoted to a goddess.

Hundreds of people come to the temple each month. Many Hindus in the Houston area visit the temple as a source for spiritual renewal. Others visit it as a place of pilgrimage. Many others come to the temple for community celebrations of Hindu festivals. Some come because they have heard or read about the temple and are interested in seeing it.

New Tradition Taking Root

As a part of a growing tradition, Hindus who settled in the Houston area in the 1970s felt a strong need to build a traditional Hindu temple for themselves and their children. They wanted to instill in their children the culture and religion that they brought to this country. They realized that it would be very difficult to maintain their religious practices without a place to worship together as a community. The temple would also foster a sharing of culture, including devotional music, dance, and drama.

PAGES 58 and 59: A perspective view of the main entrance of the Meenakshi Temple, Houston, Texas.

PAGE 60: Architectural ornaments and intricate design used on the *vimana*. Beautiful female figures are used to enhance the aesthetic value of the building and also as symbols of fertility and prosperity.

PAGE 61: View of a minor shrine. There are shrines in each corner of the precinct housing various deities.

The Sri Meenakshi Temple Society was established in October 1977, and the original property was purchased on June 20, 1978. Sri Ganesha Temple was soon constructed, and inaugurated on *Ganesha Chathurthi* day in August 1979. At that time the temple was only a small structure barely large enough for one person to stand in while performing *puja* to Sri Ganesha. Devotees could sit in front of Lord Ganesha during *pujas*, but were not protected from the weather, having neither a roof over their heads nor walls around them. From that inaugural day until a resident priest joined the temple community, dedicated Houston families alternated in performing daily *pujas* for Lord Ganesha. Later, when finances permitted it, an adjacent facility was built, and Sri Ganesha Temple was enlarged and fully enclosed.

There were several good omens, including the vision of the seer of Kanchi Kamakoti Peetham that there would be a temple dedicated to Shakti, which helped to determine the presiding deity at the temple. With the blessings of Goddess Meenakshi

and through the efforts of many Hindus, the construction of the main temple was begun soon after the original Ganesha Temple was built. Padmasri S. M. Ganapati Sthapati made two trips to Houston from Chennai, India, and drew the main temple plans. Padmasri M. Muthiah Sthapathi developed further details and helped to oversee the construction of the main temple and later additions by skilled and dedicated temple artisans (*shilpis*) from India. In addition, several very talented local Hindu architects helped with the planning, design, and construction of the temple complex, from the earliest master plans through the most recent construction. These efforts complemented the work of specialists in Hindu temple architecture.

Celebrations

The first inauguration (*Maha Kumbhabhisheka*) was performed in June 1982. At this time the deities at the main temple— Sri Meenakshi, Sri Sundareshwara, and Sri Venkateshwara—were installed according to the *Agama Shastra*. Nandi, Lord Shiva's vehicle, was installed directly opposite Sri Sundareshwara. Garuda, Sri Vishnu's vehicle, was installed opposite Sri Venkateshwara. Sri Lakshmi, the companion of Lord Vishnu and the Goddess of Wealth, is represented in the temple as Sri Padmavati and is situated near Sri Vishnu along the north wall.

The ceremonies included *Ashtabhandhana* (installation of the deity in the sanctum, the *garbhagriha*), *abhisheka* of the ritual vessel (*kumbha*) at the apex of the temple entrance towers (*gopuras*) and *abhisheka* and *archana* of the deities. A number of priests from India participated in these traditional rituals.

In June 1994, the twelfth anniversary of Sri Meenakshi Temple was celebrated in grand style. *Ashtabhandhana* was performed for the main deities. The metal idols (*utsavamurtis*), recently arrived from India, were inaugurated during that time.

An even grander celebration was held in July 1995 with a *Maha Kumbhabhisheka* marking the completion of major construction at the temple. The *Maha Kumbhabhisheka* for the east *rajagopura*, the three other *gopuras,* and four *prakara mandapas* (temples in the outer corners) was performed. With more than twenty priests from India and various parts of the United States, this was one of the most elaborate celebrations of its kind held anywhere outside India.

In September 1999, a *Kumbhabhisheka* was

held to install the black granite *koshta vigrahas* (five statues around each of the major deities set into the recesses in the inside and outside walls). Also installed were *chandikeshwara* (where items such as flowers that have been offered to Shiva can be placed), *dvarapalas* and *dvarashaktis* (guards), Nandi (bull who transports Goddess Meenakshi), and Nandi Mandapa (Nandi's temple). In addition, an offering pedestal (*balipitha*—the area where food offerings are left to be shared) and the flagpole (*dhvajastambha*) were also installed. The addition of these features makes the Sri Meenakshi Temple complete according to the sacred traditions.

Temple Deities

Goddess Meenakshi is the consort of Lord Sundareshwara (Shiva). She is the manifesting power of Shiva, both potential and dynamic. She is also symbolized as Shakti, or the power that supplies energy to Shiva. In reality, the god and the goddess are the passive and active aspects, respectively, of the Absolute Reality.

Sri Meenakshi is also thought of as symbolizing Prakriti, or Nature. She was first known as Thadathagai and is said to have appeared from a sacrificial fire to become the daughter of King Malayadwaja and Queen Kanchanamala. After her marriage to Lord Sundareshwara, she was named Meenakshi. Her name was chosen because she protects her progeny through her merciful glances, like a fish guarding her eggs. Worship of God as the Divine Mother, such as worship of Sri Meenakshi, is one of the greatest contributions of *Sanatana Dharma* (Hinduism).

The idol (*vigraha*) of goddess Meenakshi is 4.5 ft. tall and is placed on a pedestal 1 ft. high. Like the other major *vigrahas* at the temple, her *vigraha* was carved of special black granite from southern India. Artisans from a school near Madras, established to create Hindu temple sculpture, carved all the major black granite images (*murtis*) seen in the temple except for that of Sri Venkateshwara.

Other deities in the temple include Lord Shiva, who is worshiped in the Meenakshi Temple in the form of a *linga*, a simple stone shape standing on a pedestal. Shiva means "auspiciousness" and *linga* means "symbol" or "representation," so the *Shiva-linga* is a symbol of auspiciousness.

Sri Venkateshwara (Vishnu), also known as Balaji, is considered to be the protector, or sustainer, of the universe. He is shown with four arms. One hand holds a lotus (its petals symbolizing the unfolding of creation). The second hand holds a conch shell, symbolizing the primordial sound from which all existence comes. The third hand has a *chakra*, the discus that always returns to the owner after destroying an evil being. The fourth hand carries the mace (*ghada*). Both the *chakra* and the *ghada* symbolize the power to destroy all evil. The Sri Meenakshi Temple's *vigraha* of Sri Venkateshwara is made of black granite and was sculpted at the Tirupati Temple in Andra Pradesh, India. Sri Lakshmi, the consort of Vishnu, is the Goddess of

PAGES 62 and 63: Panoramic view of the Meenakshi Temple. At the far right stands the monumental *rajagopura;* in the center is the main temple with the *vimanas* above the shrines of Goddess Meenakshi, Lord Sundareshwara (Shiva), and Sri Venkateshwara (Vishnu). The second and third *gopuras* face south and north; at the left are the west *gopura* and the minor shrines. The Meenakshi Temple is one of the most traditionally built Hindu temples in the United States.

Wealth. She is represented at the Sri Meenakshi Temple as Sri Padmavati.

Deities in the northwest hall (*mandapa*) include Lord Subramanya, also known as Thiru Murugan, Karttikeya, or Skanda; he is the second son of Shiva and Parvati. Lord Rama, Goddess Sita, and Sri Lakshmana are the next group of deities. Sri Rama is considered to be a perfect man and perfect king. He is always depicted with a bow and arrows and thus represents eternal readiness to destroy both internal and external enemies.

Lord Krishna nearly always is shown with his beloved Radha. Sri Krishna is the eighth incarnation (*avatara*) of Vishnu. He is represented as a cow herd, playing on his flute. Radha, Krishna's eternal companion, is one of the milkmaids (*gopis*) who love to play and dance with him.

Deities in the northeast *mandapa* include

the Navagrahas, the nine celestial houses that are considered by many to influence every aspect of our lives. The Navagraha grouping is comprised of Surya (sun) in the center, Chandra (moon), Angaraka (Mars), Budha (Mercury), Guru (Jupiter), Sukra (Venus), Sanishwara (Saturn), Rahu (the point where the moon crosses the ecliptic or celestial equator to the north), and Kethu (the point where the moon crosses the ecliptic or celestial equator to the south).

Sri Nataraja is the representation of Shiva in the famous dance pose as the creator of the universe, the origin of rhythm, the destroyer of delusion (Apasmara,) and the purifier. Sri Bhairava is a representation of Shiva in his terrifying aspect.

Deities in the southeast *mandapa* serve a unique role. The Sri Meenakshi Temple is the first temple in the world to have a *vigraha* of Sri Jyoti. The installation and

consecration took place on June 27, 1982. Goddess Jyoti is not a new deity, but was mentioned in the *Skanda Purana*. She is thought to have been created by a spark of energy from Shakti's forehead. She was first thought of as the *vel*, the weapon of Lord Skanda (Subramanya), but later it was revealed that this *vel* is not an instrument, but a deity in her own right. Sri Jyoti is considered to be *kundalini shakti*, the energy that rises in our spine and becomes Jnanambal, or the Goddess of Wisdom, in our foreheads. Goddess Jyoti is represented in the temple as a spirit of flame that is the base for an etching of a sixteen-year-old girl known as Balambika.

Sri Durga is perhaps the most widely worshiped aspect of Shakti. Literally, Durga means "difficult to know or to approach." She is pleasant and beautiful and yet at the same time terrifying and powerful. She is described as wielding several weapons such as the bow and arrow, sword, discus, and a trident. With her weapons, she can destroy not only evil but also the sorrow in one's life.

Sri Kanyaka Parmeshwari is considered by her devotees to be a form of Sri Parvati. Vasavi, as she is also called, emphasizes virtues of love and character.

Deities in the southwest *mandapa* include Sri Ayyappan and Maha Ganapati. Maha Ganapati, of black granite, resides in this corner *mandapa* while Sri Ganesha remains in the Sri Ganesha Temple. Ganapati (Ganesha) is the first son of Sri Shiva and Sri Parvati. Sri Ayyappan is regarded as the third son of Lord Shiva and the son of Mohini, in whose form Lord Vishnu appeared. He is also called Hariharaputra—son of Vishnu (Hari) and Shiva (Hara). His most traditional temple is on top of the high hill of Sabari, or Sabarimala in Chengannur, Kerala, India. Ayyappan guards us from evil spirits. Moreover, he endows us with blessings and wisdom (*jnana*), leading to salvation.

PAGE 64, TOP: The outer walls of the Meenakshi Temple are lined with delicate pillars and finely crafted ornamentation.

PAGE 64, BOTTOM: The main deity in the temple, Goddess Meenakshi. She is the consort of Lord Sundareshwara (Shiva).

PAGE 65: Standing one behind the other, the towers of the Meenakshi Temple. The impressive *rajagopura* to the right has stepped levels decorated with miniature buildings. In the forefront is the south entrance.

Hindu Temples in North America

Paschima Kasi
Sri Viswanatha Temple
Flint, Michigan

In the late seventies a dream evolved among the Hindus settled in the mid-Michigan area to set up a self-perpetuating religious and cultural organization that could fulfill the spiritual and cultural needs of the Hindu community. An initiative toward this goal was taken up when a group of about 30 devotees gathered on November 25, 1979, at the residence of one of the devotees in Flint to discuss the possibilities. During this meeting, guided by the inspiration of Swami Chinmayananda, the group initiated the idea of establishing a Hindu temple.

As a result of this meeting, a committee consisting of eleven devotees was formed. It was decided that the organization would represent the best of their great Hindu heritage and foster and promote all aspects of the Hindu way of life, philosophy, and religion. It was decided to build a temple for worship and a study center for cultural activities. Subsequently, based on the committee's recommendations, a 12-acre site on Elms Road in Flint Township was acquired.

Inspired Work

On November 23, 1980, the ground-breaking ceremony (*Bhumi Puja*) was performed for the construction of the study center. Soon the project gained momentum, and generous donations for the building fund began to arrive. The construction of the study center progressed. Then, on April 14, 1981, ground-breaking ceremonies were performed for the construction of the worship center. To keep costs to a bare minimum, a devotee with an engineering background assumed the voluntary role of the Managing Trustee, Engineer, General Contractor, and Supervisor. After getting plans, approvals, and finances in place, the construction of the temple proceeded. The study center was completed in June 1981, and the community immediately started using the center for many of its programs.

A part of the temple was completed by October 1981, and the community immediately started using the center for religious services. After thorough research and consulting with many great masters, it was decided to dedicate the temple to Sri Vishwanatha and to give the campus the name of Paschima Kasi (Kasi West). The idols of the Sri Vishwanatha, Mother Vishalakshi, and Lord Sri Vighneshwara were ordered. The idols were crafted by renowned temple artisans (*shilpis*) in Mysore, India, and then shipped to Flint in September 1982.

In December 1981 Sadguru Sant Keshavadas visited the temple, conducted 108 *Satyanarayana Vratam*, and opened the Free Medical Clinic as a humanitarian service to the needy population in the local community. This work of service was dedicated to Lord Vaidyanatha.

During 1980, 1981, and 1982, Swami Chinmayananda had visited Flint several times and inspired the community to proceed with their temple-building plans. It was Swamiji's inspiration that brought the community together and inspired them to realize their goals. One of the devotees among the organizers took a one-month trip to India, visiting many temples there to study their organization and management.

PAGES 66 and 67: A perspective view of the portals of the Paschima Kasi Sri Vishwanatha Temple, Flint, Michigan.

PAGE 68: A view of the detailed work on the structure of the building.

PAGE 69: A view of the three *vimanas* above the main sanctum sanctorums.

These new learnings facilitated temple planning and expedited the process of temple construction. This was the third Hindu temple to be built in the United States.

The *Pratishthana* and inauguration were set for October 27 through 31, 1982. After the gala arrangements were completed, the inauguration of the temple took place in the presence of many spiritual masters and community leaders, along with thousands of devotees.

To date, this is the only Hindu temple dedicated to Lord Sri Vishwanatha (Lord Shiva) in the United States and Canada. Now being made manifest were the fruits of many years of dedicated effort, commitment, and the contributions of many concerned, devoted persons who had been inspired by many great masters and supported by the blessings of the great Sri Vishwanatha. Swami Dayananda Saraswati, a learned spiritual master, performed the *Pranapratishtha* of the temple, in the presence of Swami Chinmayananda and other Hindu spiritual masters.

The large hall (*mahamandapa*) was finished in 1984. The towered roofs (*vimanas*) over the sanctuaries for Sri Vishwanatha, Sri Vighneshwara, and Sri Vishalakshi and the Indianization of the temple were completed in 1986 by temple architects (*sthapatis*) Sri Sataiah and Sri Chidambaram from Bangalore, India.

The *Khumbhabhisheka* was performed in 1986 in the presence of Swami Dayananda Saraswati, Swami Bala Gangadharanatha, and Sadguru Sant Keshavadas.

Deities and Celebrations

The main deity, Sri Vishwanatha, is represented in the form of a *Shivalinga*, the Divine captured in a formless form. The *Shivalinga* is made of black granite, which

PAGE 70: Detailed work on one of the *vimanas*.

PAGE 71, BOTTOM LEFT: Detailed work on the main building.

PAGE 71, BOTTOM RIGHT: Line drawing of four-faced *Shivalinga* called *Mukhalinga*. *Line drawing courtesy of V. Ganapati Sthapati & Associates, Chennai, India.*

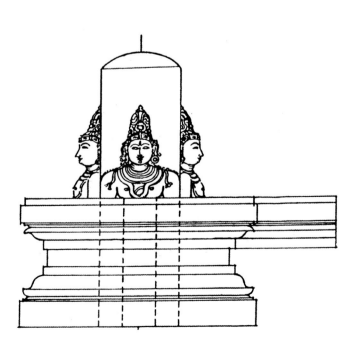

was sculpted in Mysore, India.

A *linga* has three parts. The lowest part, which is square in shape, is called *brahmabhaga*; the middle part, which is octagonal in shape, is called *vishnubhaga*, and the upper part, which is cylindrical, is the *rudrabhaga*, to which the worship is offered. *Shakti* is thought to reside in the uppermost part of the *linga*.

Shivalinga literally means "the body of Shiva" or "sign of Shiva." Next to the symbol of *AUM* (*Om*), it is perhaps the most potent, powerful, and popular symbol in all of Hinduism. In almost all the Shiva temples, worship is generally made to *Shivalingas*. Very rarely do we come across his image in human form in the sanctum sanctorum of any Shiva temple.

It is interesting to note that unlike the Vedic people, who regarded the cow as a sacred animal, the followers of Shiva venerate the bull. It is because Nandi the Bull is Shiva's vehicle. In all Shiva temples, we find that Nandi is placed right in front of the image of Lord Shiva, facing the image of Shiva and looking at him. When a devotee goes to a Shiva temple, he or she first offers salutations to Nandi and only afterward to Shiva's image.

According to Vedic legend, whenever *asuras* (demons) come to dominate the universe, Shiva is reincarnated to destroy that evil.

For believers, Shiva is also seen to be the cause of causes, and the *Shivalinga* represents Shiva as the cause of creation. This may appear as a paradox, given that Shiva is considered the destructive aspect of the Hindu Trinity. However, for something new to originate, an existing thing has to be destroyed, just as one day must end for the next day to begin or the apple blossom to die for the fruit to be born. According to Hindu thought, destruction is not ruin, but only a change of form. Hence the *Shivalinga* can be considered to be the representation of destructive construction. It is also considered to be that which survives *Pralaya*, the ultimate dissolution and end of all.

In the temple, Sri Vighneshwara and Sri Vishalakshi, as the supporting deities, are placed on the left and the right sides (respectively) of Lord Sri Vishwanatha (*Shivalinga*). If we understand the temple as the two-dimensional cross-section of a three-dimensional man, the deity, in this instance Shiva, is the *Paramatman*, the Supreme Self. Sri Vishalakshi symbolizes the cosmic energy of spiritual intelligence, and Lord Vighneshwara (Vinayaka or Ganesha) represents the discriminative intelligence of the physical personality.

Just outside the sanctum are additional deities representing various aspects of Hindu belief and tradition. The Navagrahas, the nine celestial deities, were consecrated and inaugurated in September 1999.

One of the ancient festivals of the Hindus is *Shivaratri*, "Night of Shiva." *Shivaratri*, dedicated to Lord Shiva, is celebrated on the moonless night of the month of *Phalguna*, which is the fourteenth day in the *Krishnapaksha*, or "the dark half." Owing to a special planetary conjunction, spiritual practices done on this day are considered to be especially auspicious and beneficial. There is a reference to this in one of the *Puranas*, where Shiva himself tells Parvati Devi (the Divine Mother) that this day is particularly dear to him, and that those who perform the prescribed austerities on this day will be freed from all sins.

Paschima Kasi Sri Viswanatha Temple has celebrated *Shivaratri* as a special occasion on a grand scale every year since the inception of the temple. Thousands of devotees of Lord Shiva and spiritual seekers gather to participate in the rituals—offering ablutions (*abhisheka*), worship (*archana*), and prayers, and joining in the feeling of joy at having beheld the image of the Lord on this auspicious day. At 9:00 o'clock in the evening, *Shiva Parvati Thiru Kalaman* is celebrated with grandeur, symbolizing the great significance of marriage, life, and family. After worship and prayers throughout the night, *Shivaratri* celebrations conclude with *abhisheka* and *Prabhata Puja* at 6:00 the next morning, with the devotees and spiritual seekers fulfilling their aspirations of joy at having had *darshana* of the Lord.

Auspicious Setting

The temple is on the banks of a small tributary river to the Flint River. The tributary river makes a 180-degree turn at this location, just like the river Ganga at Varanasi, lending particular sanctity to this temple.

Kasi West represents the spirit of Varanasi in Flint, Michigan—the other capital of Lord Sri Vishwanatha. The life dream for millions of Hindus is to have *darshana* of Sri Vishwanatha on the banks of the sacred River Ganga at Varanasi (Kasi), India. Today, another option can be to visit Kasi West in the state of Michigan. It is the first *Agamic* Shiva temple in the United States, with highly trained priests and staff to serve the needs of devotees. The inspiring surroundings of the temple have created a place of tranquillity for meditation, prayer, and worship. The adjacent lake and stream, the Western counterpart of the Ganges; the Midwestern cumulus clouds that can represent for us the snowcapped Himalayas; and the *shakti* of this sacred place all magically transport us to Shiva's City of Light, Kasi.

Hindu Sabha

Brampton, Ontario

In May 1975 in the city of Brampton in Ontario, Canada, five founding members established the Hindu Sabha, a nonprofit religious organization dedicated to promoting the study, practice, and development of *Sanatana Dharma*, the eternal spiritual tradition of the Hindus, which is the sum total of Hindu culture, philosophy, and religion.

For several years after the founding of the Hindu Sabha, the members of the local Hindu community used a public school venue for their weekly prayers, but by August 1979 they were able to move into their own temple facility in Brampton. Then, in 1985, the community purchased 25 acres of land in Brampton for building a new temple to serve the needs of the growing community. The site, situated within a seven-mile drive from Pearson International Airport, provided enough space for building a multipurpose temple complex. By 1991, a vision of the new temple was in place, and the ground-breaking ceremonies were conducted in May 1992.

PAGES 74 and 75: Modern design and technology of the Hindu Sabha in Brampton, Ontario, beckon to the youth and the generations to come. Exterior ornamentation is still to be added, following the design depicted in the line drawing on pages 78-79.

PAGE 76, LEFT: Mahavishnu with his consort Lakshmi.

PAGE 76, RIGHT: Sri Krishna and Radha.

PAGE 77, LEFT: Lord Shiva and Parvati.

PAGE 77, RIGHT: Durgamata.

Unique Blend of Past and Present

The design philosophy for this temple was that it must appeal to the next generation and yet reflect traditional Hindu architecture. The design called for a combination of fiberglass and glass-block construction to admit plenty of daylight through the three towers (*shikharas*). This material was tested in Toronto for the harsh Canadian climate with its freeze-thaw cycles. The cost was very economical compared to precast concrete.

The Hindu Sabha temple is different from others because its builders broke the tradition of designing a dark *shikhara* that disallows a clear view of the space above the deity image. The design called for puncturing the *shikharas* with glass blocks and fiberglass panels, while retaining the traditional shape to identify the temple as Hindu. During the early morning hours, the inner spaces are flooded with outside light, bestowing a glow on the images of the deities within. At night, the *shikharas* become the source of light flooding out in all directions, shining like jewels against the dark sky. The main *shikhara* is 120 ft. high, beckoning worshipers to the temple both day and night. With its imposing and unique presence, the temple has become a landmark in the city of Brampton.

When the temple planners studied Hindu temple architecture, they learned that the sanctum (*vimana*) that houses the deity has a circumambulatory passageway around it, so that devotees can move in homage around the *murti* (deity image). The planners decided to assemble all the deities under one *shikhara*, thus making the best use of the space available, with one circumambulatory path (*pradakshina patha*) around the entire grouping. On entering the pillared hall, one sees the deities arranged according to their roles, with the creator of the Universe at the top.

Shiva-Parvati, with their traditional abode on a mountain, also occupy a high place in the sanctum grouping. Since Ganesha is the deity one prays to first, his image is situated at the front and at eye level.

Construction and Inauguration

Construction of the temple began in May 1994, with the first phase of construction completed in a little more than one year. At this point, the lower level, main floor external shell, and most of the roof were complete (the *shikharas* were completed in 1999-2000). The temple was inaugurated with traditional ceremonies in June 1995. During his same time, the *Jagdamba Mata Murti Pranapratishtha* was performed, in the presence of His Holiness former Jagat Guru Shankaracharya Swami Satyamitranand Giriji Maharaj.

In February 1996 the *Shiva Darbar Pranapratishtha* was conducted by His Holiness Gopaldham Pithadhishwar Swami Gopal Sharan Devacharya Ji of Vrindavan. In October 1996, *Sri Rasha Krishna Pranapratishtha* was conducted, again by His Holiness Gopaldham Pithadhishwar Swami Gopal Sharan Devacharya Ji.

Many inaugural ceremonies and special celebrations followed:

August 1997: 1008 *Havan Yajna* and *Sri Ram Darbar Pranapratishtha*—conducted by His Holiness former Jagat Guru Shankaracharya Swami Satyamitranand Giriji Maharaj.

June 1998: *Vishal Bhagwati Jagran*—conducted by Sri Narindra Chanchal Ji and party from India. More than 15,000 devotees benefited from Ma Jagdamba's blessings.

June1998: *Sri Lakshmi Narayan Pranapratishtha*—conducted by Jagadguru

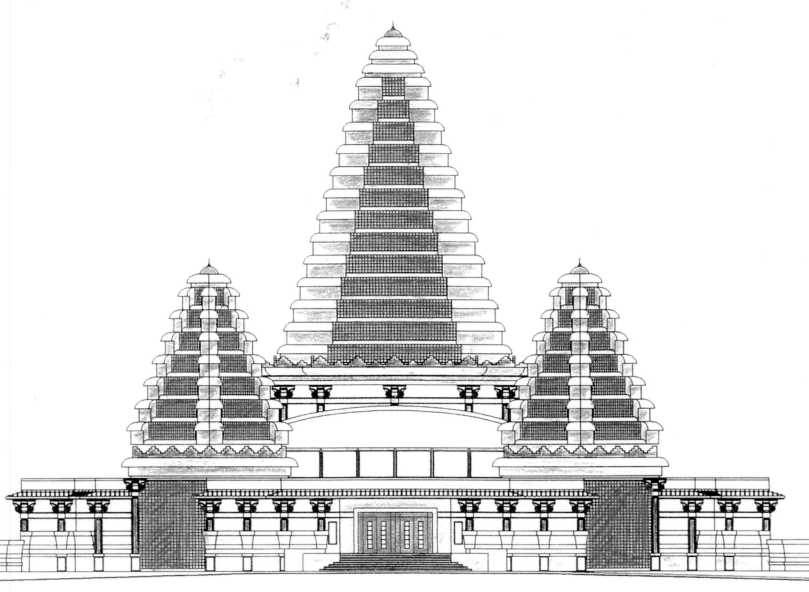

Mahamandaleshwar Shri Shri Yogiraj Swami Mohan Dasji Vairagi.

September1998: A melodious *Srimad Bhagavat Kath*—offered by Sri Mridul Goswami Krishan Ji of Vrindavan.

October 1998: *Diwali*—celebrated at the temple by more than 10,000 devotees.

July 1999: *Sri Hanumanji Murti Prana-pratishtha*—conducted by Swami Mohan-dass Ji Varagi.

The temple has approximately 32,000 sq. ft. of constructed space, including the lower level. The main floor is approximately 17,000 sq. ft., including 4,000 sq. ft. of altar space that houses the following deities: Lord Vishnu, Ram Parivar, Radha and Lord Krishna, Lord Shiva and Parvati, Durgamata, and Sri Hanuman. The main prayer hall (*mandapa*) accommodates more than 1,000 people, drawing many devotees to the temple even during normal weekday events.

All the columns, ceilings, and entablatures are to be completed with traditional sculptural motifs. This design is already complete and will be realized during the next phase of construction.

A Community Hall and kitchen on the lower level is approximately 15,000 sq. ft. in area. The lower level also offers facilities

PAGE 78, TOP LEFT: View of the temple at night. At night the structure can be seen from a great distance because of the light emanating from the *shikharas*.

PAGES 78 and 79, BOTTOM: Line drawing of the temple with ornamentation.
Line drawing courtesy of Arun W. Pradhan, Ontario, Canada.

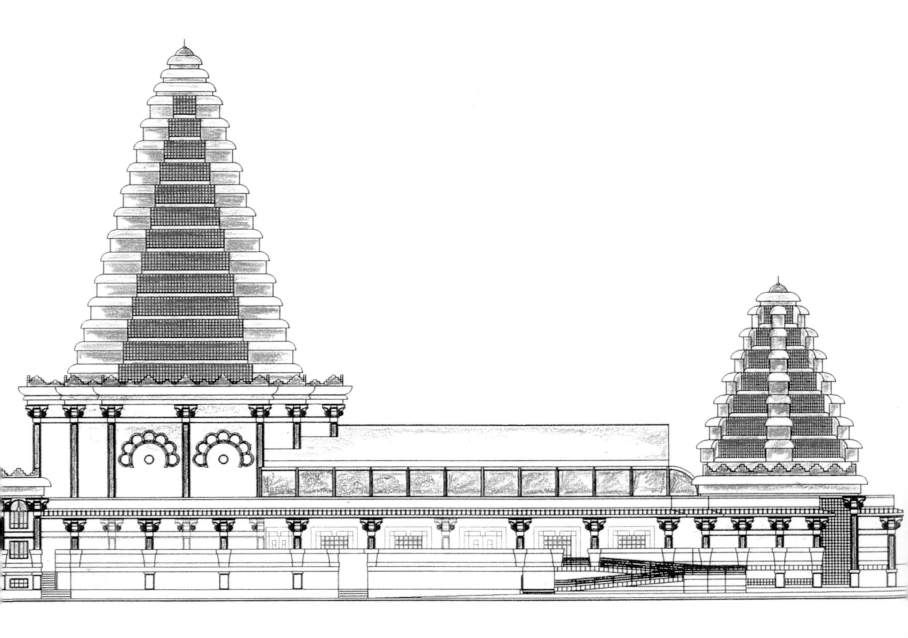

for conducting concurrent activities such as Hindi language classes, music classes, and senior citizens' meetings. A standalone multipurpose community facility is projected for construction over a period of time in the future.

Current Goals, Future Visions

Set amid serene surroundings on a sprawling site of 25 acres, the project set out to provide a setting for conducting the main Hindu sacraments and rites and a community hall for performing personal functions such as marriages. Building activity will continue for years to come to accommodate all

the needs of the current temple membership and to reflect the wishes of the growing and vibrant Hindu community in the Brampton area.

Hindu devotion is primarily individual. The halls are not for mass worship but are more a place for meeting and for listening to *bhajans*. Considering all aspects of religion and tradition, the temple planners have married the past and the present, with a futuristic view of creating a place of worship, a meeting place for the community to identify as their own, and a facility that would attract generations to come for conducting their own religious and community activities.

Hindu Community Organization Dayton
Fairborn, Ohio

The Hindu Community Organization in Dayton, Ohio, was incorporated on December 18, 1976, and it was during this time that the possibilities for constructing a place of worship for local area Hindus was considered. Before this, the Hindus in the community used to meet at a local community center on the third Sunday of each month to conduct *bhajans* and hear discourses.

In 1979 definitive ideas of building the temple began to evolve, and during 1981 the move toward looking for land began in earnest. Another institution named the Bharatiya Partnership was formed in 1982 by a group of Hindu physicians, who purchased 52 acres of land, of which 5.5 acres were donated to the Hindu Community Organization. This parcel of land in Beavercreek, near the city of Dayton, became the site for the projected temple.

The temple was designed by Chander Saxena, a leading architect from Columbus, Ohio, along with renowned temple architect Dr. V. Ganapati Sthapati from Chennai, India. From the very beginning of the project, Swamiji Brahmasri Dhayanadha Sarasvathi of Adarsha Vidyalaya also played a major role in the shaping of the Hindu temple at Dayton.

PAGES 82 and 83: A perspective view of the portals of the Hindu Temple in Dayton, Ohio. The majestic *rajagopura* looms in the foreground. At the far right can be seen the three *vimanas* over the main sanctum sanctorums.

PAGE 84, TOP: The main deity in the temple, Sri Satyanarayana.

PAGE 84, BOTTOM: Side view showing the *balipitha, dhvajastambha,* and a minor shrine.

PAGE 85: Decorated *vimana* with a *kalasha* on the top.

Hindu Temples in North America

Bhumi Puja was held on May 16, 1982, with the ground-breaking ceremony being conducted in June 1982. The ceremony was conducted over a weekend under the guidance of Sri Rangaswamy Iyengar, a priest from the Balaji Temple in Pittsburgh, Pennsylvania. On that Friday, a special *puja* was performed by a small group of devotees, who worshiped Vighneshwara in the form of an image made of turmeric powder. The following night and day were marked by heavy rains, which cleared up by Sunday, revealing a remarkable and auspicious occurrence: the Vighneshwara image, which should have been washed away, had remained intact.

It took two long years and a tremendous amount of work to acquire the formal approval of the Beavercreek's city government for construction to proceed. Once approval was in place, work started on temple construction, and the first phase was completed in late summer of 1984. The first formal service conducted was on *Janmashtami* day, August 19, 1984. This day marked the culmination of years of

effort by the local Hindu community, and the beginning of new projects that have led to the splendid structure that stands today.

Idols were then ordered from India, and the Sri Venkatachalapati image (*vigraha*) arrived in May 1985. Sri Rama and Sri Krishna *vigrahas* were received in August 1985, all of which were installed in the traditional ceremonial manner.

A major project was undertaken during 1987 and 1988 when four towered roofs (*vimanas*) were erected over the shrines of the deities. At this point, temple artisans (*shilpis*) arrived from India to provide the traditional detailing to the temple's structure. The fine and intricately detailed work on the temple is a clear reflection of the skills of Dr. V. Ganapati Sthapati and his team of *shilpis*.

After months of preparation, the temple's three towers were completed and sanctified by the grand *Kumbhabhisheka* ceremony that took place on July 15 and 17, 1988.

All the work that had been done to that

point only served to further motivate the local Hindu community. A plan to erect a tower (*rajagopura*) over the main entrance, the temple's crowning feature, was undertaken and quickly completed. The year 1993 also saw the installation of the temple flagpole (*dhvajastambha*) and pedestal of offerings (*balipitha*). It was later in the year 2000 that official priest's quarters were constructed, and the temple finally stood complete.

The Hindu Temple of Dayton, Ohio, is the first temple to have been constructed in the state, and is frequented by residents of Indiana, West Virginia, Kentucky, and people from all over Ohio. When the construction of the temple began, the local Hindu community was comprised of only 350 families, but since that time that figure has almost doubled.

This temple also bears the distinction of being one of the few temples in the United States that was constructed without any loans or interest paid to any financial institution. That fact marks this temple as the fruit of true devotion, and as a great example of the Hindu community's commitment and contribution to both strengthening and diversifying the great nation of America.

PAGE 86: View of the towering *rajagopura* in a splendid garden setting.

PAGE 87: Front view of the temple.

PAGE 88, TOP: Statuette adorning an inside wall of the temple.

PAGE 88, BOTTOM: *Mahamandapa* with the main shrine in the center.

PAGE 89, TOP: Detail of a carved wooden door of the temple with a bell at the center.

PAGE 89, BOTTOM: View of the *vimanas* over the main sanctum sanctorums.

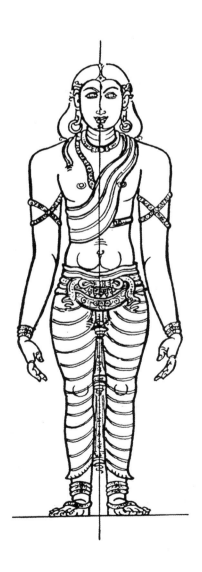

Connecticut Valley Hindu Temple Society
Middletown, Connecticut

The Connecticut Valley Hindu Temple Society was founded in Hartford in the year 1979, when a few devotees got together with the principal aim of serving the cultural, religious, and social needs of the Indian community in the State of Connecticut in particular and across North America in general. Although the genesis of a commitment to build a temple in central Connecticut occurred that same year, the idea can be traced as far back as 1971, when a few devotees were persuaded by friends to initiate and lead a *bhajan* group. Monthly meetings for recitation of stanzas from the *Bhagavad Gita* were followed by *puja* in living rooms and basements often adorned with colorfully decorated altars. The completion of all eighteen chapters of the *Gita* was followed by a great celebration in 1976, when the whole process began all over again. The celebrations of major Hindu festivals were generally held in various places such churches, community centers, and college and university classrooms.

The Society's goals were to build and maintain a Hindu temple complex in the central Connecticut Valley region to serve as a common place of worship; to organize religious and spiritual discourses, study of religious texts, and yoga and meditation classes; to offer facilities for Indian language studies and instructions in Indian classical and devotional music; to arrange for publication of material connected with Hinduism and Hindu culture, keeping in mind the special interests of children and youth as well as adults; to provide facilities and organize cultural events in cooperation with other cultural organizations in the Connecticut Valley region; and to engage in charitable and educational activities. In January 1982, the decision was made to dedicate the temple to Lord Satyanarayana. The selection of Satyanarayana as the presiding deity for the temple was unanimous, as he represents a combination of the Hindu Trinity—Brahma, Vishnu, and Maheshwara.

During 1984, many sites in different towns of Connecticut were considered. After extensive property hunting, a wonderful piece of land of approximately 8 acres was purchased on Training Hill Road, Middletown, Connecticut. This site was selected for many reasons, especially its proximity to Wesleyan University, which is famous for its classical Indian music program under the direction of Sangita Kalanidhi Tanjore Vishwanathan. Also it was central to the State of Connecticut. This action created confidence in the Hindu community that this team could achieve its dream of building the envisioned Sri Satyanarayana Temple.

Initial Planning

Poring over the drawings for the building and figuring out how to make the temple as inclusive of all Hindu deities as possible became an important issue for the members. Work started in earnest on temple plans as the team worked together with Barun Basu, an eminent architect in Connecticut with experience in building temples according to the Hindu tradition. The Satyanarayana temple is complex not only for its compliance with the edicts laid out in the ancient scriptures called the *Agama Shastras,* but also in its goal to weave together the social and community requirements of Hindus in a foreign land while endowing the facilities with the peace and dignity inherent in all temples. This temple complex of almost 30,000 sq. ft. represents

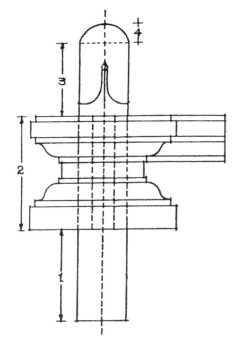

PAGE 94: *Dvarapalaka,* exhibiting elegant design and intricate detail.

PAGE 95: Navagraha (Nine Planets). The sculptures of *grahas* (planets) in Hindu temples are oriented in such a way that no two *grahas* face each other. Eight *grahas* surround Surya (the sun). Surya faces east, and each *graha* faces one of the four directions. The icons of *grahas* in Indian temples represent adoration of the cosmos as symbolized by the planets of the solar system. Performing Navagraha *homa* is very auspicious. Offerings include sesame seeds, rice, or any of nine designated grains.

Center: Surya (Sun); color is red, gem is ruby, offering is wheat, and prayers are offered on Sunday. Front of center: Sani (Saturn); color is black, gem is blue sapphire, offering is sesame, and prayers are offered on Saturday. Front left: Ketu (Nodal Planet); color is green, gem is cat's eye, offering is gram, and prayers are offered on any day of the week. Front right: Rahu (Nodal Planet); color is blue, gem is topaz, offering is urad dal, and prayers are offered on any day of the week. Back of center: Sukra (Venus); color is white, gem is diamond, offering is black-eyed peas, and prayers are offered on Friday. Back left: Budha (Mercury); color is yellow, gem is emerald, offering is moong dal, and prayers are offered on Wednesday. Back right: Chandra (Moon); color is white, gem is pearl, offering is rice, and prayers are offered on Monday. Center left: Guru (Jupiter); color is white, gem is white sapphire, offering is chana dal, and prayers are offered on Thursday. Center right: Angaraka (Mars); color is dark red, gem is coral, offering is toor dal, and prayers are offered on Tuesday.

a dedication to preserve the works of ancient craftsmen and the memory of past images of rituals by the first generation of Hindu devotees in Connecticut. The building exploits the elements of orientation for energy conservation and optimization of comfort levels, as well as employing current technologies in lighting, acoustics, and monumentality.

During the planning process a major criterion was that of growing and blending within the surrounding community, while generating reverence for the Hindu tradition and rituals. It was vital to create a place where young and old alike could be proud to identify with the temple not only for religious functions but also for cultural and social education.

The purpose of any temple is to help us to commune with God. If we delve deep into the prayers, practices, and rituals of temple worship, we will certainly reap many spiritual benefits. Everything we see the priests doing when they perform *pujas* or various rituals has a symbolic meaning. Everything that we offer to God is through the heart, meaning that we are practicing *bhakti yoga*, the path of devotion. Our *bhajans, kirtans, japa,* and *puja* are all meant to melt the heart.

The ground-breaking ceremony, *Bhumi Puja,* was performed in 1986, with the result that the adrenaline really started to pump among the community members to implement the first phase of the project. October 1989 saw the commencement of Phase I, which included the community hall portion of the construction. Swami Satchidananda inaugurated the first phase in 1989 and blessed the efforts to build a temple for Lord Satyanarayana. The community hall served as a place of worship and a place where other Hindu and cultural and educational activities could be conducted with pride and joy.

BUDHA

PAGE 96: *Vimana* with *kalasha* on the top. The large skylight above the *vimana* brings natural light into the temple.

PAGE 97: A wide view of the main sanctum sanctorum, minor shrines, and *mahamandapa* with polished wooden floor.

Temple Construction and Deity Installation

Construction of the temple itself was completed by the end of 1998. The images (*vigrahas*) of Lord Satyanarayana, his consorts Sri Devi and Bhudevi; Mahaganapati; and the Navagrahas were sculpted from granite in authentic Hoysala style by a gifted temple artisan (*shilpi*) of Katriguppa near Bangalore. The sanctum sanctorum phase of the temple was complete in 1999 by Selvaraj Sthapati and his team of eight *shilpis*, who came from India exclusively for the purpose.

The Hindu immigrant community has set a landmark in the history of the state of Connecticut. Our 20-year-old dream is now a reality. The Hindu community has been growing steadily in the state, and the increased participation in temple activities is a sure sign that the Society is serving the religious needs of the community.

The *Pratishthapana* of Sri Ganesha, Sri Satyanarayana, Sri Sri Devi, Sri Bhudevi, and Navagrahas took place on Sunday, May 30, 1999, *Purnima* (full moon) day, which was the crowning event of installation of Lord Satyanarayana. The event itself constituted an important milestone in the establishment and growth of a significant temple on this continent, fulfilling the dream of committed devotees over the last twenty years.

The installation ceremonies for Sri Rama Parivar, Sri Mahavira and Sri Subramanya, Valli, and Devayani were also held in the same year. The *Pratishthapana* for Sri Ayyappan, Sri Radha and Krishna, Sri Shiva and Sri Venkateshwara were held in 2000. Sri Durga Mata *Pratishtha*, held in June 2001, symbolizes the completion of the temple as planned 20 years ago.

Many believe that the United States of America is the land of Mahavishnu, evidenced by the fact that the national bird is an eagle (Vishnu's vehicle) and that a conch, so prominent in Hindu rituals, is featured on some editions of the quarter coin. Even though quite a few temples have been erected in the United States for Lord Vishnu or his *avataras*, this is the first time we have the installation of the celebrated form of Satyanarayana. It is not a limited form of an *avatara* but the full-fledged form of Mahavishnu in all his glory and with his consorts. In the form of Satyanarayana, Mahavishnu is auspicious, most generous, and fulfills the wishes of his devotees. Invocation and worship of Satyanarayana is the easiest route for ridding oneself of worldly worries, and for securing the desired happiness and peace of mind.

Lord Satyanarayana's grace is described in a Hindu book called *Skanda Purana*. He has four hands like Lord Vishnu; however, his fourth hand does not hold a lotus like Vishnu, but rather, it is extended upward to bless the people. He has a dark complexion. In his two upper hands he holds a discus (a symbol of power) and a conch shell (a symbol of existence). With one lower hand extended downward, he asks devotees to have faith and surrender to him for protection.

The physical beauty of the images, the buildings, and the verdant wooded estate surrounding the temple are breathtaking. They are soothing to the senses and help to focus on the higher values and truths of our existence. The sunsets on the Powder Ridge Hills suffuse the sky and imbue the arboreal features of the site with a reddish golden hue.

Connecticut Valley is now blessed with a full-fledged Hindu temple for the community to enjoy. Currently it is the only Hindu temple in Connecticut constructed according to the traditional Hindu religion and the *Agama Shastras*.

International Society of Divine Love

Austin, Texas

Established in 1990, Barsana Dham is the main U.S. Center of the International Society of Divine Love. It provides the rare opportunity to experience the true devotional environment that prevailed in the ashrams of the historic saints of Vrindaban (Vrindavan) and Barsana in India 500 years ago.

This beautiful 230-acre property in Texas is a representation of the holy land of Braj in India where Shree Radha Rani and Shree Krishn appeared 5,000 years ago. Areas of Barsana Dham have been developed to be places for devotional inspiration and meditation. All the important places of Braj, such as Govardhan, Radha Kund, Prem Sarovar, Shyam Kuti, Man Mandir, and Mor Kuti are represented at Barsana Dham, providing a peaceful and devotional atmosphere for all visitors to the site.

Divine Dream

Inspired by the grace of his supreme Spiritual Master, Bhatki-yog-rasavatar, Jagadguru Shree Kripaluji Maharaj, His Divinity Swami Prakashanand Saraswati, the Founder of International Society of Divine Love, thought of creating something very special for the people of the West where they could have similar benefits as if they were in Vrindaban.

His vision was not just to buy a piece of land and construct an edifice on it. It had to be the revelation of Radha's grace, as all holy places in India are either related to the descent of God on Earth, or they mark a place where a great saint once lived.

In 1988, during the annual intensive (spiritual camp), Shree Swamiji announced that Barsana Dham would be created in the United States. Devotees were thrilled with this news and, guided by Shree Swamiji, started looking for suitable property, a site that would include scenic wooded areas with a stream, as well as harvestable land. Shree Swamiji personally went to many places and saw a number of properties in Pennsylvania, upstate New York, New Jersey, Washington, D.C., Virginia, Maryland, Northern California, and others. None of the properties were suitable according to the divine dream of Shree Swamiji—until the perfect site was found near Austin, Texas.

The property was purchased it in 1990. On it were several houses and a 130-year-old stone building, all in a very run-down condition. The devotees renovated the stone building, built houses, a large kitchen, and a dining hall and moved in. The first intensive (spiritual camp) at Barsana Dham was held in October 1991.

In 1991 Shree Swamiji designated the most important places of Braj—the land of Radha Krishn in India—at Barsana Dham. The site for Shree Raseshwari Radha Rani Temple and ashram was decided. In the following years, Vilasgarh, Prem Sarovar, Shyam Kuti, and Govardhan Hill were established. The stream that runs across the property was named Kalindi (the Yamuna River of Vrindaban), and the hill was named Barsana Hill. Radha Kund, Man Mandir, and Mor Kuti were also located.

Shree Swamiji personally planned and designed the Shree Raseshwari Radha Rani Temple and Ashram complex, which includes at the back of the temple Radha Kund, a lotus-shaped reflecting pond with fountains and small waterfalls, and Maharas Mandal, a circular area that represents the place where Radha Krishn and the *gopis* (maiden-saints of Braj) sing and dance together.

The design and construction follow the guidelines of the *Radhikopanishad, Gopal Tapniyopanishad, Devi Bhagavatam, Bhagavatam,* and the writings of the great masters of Vrindaban. Shree Swamiji personally explained every detail to the architects. Temple artisans (*shilpis*) from India worked on all the intricate work seen in the entire building. It is an excellent blending of

North Indian, South Indian, ancient, and modern styles of architecture. The floral patterns on the entrance doors, the entrance of the shrine, and the style of columns are all artfully crafted. The building holds 84 columns and includes five levels. The shrine and the *satsang* hall are together. The graceful Radha Kund and the Maharas Mandal, which has 64 columns, are also part of the temple complex.

The temple is named after Shree Radha Rani, who has hundreds of names, of which Raseshwari is one of the most important. Raseshwari signifies the absolute sovereignty of Radha's blissful charm, beauty, love, graciousness, and kindness, which encourage a devotee to feel that he or she can receive the Grace of Radha Rani and become one of the divine associates of Radha Krishn in Vrindaban.

A unique and important feature of the temple meditation hall (*satsang* hall) is that it depicts the essence of the entire Bharatiya philosophy, so that a visitor can actually see it all at one place and determine the devotional goal of his life. The most important themes of all the important scriptures are described in a continuous panel on all four sides of the hall under a realistic depiction of the sky with scattered clouds. The theme of the *Gita* is on the east side, the Upanishads on the west side, the *Bhagavatam* toward the shrine side, and the *Puranas* and the *Ramayana* on the north side toward the main entrance. Along with the writings, extraordinarily beautiful and devotional pictures of Radha, Krishn, and Radha Krishn also glorify the panels of the hall. In this way the temple hall itself stands as a source of divine knowledge that relates to all the important aspects of devotion.

The temple is designed in such a way that it captures the hearts of devotees, filling their minds with devotional excitement. On both sides of the shrine large glass windows overlook the hill and the beauty of native flowers. The devotee, while sitting in the spacious *satsang* hall in front of the shrine can feel the devotional energy and spiritual serenity that was found in the ancient ashrams of our Vrindaban saints.

Divine Celebrations

On *Sharad Purnima* day of October 1992, the foundation-laying ceremony of Shree Raseshwari Radha Rani Temple was celebrated. Shree Swamiji had personally brought the holy waters of all the important ponds of Braj, along with the water from the Yamuna River. He also brought the holy dust (soil) of Barsana, Vrindaban,

and Govardhan, collected from very special places where Radha Krishn conducted their divine pastimes (*lilas*).

All of this was laid in the center of the temple foundation by Shree Swamiji. Devotees could feel a great surge of divine energy around the foundation area. *Sharad Purnima* is the day when Radha Krishn descended to Vrindaban in Braj and revealed the divine bliss of *Maharas*— when Radha Krishn fully revealed their divine love, which an unlimited number of *gopis* experienced while playing, singing and dancing with Radha Krishn. That's why Shree Swamiji chose that particular day for laying the foundation of the temple, and, in this way, Vrindaban and Barsana (the divine abodes of Radha Krishn) were both established at Barsana Dham. It is only through the Grace of Radha Rani and Jagadguru Shree Kripaluji Maharaj that Shree Swamiji has established this Barsana Dham in its true form, where sincere devotees of God can feel blessed in the same way as they feel when they visit Braj, the land of Radha Krishn, in India. Since the physical appearance of Barsana Dham is greatly reminiscent of Braj (Barsana) in India, it becomes very easy for devotees of Radha Krishn to remember their *lilas* in this setting.

During *Maharas*. the atmosphere of Vrindaban was perfumed with the scent of flowers from all the seasons, which bloomed together to intensify the charm of the full moon night of *Sharad Purnima*. The breeze was fragrant, the sky was clear with some scattered clouds, and the weather was pleasant. Shree Swamiji incorporated all the feelings of these writings of the *Bhagavatam* and produced it in the form of Shree Raseshwari Radha Rani Temple.

Some 5,000 years ago the world felt the divine breeze on *Sharad Purnima* night, when the Shree Raseshwari Radha Rani revealed her divine love form in *Maharas* in Braj, India. On *Sharad Purnima* of October 8, 1995, she glorified the Earth once again with the manifestation of her divine Grace at Barsana Dham. As the Brajwasis rejoiced when Shree Radha appeared in Braj thousands of years ago, devotees from around the world joyously made their journey to Barsana Dham in Texas for *Sharad Purnima* in 1995 to witness her appearance in the form of her image (*murti*) in the newly completed Shree Raseshwari Radha Rani Temple.

The deity establishment ceremony, *Murti Pratishtha Mahotsav*, of Shree Raseshwari Radha Rani began on October 6 with recitations from the Vedas. On October 7,

PAGE 104, BOTTOM: Detail work on the walls and pillars of the temple. The vivid colors are derived from the traditional decorations of Hindu temples. In the main hall, on each of the four walls, there are two decorative bands depicting the divine pastimes (*lilas*) of Radha Krishn and other details from the sacred scriptures.

PAGE 105, BOTTOM LEFT: Detail of ornamental and decorative work on the pillars that line the front veranda.

PAGE 105, BOTTOM RIGHT: The *shikhara* of the Shree Raseshwari Radha Rani Temple. The *shikhara* rises just above the sanctum sanctorum housing Shree Raseshwari Radha Rani.

throughout the day, international spiritual leaders (*mahatmas*) delivered inspiring discourses about the significance of Shree Raseshwari Radha Rani and the path of *raganuga bhakti* (divine-love-consciousness) that Shree Swamiji is teaching to the world.

During the evening program of devotional chanting, the devotees, dignitaries, and visiting *mahatmas* experienced an extraordinary bliss and Grace in the remembrance of the divine names of Radha Krishn. In the anticipation of the next day's ceremony, many devotees spent almost the whole night celebrating and garlanding the temple, and those who were able to sleep dreamed of the celebrations to come. The morning of *Sharad Purnima*, October 8, 1995, began with the grand chariot procession (*rath yatra*), in which the 3-ft. deity of Shree Raseshwari Radha Rani, wearing all her jewelry, rode a beautiful chariot that was decorated with roses and marigolds grown at Barsana Dham.

The devotees, their hearts thrilled with their first *darshana* of the deity, chanted, played musical instruments, and danced as they followed the chariot along the procession route. Shree Swamiji performed the first *arati* at the temple entrance, followed by *arati* by all the guest *mahatmas*.

All along the procession of Shree Raseshwari Radha Rani, a helicopter flying overhead showered flowers from the sky. It was like the celestial gods and goddesses overjoyously showering hundreds of thousands of flowers on Radha Rani as a sign of their deep gratitude to her.

The procession to the temple, led by Shree Swamiji, stopped at the main entrance of the temple. Flowers were still being showered from the sky, and devotees standing on the roof of the portico were also showering flowers on Radha Rani and on the dancing crowd of *mahatmas* and other devotees. All the guest *mahatmas* were singing "Radhey" and dancing hand in hand with Shree Swamiji. The scene was unlike anything anyone had ever seen before. The *mahatmas* were dancing on a path covered with flowers, amid more flowers being showered down upon them from above, their hearts filled with the joy of the gracious celebrations of Shree Raseshwari Radha Rani.

The long-awaited moment had come for Shree Swamiji to reveal the vision of Radha Rani within the temple sanctum. He

entered the main temple first and came out again after a few minutes. The sanctum was now open for everyone's *darshana*. Guest *mahatmas* had the first *darshana*, followed by all the devotees.

Shree Swamiji, at the request of devotees, graced the occasion by delivering a speech, first in English and then in Hindi, describing the secret of the Raseshwari name. He also said that the prime aim of all religions is to experience the blissfulness of God, which is divine and undivided. He explained that religious diversities would automatically disappear if (keeping aside the ritualistic and cultural differences) people began to desire to experience that undivided love of God.

Abode of Radha Krishn in America

Barsana Dham was established under the auspices of the International Society of Divine Love (ISDL), a registered nonprofit, religious, educational, and charitable organization. ISDL was founded by His Divinity Swami Prakashanand Saraswati in India in 1975, in New Zealand in 1978, and in the United States in 1981.

ISDL has two main objectives: to reveal the eternal knowledge of the Vedas, the *Gita*, *Bhagavatam*, and other holy scriptures to interested souls, and to impart the practical process of divine upliftment called "divine love-consciousness," which is based on the ancient path of *raganuga bhakti*.

ISDL has established ashrams in India, New Zealand, and the United States. ISDL centers throughout the United States hold regular *satsangs* on Wednesdays and Sundays for the general public, who are welcome to come and receive the knowledge of divine love and experience the bliss of the chanting of the divine names.

The dawn of the divine energy, Barsana Dham has played a key role in that rejuvenation. The installation of the deity of Shree Raseshwari Radha Rani at Barsana Dham signifies the introduction of harmony and peace in the world. The deity represents the presence of Shree Raseshwari Radha Rani on the land of the United States of America, and Barsana Dham represents the divine abode of Radha Krishn. Since the temple was constructed with consideration for all aspects of the devotional feelings of devotees, it has become a place of pilgrimage for countless devotees living in the Western world.

Hindu Temple and Cultural Society of USA

Bridgewater, New Jersey

In the 1980s, a group of devotees pondered the idea of building a full-fledged Hindu temple in central New Jersey because of the heavy concentration of Hindus in that area and easy accessibility to many potential worshipers living in the Tri-State area of New York, New Jersey, and Pennsylvania. The result of those early plans is the beautiful Venkateswara Temple in Bridgewater. It is centrally located in the state of New Jersey, off Routes 202/206, and is easily accessible from highways I-287, I-78, the New Jersey Turnpike, and the Garden State Parkway. The temple draws the majority of its devotees from New Jersey, New York, Pennsylvania, and Connecticut. However, visitors from all over the world visit it regularly.

The temple has received recognition as one of the premier temples in North America. The institution is proud to be able to satisfy religious, cultural, and community service needs of the Hindus in the area.

A Temple for All

The Hindu Temple and Cultural Society of USA, Inc. was incorporated in September 1989 to build a temple and cultural center to serve the religious, cultural, educational, and community needs of the region. Several devotees initiated a gift certificate program in order to raise funds and to spread the message to the community. Soon thereafter, religious services were conducted by a group of volunteers at devotees' homes to serve the religious needs of the community and to raise awareness of this temple organization.

A building with about 9 acres of land was purchased on January 28, 1992, and the temple was inaugurated on February 29, 1992. Religious functions have been conducted since then according to authentic Hindu tradition.

Dr. V. Ganapati Sthapati of Chennai was consulted for temple design, and the architectural drawings were finalized to build a Hindu temple with Sri Venkateshwara as the presiding deity. The design was based on the ancient Dravidian (South Indian) style of architecture.

The main temple is 11,000 sq. ft. in area. The Venkateswara Temple is truly a temple for Hindus, where they can worship all the main Hindu gods and goddesses. The granite idols were brought from South India, and the marble idols, from North India. Lord Sri Venkateshwara (Balaji) is the main deity (*mula vighraha*), whose granite image measures 7 ft. in height and stands impressively on a 15-in. pedestal (*pada pitha*). Other granite idols include Sri Devi, Sri Bhudevi, Sri Maha Ganesha, Sri Shiva, Sri Ambika, Sri Ayyappan, Sri Subramanya, and Navagrahas. Shrines in the temple with marble idols include Sri Durga, Sri Lakshmi Narayana, Sri Radha Krishna, Sri Rama Parivar, and Sri Hanuman. Shrines for Sri

PAGES 106 and 107: Front view of the Venkateswara Temple in New Jersey. Elegant outlines, classical statuary, and rich traditional artforms characterize this temple.

PAGE 108: Impressive silhouette of the monumental *rajagopura*, which gives access to the main temple.

PAGE 109: Side view of the temple, showing the *rajagopura* and three *vimanas* above the sanctum sanctorums.

PAGE 110: The main *vimana,* swarming with ornamentation, typifies the art of the *shilpi.*

PAGE 111: Side view of temple.

Satyanarayana and Sri Lakshmi and Sri Saraswati are also present.

Modern Construction

The ground-breaking ceremony, *Sanku-shthapana* (or *Bhumi Puja*), was performed on June 9, 1995. Construction of the traditional temple started on May 16, 1996.

The exterior building and the superstructures of the temple were built with new state-of-the-art glass-reinforced concrete (GRC) technology. GRC has many advantages over traditional temple construction. First, the GRC process ensures longevity and is applicable to extreme temperature variations experienced in northeastern United States. Computer-aided-design (CAD) techniques were used to preview the sculptures and designs before molding the finished product. Once the designs were approved, the columns, domes, and sculptures were produced in Bahrain by Indian temple artisans (*shilpis*) using precast molds and then shipped to the site for assembly. This method enabled us to build the temple in a record two years. From a structural standpoint, the technology meets the seismic codes. Our temple is a pioneer in setting a new standard in temple building, combining the ancient tradition with modern science. This is the first temple with South Indian architecture built with glass-reinforced concrete technology.

Kumbhabhisheka was celebrated in grand

style on June 7, 1998, under the auspices of H. H. Sri Sri Sri Tridandi Chinna Srimannarayana Ramanuja Jeeyar Swamiji. Thousands witnessed the once-in-a-life-time event, while a helicopter showered flowers on the temple and on the entrance-way towers (*gopuras*).

The main entrance tower (*rajagopura*) and the temple flagpole (*dhvajastambha*) were inaugurated on July 3, 1999, under the auspices of H.H. Sri Sri Sri Vidyananda Swamiji.

Future Plans

Plans are in place to construct a concrete courtyard (*prakara*) around the Sri Venkateswara Temple so that devotees can circumambulate the temple (do *pradakshina*).

The proposed *prakara* will be about 15 feet wide and will cover a total length of approximately 1,500 feet. This project is expected to be completed in two phases. Construction of concrete pillars and slabs with a small parapet wall will be part of the first phase. The second phase will involve Indianization of the structure.

A traditional Hindu temple is a miniature representation of the divine cosmos, and walking around it is equivalent to worshiping the entire cosmos. To this end, devotees walk in the *prakara* before entering the temple. The *prakara* will also provide for *ratha* (chariot) *pradakshina* and *anga pradakshina* (a form of worshipful prostration and circumambulation while lying prone on the floor with arms outstretched, circumambulating the temple by rolling).

PAGE 112, TOP: Detail work on the entrance wall shows Garudar, a mythical bird that serves as the vehicle (*vahana*) of Lord Vishnu.

PAGE 112, BOTTOM: Detail design showing Yali (mythical temple protector) on each design element adorning the outer walls.

PAGE 113, TOP: A decorative *mandapa* in the garden.

PAGE 113, BOTTOM: Details of the *rajagopura*, with two d*varapalakas* at the center.

Hindu Temple of Greater Chicago
Lemont, Illinois

Thousands of Hindu families migrated from India to the United States from the early 1960s seeking higher education and challenging careers. As the families grew and settled down, it became apparent that there was a necessity to actively encourage continuation of the traditional religious and cultural values of India. Several Asian Indian organizations sprung up during this period, providing some cultural avenues, but there were no religious institutions that the Hindus could call home.

It was the year 1977 when the then president of theTelugu Association of Greater Chicago discussed the possibility of founding a religious organization and building a temple. An ad hoc committee was formed, with the result that the Hindu Temple of Greater Chicago was established as a not-for-profit organization to serve the needs of all Hindus. The first General Body meeting was held in December 1977, and the first Governing Body for 1978 was elected.

PAGES 114 and 115: Front view of the Hindu Temple of Greater Chicago, Lemont, Illinois, also known as the Rama Temple. Dedicated to Lord Rama, this temple is one of the more traditional temples built in the United States, displaying elegant outlines and classical statuary. It is one of two temples built on the same precinct.

PAGE 116, BOTTOM LEFT: A sculptured panel inside the main temple depicting Lord Rama.

PAGE 116, BOTTOM RIGHT: A sculptured panel inside the main temple depicting, from left to right, Dasharatha, father of Sri Rama, Sita, and Sri Rama.

PAGE 117: In the foreground, a view of the *vimana* over the main sanctum sanctorum, with the *rajagopura* to the right.

Panoramic Vision

The first president and other enthusiasts had a macro-vision to integrate all the Hindus from various parts of India. Their panoramic vision included a place of worship, a place of cultural and fine arts activities, religious and language schools, and a library.

In order to meet the religious needs of all Hindus from various parts of India, it was decided to have as the presiding deity (*pradhana devata*) Sri Rama along with Sita Devi, Sri Lakshmana, and Hanuman; and Lord Vinayaka as the main deity. The next challenge was to find an appropriate site to build a traditional temple. Over 30 possible locations in the Greater Chicago area were surveyed. After considering all options, the group selected a 17.6-acre site in Lemont—a beautiful, wooded hillside property, with adjacent waterfalls.

As enthusiasm and momentum gathered, other organizations began to show interest. Architects from India and United States were chosen to draw up a master plan, and a 17-member building committee struggled hard to design a structure to satisfy all regional Hindu groups. It was a monumental achievement to have the master plan finally approved in December 1981. Padmasri S. M. Ganapati Sthapati from Andhra Pradesh was appointed chief temple architect. During May 29 to 31, 1982, a model of the temple complex was exhibited at the Second Convention of Asian Indians in America at the Palmer House in Chicago.

H. H. Gurudeva Sivaya Subramuniyaswami from Hawaii met with a few dedicated volunteers on November 3, 1982. Impressed with the enthusiasm, he promised a statute of Lord Vinayaka, which was promptly delivered on November 12, 1982. The Vinayaka was initially housed at a private residence in Lombard, where worship ceremonies commenced on Friday, November 19, 1982. In the absence of a formal priest, many members of the religious committee offered their assistance. On January 12, 1983, a statue of Lord Vinayaka, which had been originally requested, arrived from Andhra Pradesh. As worship services were moved to larger locations, ever larger numbers of devotees joined, with the *Ramanavami* celebrations drawing 400 people.

On June 17, 1984, Sri N. T. Rama Rao,

then Chief Minister of Andhra Pradesh, laid the foundation stone for the temple. More than 800 Hindus congregated to witness this historical event. On January 25, 1985, on a cold wintry day, the consecration ceremonies (*Pratishthapana*) of Sri Gnyana Vinayaka took place at the Ganesha Mandir. Two priests were made available for all religious services, and the temple had its doors open from 9 a.m. to 9 p.m.

In 1985, the temple celebrated all main Hindu festivals—*Mahashivaratri, Holi, Janmashtami, Hanuman Jayanthi, Ganesha Chathurthi, Varalakshmi Puja, Navaratri,* and *Diwali*. Several dignitaries, including Sri Morarji Desai, Swami Chinmayananda, and Sivaya Subramuniyaswami, contributed in various ways to enrich the diversity of the temple. Lata Mangeshkar, the nightingale of India, formally inaugurated the Ganesha Mandir on June 11, 1985.

Construction Phases

Phase 1 of the construction, which comprised an area of 8,000 sq. ft., included a sanctum (*garbhagudi*), entrance portico (*ardhamandapa*), and a large community hall (*mahamandir*). Due to the generous contributions from devotees and the support of various organizations, Phase 2 work was then undertaken, which included the *anivottimandapa*, the hall in front of the main deity; the Hanuman shrine; a 95-ft.-tall main tower (*rajagopura*); and Lord Venkateshwara, Sri Devi and Bhudevi, and Radha-Krishna shrines. In 1985 additional land with a house was purchased, bringing the total area to 20 acres.

The year 1986 was a landmark in the history of the temple. On May 3, 1986, the *Shivalinga Pratishthapana* was performed, made possible due to a generous donation from H. H. Sivaya Subramuniyaswami. During 1986 the temple artisans (*shilpis*) work long hours under the guidance of Dr. V. Ganapati Sthapati. The *Kumbhabhisheka* of the Sri Rama Temple was celebrated between June 27 and July 6 with full religious ceremonies.

In 1987, we focused on increasing attendance and organizing the inauguration of the Radha Krishna shrine. The *Diwali* celebrations attracted thousands of devotees. The Indianization of the Ramalaya *rajagopura* was completed. The temple made further progress in 1988, as the marble deity of Durga Devi was delivered, and the *Devi Jagran*, an all-night vigil with devotional singing, attracted a considerable numbers of devotees. This activity helped in raising funds toward the expansion of the Ganesha-Shiva-Durga temple. Additional adjoining land with a house

PAGE 118: *Vimana* of the second temple on the grounds, known as the "GSD" (Ganesha - Shiva - Durga) temple complex, built in the Kalinga dynasty style.

PAGE 118, LEFT: Line drawing of Sri Anjaneya. *Line drawing courtesy of V. Ganapati Sthapati & Associates, Chennai, India.*

PAGE 119: A view from the rear of the temple.

was purchased, bringing the total land area to 22 acres.

The year 1992 saw the expansion of the Ganesha-Shiva-Durga temple and also of the parking lot. The *Ratnagarbhanyasa* of Ganesha-Shiva-Durga (ceremony for laying gems in the foundation) was performed in 1993. In 1994 focus was on Indianization of the Ganesha-Shiva-Durga temple. In the summer of 1994, The *Kumbhabhisheka* ceremonies for Lord Ganesha, Lord Shiva, Lord Subramanya, and Devi Parvati were performed. In 1996 the *Kalashastapana* for the Durga shrine and *Kumbhabhisheka* of Ganesha-Shiva-Durga temple were celebrated, and the initial phase of the main gate project was completed.

In 1998 a magnificent bronze statue of Swami Vivekananda (10ft., 2in. in height) was installed on the temple grounds—the only statue of the Swamiji outside India to date. Work is underway to construct a Vivekananda Center with a meditation hall, library, and a lecture hall. A grand Community Center was constructed in 2001 to facilitate community celebrations of weddings and other social and cultural celebrations.

Hindu Heritage

The deities in the temple complex stand to guide the members of the Greater Chicago Hindu community in preserving their time-honored Hindu heritage. The main deity in the Rama Temple complex is Sri Rama and includes Sita and Lakshmana, Sri Ganesha, Sri Hanuman, Lord Venkateshwara (Balaji), Sri Mahalakshmi, and Sri Krishna and Radha. The main deities in the Ganesha-Shiva-Durga temple are Sri Shiva, Sri Ganesha, Sri Durga Devi, and also include Sri Subramanya, Sri Devi Parvati, and the Navagrahas.

Thus far the temple planners have done all they can to realize some of the goals set forth earlier to serve the needs of more than 13,000 Hindu families in the Greater Chicago area and beyond. The Hindu Temple of Greater Chicago continues to stand as a symbol of the Hindu heritage of its many members.

PAGES 120 and 121: The "GSD" temple complex is one of the most famous examples of the Kalinga dynasty style of architecture in the United States. It is renowned for its design and perfect balance.

PAGE 121, TOP: Line drawing of Sita, Lord Rama, and Lakshmana.
Line drawing courtesy of V. Ganapati Sthapati & Associates, Chennai, India.

PAGE 121, BOTTOM: The entrance portal of the "GSD" temple.

Hindu Temple of St. Louis
Ballwin, Missouri

As first-generation Indians, we all came from our *karma bhumi* (land of action) and landed in this *bhoga bhumi* (land of material comforts). After leaving the shores of our *janma bhumi* (land of birth), seeking the promised land of prosperity and plenty, we have settled in the United States of America halfway around the world. After our immediate goals were realized, we felt a spiritual vacuum. To fill the void, a group of us met in September 1987 and discussed building a temple in St. Louis. An ad hoc committee was formed to draft the constitution. The Hindu Temple of St. Louis was formally registered as a not-for-profit corporation in the State of Missouri on March 7, 1988. After visiting several sites, the present site was selected for its prime location across Queeny Park in Ballwin, Missouri, near the city of St. Louis.

A humble beginning in 1987 has blossomed into a remarkable achievement. Swami Chinmayananda inaugurated the formal activities of the temple on August 7, 1988.

PAGES 122 and 123: Front view of the Hindu Temple of St Louis, St. Louis, Missouri. Dedicated to Lord Venkateshwara, this temple displays intricate detail, elegant outlines, and classical statuary.

PAGE 124: Another architectural wonder can be seen on the outside wall of the entrance, with depictions of Sita-Rama *kalyana* (wedding) and Meenakshi *kalyana*. The photo shows Meenakshi *kalyana* in exquisitely carved detail.

PAGE 125: One of many artistically designed and intricately carved pillars in and around the temple complex.

One of the basic tenets of Hinduism is that God can be realized through different paths, and the path of devotion (*bhakti yoga*) is the simplest and more practical in this time of the *Kaliyuga*, the "Dark Age." In *bhakti yoga* the all-pervasive and formless God is given a physical form with which the spiritual aspirant can establish an intimate one-to-one relationship and direct communication with his chosen deity (*Ishta Devata*). The St. Louis temple is dedicated to that vision.

The ground-breaking ceremony (*Bhumi Puja*) was performed on April 21, 1990, by His Holiness Sri Ganapathi Sachchidananda Swami of Mysore, India. It was a memorable sight to see Swamiji and several devotees carrying the blessed bricks over their heads to the present temple location. *Shankushthapana* (installation of the first brick for the temple structure) was laid by Sri Swamiji amid Vedic chanting.

Two Phases

The architectural plans were drawn by the famous Dr. V. Ganapati Sthapati and Associates of Chennai, India. After obtaining the necessary building permit from St. Louis County, the construction of the temple was started on May 15, 1991, and completed by November 8, 1991. After the completion of this first phase, the formal inauguration of the temple was conducted on November 9, 1991, by Swami Chetanananda of Vedanta Society of St. Louis. The original building, with 2,740 sq. ft. in the upper level and 2,000 sq. ft. in the basement, proved to be inadequate within a very short time.

Formal inauguration of Phase 2 activities took place on May 2, 1993 in the presence of Sri Ganapathi Sachchidananda Swamiji with *Ganapati Homa* in a specially erected tent on the temple grounds. Priests' quarters to accommodate three families were completed by January 29, 1994.

Initiation (*Samprokshana*) of the metal idols (*charabimbas, utsavavigrahas*) was celebrated on January 21, 1995. These *panchaloha vigrahas* (images made of a five-metal alloy) were made by Tirumala Tirupati Devasthanams at Tirupati, India. The construction of the new building was started on the auspicious *Guru Purnima* day on July 12, 1995. The basement of the

present temple was completed in December 1996. With the arrival of eleven temple artisans (*shilpis*) from India on January 21, 1997, the work on the sanctum sanctorums (*garbhagrihas*) was started. The work on the entranceway towers (*gopuras*) was initiated in May 1997.

Working almost 12 hours a day for 28 days a month, the *shilpis* completed Phase 2 in record time. The *Kumbhabhisheka* celebrations and consecration ceremonies, the *Pranaprathistha*, of the presiding deities (*mulavigrahas*) took place on July 6, 1998. Dr. V. Ganapati Sthapati, his associate Sri R. Selvanathan, and Shiva and his team of *shilpis* had done magnificent sculptural work. These master craftsmen have produced a structure of unique architectural beauty. With divine blessings, the Hindu Temple of St. Louis celebrated the dedication ceremony of the main entranceway tower (*rajagopura*) on July 8, 2000.

Architectural Marvel

The Hindu Temple of St. Louis is an architectural marvel and reflective of the artistic skills of the erstwhile designer and the *shilpis* who painstakingly executed the job. The temple belongs to the South Indian style of temple architecture, incorporating the basic structure of the *garbhagriha*, where the idol of the main deity is kept. A porch covers the entrance to the temple, which is supported by carved pillars. A prominent towered roof called the *shikhara* surmounts the top of the *garbhagriha* and dominates the surroundings. The *shikhara* of the temple is made of distinct horizontal levels that decrease in size as they rise upward, forming a pyramidal structure. Each level is decorated with miniature designs. The temple has a tall sanctum tower (*shrivimana*), which conforms to the principles of South Indian temple architecture. Another architectural wonder is seen on the outside wall of the entrance. Two beautiful depictions of Sita-Rama and Parvati-Shiva weddings (*kalyanams*) can be seen. The design and carving have been executed with a great amount of professionalism.

The main deity is Lord Venkateshwara. Venkateshwara, another form of Lord Vishnu, is one among the Trinity, representing the power of sustenance. He is regarded as *Kaliyuga Varada*, the "Giver of Boons" in this dark and degenerate Age of Kali. He is always close to his devotees and ever ready to bless and protect them. He is also called Balaji and Govinda.

As this is a multi-deity temple, it includes Sri Mahalakshmi, Sri Shiva, Sri Parvati, Sri Ganesha, and Sri Karttikeya carved out of black granite by Dr. V. Ganapati Sthapati and Associates at Mahabalipuram in India. The marble idols of Sri Sita, Sri Rama, Sri Lakshmana, Sri Hanuman, Sri Radha and Sri Krishna, Sri Ganesha, Sri Durga, and Sri Dattatreya were sculpted in Jaipur by the famous Pandey Moorthi Bhandar.

PAGE 126: Main temple entrance door carved in wood with decorative work.

PAGE 127, TOP: Decorative *vimana* showing Lord Vishnu.

PAGE 127, BOTTOM: Top portion of the *rajagopura*, with a series of *kalashas*. The number of *kalashas* normally represents the height of the *rajagopura*.

PAGE 128: *Vimana* showing Yali (temple protector) at the top, with goddess Lakshmi seated below and a lion at her side. The goddess is placed in front of a gap in the *vimana*, which occurs on each of its four sides. The intricate work is a tribute to the *sthapati* and *shilpi*.

PAGE 129, TOP: View from the *mahamandapa* of the main sanctum sanctorum.

PAGE 129, BOTTOM: Rama Parivar on one of the *vimanas*.

Hindu Temples in North America

New Mathura Vrindavan and Golden Palace

Moundsville, West Virginia

West Virginia is renown for its natural beauty—verdant hills and mountains—but who would expect to see at the end of one of those winding Appalachian roads a palace of gold? On seeing its domes and stained-glass windows, the visitor may stop a moment to wonder whether he's been suddenly transported to mystical India.

Prabhupada's Palace of Gold stands as one of the most amazing testimonials to the transplanting of Vedic culture from its ancient roots in India to the fertile soil of America. Its conception, design, construction, and use reflect more the workings of an all-knowing God than the glories of expert designers, architects, engineers, and craftsmen!

The odyssey begins in 1896 with the birth of Abhay Charan De into a family of Krishna devotees in Calcutta, India. Astrologers predicted that the child would become a great exponent of Krishna's teachings, cross the ocean, and open 108 temples. In 1922, Abhay met his spiritual master, Srila Bhaktisiddhanta Saraswati, who inspired him to spread Krishna consciousness in the English language. At the advanced age of 70, Srila Prabhupada boarded a cargo ship to America with a crate of his English translation of the *Srimad Bhagavatam*, a set of cymbals (*karatals*), and seven dollars.

PAGES 130 and 131: On the verdant hills of West Virginia one finds this labor of love called the Palace of Gold, built without blueprints by young devotees using do-it-yourself books as their guide.

PAGE 132, TOP: Radha and Sri Krishna housed in the Temple of Understanding.

PAGE 132, BOTTOM: At the south entrance of the temple hall stand teakwood doors embellished with carvings of elephants, lotus stalks, and flowers. These doors, as well as all the other woodwork, were carved in Mumbai, India.

PAGE 133, TOP: At the front and back of the Palace of Gold, four royal peacock windows contain more than 1,500 pieces of hand-fashioned stained glass. Peacock and lotus motifs pervade the palace, etched into numerous windows and carved into doors.

PAGE 133, BOTTOM: In the west gallery there are some two-dozen semicircular stained-glass windows diffusing sunlight in various colors and shades. These hues are reflected by the dark green marble and red travertino of the floors and a ceiling of mirrors.

PAGES 134 and 135: The main entrance to the Palace of Gold. Surrounding the palace are two levels of terraces replete with flower gardens and bordered by waterways with more than a hundred ornate fountains. The Garden of Time, to the east of the palace, is resplendent with color from spring to late fall. Walkways divide the flowers into islands that surround the central fountain, like calibrations on a sundial. A lion, flanking the main stairway, roars salutations.

In America, he attracted young followers by his purity and love for God. They helped him start the International Society for Krishna Consciousness (ISKCON) in 1966 in New York. Inspired by successfully teaching Americans to become Krishna devotees (*bhaktas*), ISKCON began to spread around the world.

New Vrindavan

In 1968, disciples purchased 113 acres of farmland in West Virginia and asked Srila Prabhupada what to do with it. He replied, "In America, there are so many new things—*New* York, *New* Jersey, *New* Mexico, why not turn this land into *New* Vrindavan!" Inspired by this vision, his disciples began by establishing a place for worship of Krishna in an old battered shack, and by growing crops and protecting cows.

Feeling a need for the guiding presence of their spiritual master, the disciples wanted to build a home for Srila Prabhupada. A

hilltop location was chosen for its potential beauty, hardly apparent at the time because the land was being used as a dump. Devotees began by removing the debris and clearing the land. It was only years later that it was discovered that the site was perfectly in line with the *Vastu Shastra*, a ancient Sanskrit treatise on sacred architecture.

In 1973, a rough plan was sketched on a scrap of paper and construction began on a simple house. There was no budget, no contractors, nor even any skilled workers. The young devotees themselves began to learn how to do everything by reading do-it-yourself books. In the next few years as their talents developed and the possibilities expanded, plans evolved to include stained glass, inlaid marble, intricately hand-carved wood, and crystal chandeliers.

In 1976, at the age of 80, Srila Prabhupada toured the palace under construction and lovingly approved of the devotees' labor of

love. The following year Prabhupada became very ill and when asked when he would like to move in to his palace, said, "Let us see which palace Krishna wants me to go to." On November 17, 1977, Srila Prabhupada left this mortal world. However, his disappearance did not deter the devotees from completing the palace. Rather, they now saw the palace as a fitting memorial to the greatest preacher of Krishna consciousness in modern times!

Architectural Wonder

Gold leaf detailing, inlay work in marble and onyx, beautiful water fountains, and colorful flower gardens were the finishing touches to the palace. Like the famous palaces of India, Prabhupada's Palace glories in its marble work, totaling 254 tons. For the inlay work on the walls and floors, 50 varieties of marble and onyx were imported from France, Italy, Canada, and the Middle East. The raw slabs were cut into more than 20,000 pieces, polished, and then shaped into unique designs. In the main temple room, the marble pillars are topped with gold-leafed capitals.

Among the many attractions at the palace are teakwood doors at the south entrance, beautified by carvings of elephants, lotus stalks, and flowers. These doors, as well as all the other palace woodwork, were carved by Mistri Dhirijam and Sons of Bombay, a devotee family famous throughout India for this art. On the archway above the doors is abundant gold-leaf tracery that ornaments the palace within and without. Laid in leaves one one-thousandths of an inch thick, the 22-carat gold leaf covers a total of 8,000 square feet.

The final finishing touches on the palace led to the Grand Opening in September 1979. Major media, including the *New York Times*, *Newsweek*, and the *Washington Post*, hailed the palace as a major architectural and spiritual wonder. Since that time, thousands of visitors from around the

PAGE 136, BOTTOM LEFT: The lower terrace with fountains, water lilies, and *chatra* (umbrella), a covered sitting place often constructed by ancient Vedic kings for holy men to use in prayers and meditations.

PAGE 136, BOTTOM RIGHT: Sri Krishna in the Puri Janganath style as seen in the Temple of Understanding.

PAGE 137, BOTTOM: Like the famous palaces of India, the Palace of Gold glories in its marble work—some 35,000 feet, weighing 254 tons. For the inlay work on walls and floors, 50 varieties of marble and onyx were imported from France, Italy, Canada, and the Middle East. The raw slabs were cut into more than 20,000 pieces, polished, and then shaped into unique designs. Here, in the main temple room, the marble pillars are topped with golden capitals. The walls are made of a subdued white Italian creamo, and the floors combine intricate designs reminiscent of both Jaipur and Versailles.

world have toured the palace, shopping at the palace gift store, dining at its vegetarian restaurant, and strolling in the palace's award-winning rose gardens.

With the influx of thousands of visitors, a great need arose to provide facilities for large crowds to worship and stay overnight. By 1984, a new Radha Krishna Temple was completed just a quarter of a mile from the Palace of Gold. The new compound, replete with manmade lakes, gardens, and walkways, included the Palace Guest Lodge and Cabins, amphitheater, resident apartments, schoolhouse, and recreation area.

All the skills and talents developed by the devotees were utilized in creating the beauty of Sri Sri Radha Vrindavana Candra's Temple. The temple is the home for the deities Radha Krishna, Sri Nathji, Jagannatha, Narasingadeva, and Gaura Nitai. The opulent interior features the largest stained-glass ceiling in North America, a unique hand-carved teakwood deity cart (*ratha*) and swing (*jhulan*), silver- and gold-plated deity houses (*shringasana*), wrought-iron gates, and original oil paintings of Krishna's pastimes.

The New Vrindavan Community celebrates annual religious festivals as well as conducting many regular rituals on a daily and periodic basis. The 4000 sq. ft. temple room can easily accommodate more than 500 people for *arotika* (or *arati*), *kirtan*, *bhajans*, scriptural discourses, dramas, and classical Indian dance performances. *Arotika* is held six times a day, and free meals are served three times daily all year round.

Hindu Community and Cultural Center
Livermore, California

In the mid-1970s, the Hindu community of the San Francisco Bay Area was small, consisting of many young professionals making their presence felt in the new land of opportunity. For them, establishing roots in this new land also meant preserving their identity and tradition. Many individuals and groups felt the urge to do something to achieve this. Against this backdrop, the concept of the temple materialized as a few such individuals came together, representing three different kinds of vision aimed at providing the children of Indian origin knowledge of their own languages and culture. One devotee had been working to create an Indian Cultural School in 1974. Another devotee, striving to nourish Indian art forms in the Bay Area, had been working with other music lovers on the creation of what is now the South India Fine Arts organization. Meanwhile, other devotees, who were collecting donations for the Hindu Jain temple in Pittsburgh, had convinced themselves of the need for a temple of their own in the Bay Area.

As one might expect, these three groups soon came to know of each other's existence and met for the first time early in 1977. There was an immediate meeting of the minds, and the vision for a Hindu temple was established. The idea began to spread and others joined the cause. In July 1977 the Hindu Community and Cultural Center was incorporated as a nonprofit organization.

The group set to work and actively solicited community involvement. By making presentations at community gatherings, the sincerity of purpose, the practicability of building a temple, and the determination of the group in pursuing its cause were conveyed to the community at large. The enthusiasm caught on as others joined in. Through periodic meetings, picnics, and other get-togethers, the group began giving form to its dreams. Initially, energies were directed in four general directions: the type of the temple to be erected, its location, mobilization of resources, and the governance structure.

Initial Temple Plans

The type of temple to be built was defined by the character of the group of individuals involved. Because the group included Hindus from different parts of India and outside, the temple was visualized as one that would satisfy the spiritual needs of all Hindus, regardless of denomination or region. As a practical reality, it was felt that the temple should offer traditional forms of worship for Shiva, Vishnu, Shakti, Ganesha, Karttikeya, Krishna, and Rama, with Shiva and Vishnu as presiding deities. The vision was that the temple would be built strictly according to the ancient traditions of Hindu architecture.

The search for suitable land began. Because the Hindu community was dispersed throughout the Bay Area and had limited monetary resources, the land had to be large enough to accommodate a traditional Hindu temple, reasonably equidistant from all parts of the Bay Area and be in an area where the price was within reach. Many sites were looked at, discussed, and discarded. An acceptable piece of land was identified in Pleasanton in June 1978 and efforts were mounted for its purchase. This venture gave the planners a valuable lesson on how democracy functions in America. Before the land purchase, permission had to be obtained from the County of Alameda for constructing the

proposed temple. To this end, precious funds were spent toward a soil survey of the site and the drilling of a well for water supply. Although the county was sympathetic to the cause, there was strong public opposition, presumably stemming from concerns about traffic and lack of sufficient sewage facilities. The permit was denied in 1979. Briefly, the group felt devastated. But not for long.

As for resources, funds had to be generated entirely as donations from the Hindu community. While the search for land was going on, funds were collected and saved toward land purchase. The first major fund-raising effort was a music concert in Oakland by Srimati M. S. Subbulakshmi.

About this time, ideas were also being formulated on how the Hindu community and Cultural Center would be administered. Long hours were spent in formulating appropriate principles of self-governance. Many sensitive topics such as regional differences, linguistic groups, and styles of worship were brought out and discussed. The ideas gradually evolved toward an institution whose steward would be a Steering Committee consisting of some two hundred members who had demonstrated an

abiding interest in the welfare of the temple. A Board of Directors and an Executive Committee, elected from the Steering Committee, would administer the temple. The importance of diversity for the health of the temple was recognized. The group felt that the best way to nourish diversity was to have a diverse, enlightened Steering Committee with properly conducted elections. The vision was that the vitality of the organization would be maintained by a continuing influx of new blood into leadership roles.

The disappointment with the Pleasanton failure was soon forgotten, and the search for a new site continued with vigor. Indeed, better things were in store. In November 1980, a 4-acre rectangular piece of land was identified on the outskirts of the city of Livermore. Remarkably, it was laid out exactly east-west, ideal for a Hindu temple! The price was within reach and everyone was energized.

This time the temple planners were better prepared to succeed with the democratic process by working with the city of Livermore as well as the local population. Special efforts were made to inform the public about Hinduism and the Hindu

community, and what the temple would bring to the area. A local Unitarian Fellowship opened its doors for informational meetings for local residents. The Valley Covenant of Ministers, an interfaith leadership group, heard about the project and wrote a glowing letter in support of the proposed temple, pointing out that the spiritual diversity of the area would be enhanced. One evening in August 1983, the Livermore City Council, after a public hearing, issued a permit to the Hindu Community and Cultural Center to erect a Hindu Temple at the site. The Hindu community had ascended to a new plateau in their historical journey.

Even as momentum was gathering to raise funds for temple construction, Gurudeva, Sivaya Subramuniyaswamy of the Palaniswamy Temple in San Francisco gave, in October 1982, two beautiful idols of Ganesha and Subramanya with encouraging words that *pujas* for these deities be performed and that temple plans would soon be realized. Dutifully, these two idols began visiting the homes of devotees, one week at a time and daily *pujas* were performed by the families. On weekends, community sense was fostered and the circle of devotees enlarged when the host families invited other families to participate. Lack of ritualistic knowledge was compensated for by sincerity and devotion.

Soon after obtaining the permit, preparations for the ground-breaking ceremony, the *Bhumi Puja*, began in earnest, and the land was consecrated in November 1983. The historic function was attended by more than 200 devotees, although there had been heavy rains the previous day. The ceremonies were blessed by many religious leaders of the Bay Area. To serve the immediate needs of the community, an interim temple was started in a temporary structure constructed behind the house in April 1984, and the first permanent priest was appointed. In June 1984 the foundation stone for the Shiva-Vishnu Temple was laid by the then Chief Minister of Andhra Pradesh, Sri N. T. Rama Rao.

Activities gathered momentum on many fronts. By September 1984 loans were approved by the State Bank of India and the Tirumala Tirupati Devasthanams. The city of Livermore granted a construction permit. Preparation of the land started in October 1984, and the temple artisans (*shilpis*) from India commenced work on the temple structure in June 1985. In

October 1985, ground was broken for the Community Center by Ustad Ali Akbar Khan and the foundation stone laid by Pandit Ravi Shankar.

Final Phases

The design of a Hindu temple in accordance with the *Agama Shastras* was entrusted to Padmasri M. Muthiah Sthapathi, and the Project Manager for the temple was Bhupinder Gosain. The unique structure would combine northern and southern Indian styles of architecture to reflect India's cultural diversity. The temple enclosure of 100 ft. by 100 ft. would have two principal entrance towers (*gopuras*), one for Kashi Vishwanatha, in the Kalinga style of the Bhuvaneshwar temple, and one for Venkateshwara Balaji, in the Chola style of the temple at Tirupati. Associated with the principal deities would be shrines for Durga, Ganesha, Visalakshi, Karttikeya, Sri Devi, Bhudevi, Krishna, Rama, and the Navagrahas. The idols of Durga, Krishna, and Rama are all made of white marble from Rajasthan, while the rest of the idols are fashioned out of black granite from southern India. The idols of Venkateshwara, Sri Devi, and Bhudevi were donated by the Tirumala Tirupati Devasthanams, while the rest of the granite idols were gifted by the Government of Tamil Nadu.

As the construction of the temple began, limitations of time and monetary resources necessitated the completion of the initial phase of the temple without a roof over the main enclosure. To everyone's delight, the important initial phase came to fruition on July 13, 1986, on the auspicious day before the onset of *Dakshinayanam*, when all the deities were ceremoniously installed and the *Kumbabhisheka* was performed with great joy. The function was rendered colorful with a ceremonial elephant and the showering of flowers from a helicopter. With twelve priests officiating the ceremonies, more than 3,000 devotees from the greater Bay Area participated in the historic occasion, along with the Honorable Leo McCarthy, Lieutenant Governor of California.

Worship in the open enclosure was causing particular hardship to devotees because of extreme weather conditions in summer and winter. The much-needed roof was soon installed over the main enclosure, protecting the devotees from the elements. A house adjacent to the priest's residence was acquired to house the *shilpis*, the compound walls erected around the periphery of the temple site, and the landscaping done. A Community Center was completed and dedicated in 1997.

New England Hindu Temple

Ashland, Massachusetts

The vision of a Hindu temple in New England appeared in the minds of a few people in the year 1978. Driven by this inspiration, an ad hoc committee was established in March 1978, when every member made a donation to assiduously pursue the goal of building the temple. A formal constitution was drafted, and an application for incorporation was duly filed with the Commonwealth of Massachusetts.

The early days of the organization were devoted to establishing its by-laws and to discussing the scope and nature of the project of building a temple. Foremost in the minds of everyone was the desire that the temple be a place of worship for all the Hindus living in and visiting this area. On August 12, 1978, the committee decided to dedicate this temple to Sri Lakshmi as the presiding deity, since most of us have come to this country in search of the prosperity and happiness bestowed by the grace of Mahalakshmi.

The inaugural function of New England Hindu Temple, Inc. was conducted with *Mahalakshmi Puja* and *Diwali* celebrations on October 28, 1978, at the Knights of Columbus Hall in Melrose, Massachusetts. Exuberance and excitement filled the hearts and minds of everyone in the large congregation as they witnessed and experienced an authentic *puja* to Sri Lakshmi. That the spiritual needs of those gathered were being satisfied was easily seen as pledges and donations started pouring in even before nonprofit status was secured for the organization, which happened one month later, on November 28, 1978. The place of congregation was soon changed to a new location that was more centrally located.

Temple Construction

In the summer of 1981, about 12 acres of land in the town of Ashland, Massachusetts, were acquired for constructing the temple. The services of Dr. V. Ganapati Sthapati from the Institute of Architecture and Sculpture in Tamil Nadu were sought for designing the temple according to the *Vastu* and *Agama Shastras*. He visited in November 1982 and provided detailed plans for the temple. In early 1983, a local engineering company was engaged to prepare the engineering design and drawings, which were submitted to the town of Ashland for approval. The land

was cleared in the fall of 1983, and in the following spring the excavation work was carried out. The contract for the foundation and structural work for the building was awarded to a local firm in the summer of 1984. The ground-breaking ceremony was observed on June 19, 1984, with a grand celebration of the *Ganesha Puja*.

In the fall of 1984 the temple applied to Tirumala Tirupati Devasthanams in India for a loan to help hasten the construction of the temple. The application was duly approved, and the first installment of 5 lakhs (500,000) of rupees was received in July 1985. When the initial contract with the engineering firm for the foundation and infrastructure was completed, the first *Ganapati Homa* (fire ritual) in the temple was performed in September 1985. The first floor held a large hall (*mahamandapa*) measuring 60 by 50 ft., with a palanquin (*alankaramandapa*) for Lord Nataraja and his consort Shivakami (for taking their metal idols, *utsavamurtis*, in procession).

A paved driveway to the temple from Waverly Street with parking spaces for 100 cars was also provided. A grand opening ceremony was celebrated on September 6, 1986. Sri Janakiram Sastrigal of Rajarajeswari Peetam in Stroudsburg, Pennsylvania, graciously performed the inaugural *puja* together with our local part-time priests.

PAGES 146 and 147: Front view of Sri Lakshmi Temple, Ashland, Massachusetts.

PAGE 148: Main entrance to the temple. Elaborate detailing on the *rajagopura*.

PAGE 149: Back view of the temple with the four *vimanas* and the *rajagopura* at the far left.

149

Extending from the large hall (*mahamandapa*) by another 30 feet, sanctums for the principal deities—Ganesha, Mahalakshmi, and Venkateshwara—were constructed beginning in September 1987. As the time approached for the Hindu architectural ornamentation of the sanctums with towered roofs and pinnacles (*vimanas* and *shikharas*), the services of Padmasri M. Muthiah Sthapathi of Tamil Nadu were contracted in 1988. In the same year, Sri Shadrinarayana Bhattar was appointed as the first full-time priest of the Sri Lakshmi Temple to provide regular services within the temple as well as services for weddings, housewarmings (*grihapravesams*), name-giving ceremonies (*namakarana*), and others, as required by the Hindu community.

The spring of 1989 saw the arrival of ten artisans (*shilpis*) from India skilled in the architectural work of temples. With their arrival, the exquisite magnificence of the sanctums with their *vimanas* began to take shape. Their patient and devoted work under adverse weather conditions brought us to planning the consecration, *Rajagopura Kumbhabhisheka*, of the main entranceway tower. Plans for the *Kumbhabhisheka* were initiated in the fall of 1989. Sri Sampathkumar Bhattacharlar of Bangalore and Sri Sambamoorthy Sivachariar of Madras were chosen as chief priests to perform the *Kumbhabhisheka*, with a host of other priests assisting them in this consecration ceremony.

Granite idols of Ganesha with his divine mount Mushika (mouse) and an offering pedestal (*balipitha*), Mahalakshmi, Venkateshwara, Garuda, and door-keepers (*dvarapalakas*), along with the bronze *utsavamurtis* of Ganesha, Mahalakshmi, Venkateshwara, Sri Devi, Bhudevi, and Shivakami were designed by Dr. V. Ganapati Sthapati of the Institute of Architecture and Sculpture of Tamil Nadu and fabricated by the artisans at the institute. The bronze *utsavamurtis* of Nataraja, Subramanya, Valli, and Devasena were designed by Padmasri M. Muthiah Sthapathi. The ornamental designs of the sanctum and the *vimana* were skillfully executed according to the Hindu *Agama Shastras* by the Indian artisans.

What was envisioned as a concept in 1978 took twelve years to blossom. Measured steps were taken during every phase, mostly due to the newness of the project. Through the grace and guidance of Goddess Sri Lakshmi, an important phase of temple construction had been completed. Sri Lakshmi Temple now joins the ranks of other Hindu temples built in different cities across the country.

It will be left to future generations to foster the growth of the Sri Lakshmi Temple and other temples, to uphold the ethical and moral values taught by our religion, and to promote Hindu culture. The temple hopes that this small step goes a long way in instilling the responsibility in our future generations to prepare them for the task of continuing our tradition and upholding the principles of our religion.

Temple Features

Sri Lakshmi Temple at Ashland has the following principal sanctums: for Sri Maha Ganapati, Sri Mahalakshmi, Sri Venkateshwara, Sri Nataraja with his consort Sri Shivakami, Sri Subramanya with his consorts Sri Valli and Sri Devasena, Sri Hariharaputra, Garuda, and the Navagrahas.

Sri Narayana, or Mahavishnu, is known for looking after the welfare and well-being of the phenomenal world. The energy of Sri Narayana is represented by Sri Lakshmi. Mother Lakshmi is always identified with the Lord, and hence they are known as Sri Lakshmi Narayana. Mother Lakshmi is the mother of prosperity, peace, and illumination. Without her grace one cannot have inner peace or perennial joy.

Lakshmi is commonly known as the Goddess of Wealth. She is the source and provider of the following sixteen types of wealth, both material and nonphysical: fame, knowledge, courage and strength, victory, good children, valor, gold and other gross properties, grains in abundance, happiness, bliss, intelligence, beauty, higher aims, high thinking and higher meditation, morality and ethics, and good health and long life.

Swami Sivanandaji Maharaj lists eighteen values that lead us to immortality. These are the greatest wealth that Mother Lakshmi bestows on us: serenity, regularity, absence of vanity, sincerity, simplicity, veracity, equanimity, fixity, non-irritability, adaptability, humility, tenacity, integrity, nobility, magnanimity, charity, generosity, and purity.

The perennial, unchangeable, and eternal truth is the supreme blessedness that Mother Lakshmi, Adishakti, represents. She is the origin. She is the light. She is the power, the wisdom, and the strength. She is the source of our peace, bliss, and illumination.

152

Hindu Temple Society of Canada
Richmond Hill, Ontario

Language and religion have been the main compo-
nents of heritage preserved and propagated in every
society throughout the generations. Hindus have
passed on the torch of knowledge to successive generations whenever and wherever the society has been
moving around. In Canada, by the late 1960s, the
need for community worship was strongly felt
among the few hundred Hindus of South Indian tradition who had migrated from all parts of the world.
For many years, the old traditions were kept alive
with *bhajan*-singing in private homes. This activity
evolved into about 100 Hindu families coming
together to form the Hindu Temple Society of
Canada with the express objective of building and
maintaining a Hindu temple following the *Agama
Shastras* and other scriptures. The Society was char-
tered in 1973, with the original trustees coming
from different backgrounds—representing many
language groups from India and Sri Lanka. For about
ten years, there was not much progress on the project because of various social and financial constraints, but the members kept the idea of the temple alive by patient planning and ardent praying.

Construction and Consecration

In the early 1980s, there was a big surge in the Hindu population of Canada, mainly because of the arrival of a large Sri Lankan Tamil community of devout Hindus. To support the needs of that growing community, land was purchased, after a lengthy search, in the town of Richmond Hill, north of Toronto. Only faith in the grace of the Lord encouraged the Society to embark on this multimillion-dollar venture, with very little in hand. The initial finances were arranged through a loan, with five trustees standing as personal guarantors. The site was consecrated in October 1983. The difficult but rewarding task of building the temple was launched with the installation of the premier deity of Hinduism, Lord Ganesha, at a temporary altar in April 1984. Thereafter, in October 1984, a "Trailer Temple," again a temporary temple built on two flatbed trailers, was constructed with about 1,000 sq. ft. of worshiping space to house Lord Ganesha and Goddess Durga. The important aspect of this phase of the construction was that a Hindu temple was built entirely through the volunteer labor of men, women, and children. Everyone had a significant part in building "their" temple. A priest, Sri Balakrishnan, was brought from India to perform the *pujas*.

During 1987-88, the main complex was designed and the construction started,

financed through a loan, this time with fourteen trustees giving personal guarantees. The multimillion-dollar construction was supervised and managed by a devotee, an experienced construction supervisor who took leave from his regular job to undertake this work. Many volunteer services went into the construction, thus reducing the overall cost and giving the community a sense of belonging and pride in the achievement. The services in the main temple started with the installation of Lord Murugan in his present abode on July 2, 1988.

The temple complex on Bayview Avenue in Richmond Hill is one of the largest Hindu temples in North America built and run according to the *Agama Shastra* tradition. The overall design was done by V. Janakiramana Sthapati, an Indian temple architect (*sthapati*), whose family, for generations, has specialized in designing and building Hindu temples. They come from the lineage (*parampara*) of builders who built the famous temple in Tanjore (Thanjavur) in South India during the Chola period. V. Janakiramana Sthapati designed and helped build the Canadian temple, together with his sculptors (*shilpis*), supported by consultations with and advice from many religious experts and leaders, including the senior Shankaracharya of the Kanchi Kamakoti Pitam. The *sthapati* prepared the granite statues of all the deities installed in the

PAGES 154 and 155: Front view of the snow-covered Ganesha Temple, Toronto, Canada. This temple is designed to withstand the harsh winter conditions of Canada. The *vimanas* on this temple were designed and manufactured with glass-reinforced concrete in Bahrain, Middle East, and assembled in Canada.

PAGE 156: One of the main shrines for Lord Murugan. The shrine and *vimana* are highly decorative in the style and colors like those found in Tamil Nadu, South India.

PAGE 157: Minor shrine for Lord Shiva, with *vimanas* in contrasting colors and intricate detailing.

157

PAGES 158 to 161: *Minor shrines and vimanas.*

temple, and his team of fifteen *shilpis* did the beautiful artwork on the thirteen altars and associated structures. The beauty and the greatness of the fine artwork are beyond description in words, and can be appreciated adequately only by a personal visit to the temple.

By 1989, all the remaining altars were opened for service with *Pratishtha* ceremonies conducted according to the *shastric* tradition. The congregation grew steadily, along with the services at the temple, and by the end of 1990 the temple had grown to a size that compared favorably with some of the largest Hindu temples in the United States.

There is a very significant difference in the experience of this temple compared to other large Hindu temples in North America. This temple is truly a people's temple. More than 90 percent of the income is generated from the services rendered—from individual *pujas* (*archanas*), consecrations (*abhishekas*), and various fire (*homa*) rituals throughout the year. The

Hindu community, more specifically the vast Sri Lankan Tamil community, has rallied around the temple and has helped to build and maintain it to this grand level, at a record pace of improvement and expansion. For nearly 200 days in any year, one festival or another is celebrated, with devotees attending in large numbers, making this one of the most active Hindu temples in the Western Hemisphere.

IIn 1992, two towered roofs (*vimanas*) were built over the sanctums, crowning the altars of Lord Murugan and Lord Venkateshwara. *Vimana Kumbabhisheka* was performed in late 1992. The temple itself had a *Mahakumbabhisheka* in August 2001, when more than 30,000 devotees attended a week-long celebration. More than 40 priests—Shivachariars and Bhatters, as well as priests from the *Agamic* and Vedic traditions—conducted the festivities when the entranceway tower (*rajagopura*) for Ganesha and the two *vimanas* for Murugan and Perumal were consecrated to the chanting of Vedic hymns. Renowned Shivachariars and Bhatters from Canada,

United States of America, India, Australia, Sri Lanka, and Germany were present. In an *Agamic* temple, the *Kumbabhisheka* ceremony is usually conducted every twelve years, in order to maintain the concentration of divinity that has been kept alive the previous twelve years. It can also be performed after the completion of a major addition, such as this one.

On the final day a *Pratishthapana Homa* was performed, when life was literally invoked in the deities. This ceremony is usually performed by a priest who has the knowledge and the ability to discern the different currents of subtle electromagnetic energy that operate in his own central and spinal nervous systems and the ability to be in full and complete control of the power generated by them.

Temple Deities

The temple houses Lord Ganesha, also known as Vinayaka, or Pillaiyar in Tamil. The Ganesha is named Varasiddi Vinayakar, meaning "the one who grants all boons to the devotees."

Lord Murugan, also known as Subramanian (Subramanya) or Karthik (Karttikeya), is the second son of Lord Shiva and is considered the Commander-in-Chief of the divine army. He is the main deity worshiped by the Tamil-speaking community all over the world. The image (*vigraha*) of Murugan is made of blue granite and is the tallest Murugan *vigraha* in the world. The Toronto Murugan is named Shivasubramanian, based on the unique design of the statue.

Lord Shiva, one of the Hindu Trinity, is worshiped in the form of *Shivalinga* to signify the formlessness of God—that he is beyond any form attributed to him. The image (*murti*) is named Chandramaulishwara.

Parvati is the consort of Lord Shiva. Her *vigraha* is a beautiful granite one—divine grace and beauty personified. She is called Thirupurasundari, meaning "the most beautiful damsel in all the three worlds."

Nataraja is Lord Shiva depicted as King of

Dance. He is the Cosmic Dancer, whose dance generates life in the universe.

Sri Venkateshwara is the most popular form of Vishnu to be worshiped all over the world. His consort is Lakshmi (Sri Devi), fondly known as Thayar, "Mother." Mother Earth in the form of Bhudevi is considered the earthly consort of Vishnu and is depicted as Andal. In this temple Venkateshwara is installed as a very beautiful *murti*, standing majestically 8 ft. in height, bestowing his divine grace on all the devotees. One of the most beautiful services at this altar is called *Pulangi Seva*, when the Lord is adorned in a dress made entirely of flowers.

Goddess Durga has a special place in the Hindu pantheon, and in this temple she is depicted as Mahishasura Mardhini, "victorious virtue over 'bull-headed' ignorance and evil." The *vigraha* is a very beautiful maiden standing on a buffalo head in the form of Vishnu-Durga, the most peaceful and gracious form of Durga Devi.

Valli and Devayani, according to the traditions in South India, are the two consorts of Murugan. Valli signifies the Earth, or *kriya shakti*, while Devayani signifies the Heavens, or *ichcha shakti*. Another unique feature of these two altars in the temple is their location. In many temples in India and Sri Lanka, the two *devis* of Murugan are located by his side, either at the same altar or in separate altars by his side. At this temple, Lord Murugan is in a west-facing altar, which is rare by itself, and the two *devis* are located in two altars situated in front of Murugan's altar, facing east, which is proper according to the *Agama Shastra*, but very unique among Murugan temples.

The Navagrahas represent the heavenly bodies that Hindus traditionally believe have considerable influence on the life of man-kind: the planets, Sun, Moon, Mars, Mercury, Jupiter, Venus, Saturn, and two other celestial features known as Raghu and Kethu. They are worshiped in all Shiva temples. Bhairavar is one of the manifestations of Lord Shiva, and in this form he is the patron deity of Kashi. Chandikeshwara is a saint known for his extreme devotion to Lord Shiva; he became the Chief of the Shiva Ghanas, who guard the abode of Shiva. Skandachandamurti's *murti* has the same function of as that of Chandikeshwara.

Lord Venkateshwara is the most popular form of Vishnu to be worshiped all over the world. His consort is Lakshmi (Sri Devi), fondly known as Thayar, "Mother." Mother Earth in the form of Bhudevi is considered the earthly consort of Vishnu and is depicted as Andal.

Lord Rama—Rama Parivar—according to Hindu tradition and later-day interpretation of the epics, is considered as the sixth incarnation of Vishnu and the ideal example for mankind to follow.

Sudarshana (Chakra), the wheel in the hands of Vishnu, is considered a separate deity named Sudarshana (Chakrathalwar) and is installed and worshiped at a separate altar.

Garuda, the King of Birds, is usually installed as the vehicle (*vahana*) of Vishnu. He is installed at a small altar directly across from the Vishnu altar and is worshiped regularly.

Sri Ranganatha Temple
Pomona, New York

Deep in the wooded valley of Pomona in Rockland County in the state of New York stands a beautiful temple dedicated to Sri Ranganatha. This is one of the few temples in the United States dedicated to Vaishnavism. It is dedicated to the practice of Sri Vaishnavam and Sri Vishishtadvaita philosophy of Bhagavad Ramanuja, as elaborated by Sri Vedanta Desika and as currently practiced by the Jeeyar of Sri Ahobila Mutt. Built in the traditional style of ancient Sri Vaishnava temples, Lord Ranganatha Temple follows the traditional knowledge (*sampradaya*) of the Sri Ahobila Mutt and Srirangam Temple in Tamil Nadu, South India.

Plans for the Sri Ranganatha Temple were started more than fifteen years ago at the express command of the 44th Jeeyar (head) of Sri Ahobila Mutt, Srimate Srivan Sathagopa Sri Vedanta Desika Yateendra Mahadesika, to propagate the Vedic concept of absolute surrender at the lotus feet of Sriman Narayana as the sure means for salvation at the end of this birth for anyone and everyone.

PAGES 162 and 163: View of the Sri Ranganatha Temple, set in a wooded area in Pomona, New York. One of the few temples in the United States dedicated to a single deity.

PAGE 164: *Vimana* with detailed work showing Narasimha Avatara.

PAGE 165: Side view of temple.

The principal deity, Lord Ranganatha, is in the posture of repose (*sayana*) on the bed of a five-headed serpent, Adisesha, a primeval serpent, mythologically conceived to hold the world on his 1,000 hoods. The idol is a replica of the deity in the Srirangam Temple in India. The Pomona place of worship is the first temple for Lord Ranganatha in North America.

Early Developments

The idea of having an exclusive place of worship for Sriman Narayana had been initiated by a group of devotees during the birthday celebrations of the 44th Jeeyar in New York in August 1985. Later, representatives of these devotees approached the 44th Jeeyar of Sri Ahobila Mutt with the predicament of not having a shrine in the United States totally dedicated for the Supreme Lord Sriman Narayana. The beloved Founder Acharya commanded the devotees to build a temple for Lord Sri Ranganatha to propagate the concept of *saranagati* (surrender and pure, devotion service).

Subsequently, a not-for-profit organization called Sri Ranganatha Seva Samithi was registered in the State of New York on October 8, 1987. In the early days, there were mainly a lot of *satsangs* to commemorate the birthdays of *Azhwars* (Vaishnavite saints) and *Acharyas* (teachers). Also, important religious festivals were observed in various devotees' homes. The first deity image (*vigraha*) of the "temple" was a small 2-in.-high *panchaloha* icon (image made out of a five-metal alloy). In contrast, the consecrated presiding deity (*mulavigraha*) of Sri Ranganatha at the temple today is 10 ft. high and weighs 9 tons.

A devotee came forward to sponsor the metal idols (*utsavavigrahas*) of Sri Ranganatha, Sri Devi, Bhudevi, Mahalakshmi, and Andal. The consecration for these deities, the *Vigraha Pranapratishtha*, was performed at the Dasavataram Samithi in Sri Rangam, India, by the officiating priests of Sri Ahobila Mutt in the divine presence of the 44th Jeeyar. Later, these *vigrahas* were air-lifted to New York and blessed by a devotee by holding devotional services (*aradhana*) every day for the next twelve years at his residence

Soon thereafter, a devotee sponsored the *utsavamurtis* of Sri Rama, Sita, Lakshmana, and Hanuman. These *vigrahas* were brought to the United States personally by a devotee after due *Pranapratishtha* in Sri Ahobila Mutt in India. Later, in October 1993, the *utsavavigrahas* of Sri Krishna, Shrinivasa, Sri Devi and Bhudevi, Sudarshana and Yoga

164

Narasimha, Bhagavat Ramanuja, and Sri Vedanta Desika were air-lifted to New York, including all twelve *Azhwars* and Lakshmi Hayagriva (Lord Narayana in the form of the Lord of Education, who saved the Vedas).

While the daily worship of the *utsavavigrahas* was being performed without interruption, the search was on for a suitable plot of land where a temple could be built. At this point, a devotee arranged for the purchase of a foreclosure property of nearly 5 acres of land in Pomona, in Rockland County, New York.

At the command of the 44th Jeeyar, Sivaprakasam Sthapati of Sri Rangam drew up the construction plans for the temple. During the next twelve-year period, a devotee traveled all over the United States, and raised much-needed funds for the construction to begin. During this period, he performed more than 300 *Satyanarayana Pujas*, 100 *Sudarshana Homas*, 100 *Kalyana Utsavams*, and delivered lectures on *Shrimad Bhagavatam* (seven *saptahas*), *Bhagavad Gita*, and Valmiki *Ramayana*. During these years, a number of devotees volunteered immeasurable amounts of their free time for the performance of daily worship and weekly *thirumanjana* (ritual bath).

Design and Construction

Sri Ranganatha Temple was designed by temple architect (*sthapati*) M. S. Sivaprakasam, who was selected by the 44th Jeeyar of the 600-year-old Ahobila Mutt for this important assignment. In 1987, this Jeeyar had designed and built the southern tower of the Srirangam Temple. The Srirangam structure is recognized as having the tallest temple tower (*gopura*) in Asia.

The ground-breaking ceremony was performed in 1997, and the first phase of the construction work began. Ten temple artisans (*shilpis*) arrived from India to fashion the sanctum sanctorum (*garbhagriha*), the towered roofs over the sanctums (*vimanas*), and *gopuras*. For 20 months, from May 1999 to January 2001, the *shilpis* worked diligently and completed all the traditional artwork, supervised by Sri Surendra Babu Sthapati. The *pranavakara vimana* on top of the main sanctum sanctorum is a sight to behold.

As the construction was proceeding, devotees from all across the United States continued to support and worship Lord Sri Ranganatha and Mahalakshmi. In 1997, the 600th Anniversary of Sri Ahobila Mutt was celebrated in the presence of Sri Ranganatha at the Pomona temple.

The second phase of the construction required a fresh infusion of funds. Many devotees came forward and helped, making possible the initiation of this phase. With the untiring efforts of the trustees of the temple and many volunteers, the construction work was completed on February 14, 2001.

This great temple could not have been built but for the goodwill, support, donations, and sacrifices of countless devotees from all over United States. With such a broad national base of supporters, there is no doubt that this temple will continue as a beacon of spirituality for centuries to come.

The final consecration, *Samprokshana* (*Kumbhabhisheka*) was performed on May 27, 2001. All the main deities were consecrated in *Pranapratishtha* ceremonies. The ceremonies had begun 48 days earlier with *Dhanyadivasam* on April 6, 2001. Elaborate functions spreading over five days culminated on May 27, 2001, with *Kumbhabhisheka*. After the conclusion of *Mahakumbhabhisheka*, *Mandala Abhisheka* for 48 days followed for all the deities.

Ancient Roots

The Pomona temple is modeled after the famous Sri Ranganatha Temple of Srirangam in Tamil Nadu, India. Located near the city of Tiruchirappalli, on a small island between branches of the rivers Kaveri and Coleroon, stands the massive temple of Srirangam. The most ancient and revered of the 108 pilgrimage shrines of Vishnu and the largest temple complex in all India, it is surrounded by seven concentric walls (the outermost wall having a perimeter of more than 3 km.) and 21 *gopuras*. Srirangam enshrines a statue of Vishnu reclining on a great serpent. A legend tells that this idol, known as Sri Ranganatha, was being transported across India to Sri Lanka by the king of Lanka, Vibhishana. Resting from his efforts for a while, he set Sri Ranganatha with his *vimana* on the ground, yet when he tried to lift it to continue his journey to Lanka, Vibhishana found that the *vimana* had magically bound itself to the earth. A hundred hands could not budge the *vimana* and the Lord inside, so a small temple was built around the *vimana*. That temple complex has since grown around Lord Ranganatha and has been rebuilt and enlarged many times over thousands of years. Its original date of founding is unknown to archeologists. Most of the temple complex standing today, including a grand hall of 1,000 beautifully sculptured pillars, was constructed between the fourteenth and seventeenth centuries.

The *Nanmugan Gopura*, built by the Jeeyar of Ahobila Mutt at Srirangam, is thirteen stories tall and is completely covered with intricately carved, brightly painted statues of the many incarnations of Vishnu. More

PAGE 166: A replica of the *vimana* at the famous Srirangam Temple in South India. The intricately designed arch around Vasudevan is called *truvachi*, which is a stylized rendering of the open mouth of a crocodile. Exquisite *hamsa* figures (birds) form the base of the arch.

PAGE 167: Front view of the temple with rolling hills in the background.

PAGE 168, TOP: Vamana Avatar depicted on one of the *vimanas*.

PAGE 168, BOTTOM: View of the *vimanas* with elegant decorative work.

PAGE 169: Sri Krishna on one of the *vimanas*.

than being just an extraordinary expression of art, these sculptures function as three-dimensional storybooks of Hindu mythology:

Vishnu, the second deity of the Trinity of Hindu gods, is responsible for the sustenance, protection, and maintenance of the created universe. A gentle, loving god representing the heart, he is the focus of intense devotional worship by a large percentage of the Indian population. To ward off the extraordinary perils that threaten creation, Vishnu frequently incarnates himself. He has appeared as Rama, Krishna, and other incarnations.

In his *Vishnu Purana*, Sage Parasara describes the Supreme Reality as Sriman Narayana, who is visualized as resting in yogic sleep in the milky ocean on a serpent bed. Deep in the recesses of our heart lotus (*vaikuntha*) lies the Infinite Truth (Vishnu) with His divine consort (Mahalakshmi) on a serpent bed (Adisesha), who is depicted as thousand-headed. He is the *antharyami* (indweller) of our heart lotus. This is the essence of Sri Ranganatha—Sri Ranganatha *tattva*.

Apart from this popular view, the image of Sri Ranganatha/Vishnu conveys a deeper meaning as held by the *Vastu Shastra* and practiced by the *shilpis* of India. According to the *Vastu Shastra*, *vastu* represents the subtle space, otherwise called *akasha*, and *vāstu* represents the gross space, or the earth (*prithvi*). *Akasha* is a living entity, which is energetic space containing matter, and the earth is also a living entity, which is matter containing energetic space. Therefore, Lord Shiva is the embodied representation of *Vastu Purusha*, the energy of the *akasha*, and Lord Vishnu is the embodied form of *Vastu Purusha*, the inherent energy of the earth. In short, Shiva represents energy and Vishnu represents matter. 🔱

Sri Siva Vishnu Temple
Lanham, Maryland

The seed for the idea that a Hindu temple should be built in the nation's capital was planted in 1976 among a few friends who were thinking about this goal since the early 1970s. By 1980 that idea had been nurtured and shared with others, and the Sri Siva Vishnu Temple Trust was formed. Its goals seemed fitting for immigrants thousands of miles from their ancestral home: to unite Hindus in America, individuals diverse in their customs but unified in their devotion and values, and to offer a place where Hindu culture could thrive among immigrants, their children, and their children's children.

The Sri Siva Vishnu Temple, located in Lanham, Maryland, is about 12 miles from Washington, D.C. What started off as a very small idea, in the living rooms of a few devotees in the late 1970s, has now blossomed into being one of the largest temples in the Western Hemisphere. Temple construction began in 1988, incorporating the Mayan, Pallava, Vijayanagara, Kerala, and South Canara styles of temple architecture. The temple houses seventeen shrines (*sannidhis*) with a number of deities, which were consecrated between the years of 1990 and 1995.

In 1984, the Sri Siva Vishnu Temple Trust acquired a plot of land with a small house in suburban Washington. This house was the Balalaya, where the shrines were initially installed. As more people began to share in the vision for a grand temple of traditional architecture and sculpture, plans were drawn up, with the blessings of the Shankaracharyas, under the direction of eminent temple architect Dr. V. Ganapati Sthapati.

In 1990, 1,400 people witnessed the consecration and installation of the first shrines in the temple building we see today. In 1991, the temple held its first *Kumbhabhisheka*, as shrines for several deities were built and consecrated. Over the years, Sri Siva Vishnu Temple adapted to the growing needs of the congregation, acquiring more land and adding shrines for Venkateshwara and Ayyappan. In addition to these shrines, a community hall was built for concerts, weddings, and other special events.

Today, the temple is the enterprise of dedicated volunteers, administrative staff, and nine priests, and the symbol of a community's joint aspirations and efforts. It is this combined strength that must be marshaled to fully complete the temple by carrying out one urgent, remaining task: the construction of the main tower (*rajagopura*) and the temple flagpoles (*dhvajastambhas*). With the support of an ever-growing congregation, this dream will be realized by June 2003.

Temple Deities

The three principal deities (Hindu Trinity) are Brahma, Vishnu, and Shiva. In the Sri Siva Vishnu Temple, Sri Shiva is in the form of a *Shivalinga*, a *linga* being a representation that strives to give concrete shape and form to an abstract, infinite, all-pervasive God who is beyond shape and form. The *linga* is believed to survive *Pralaya*, the ultimate dissolution and end of all creation. The *Shivalinga* for the Washington, D.C., temple was brought from the river Narmada and is the representation of Sri Ramanatha Swami of Rameswaram (a temple built around the twelfth century), who was worshiped by Lord Rama before he crossed the ocean to destroy Ravana and free Sita. The sanctum and sanctum tower (*vimana*) of the Shiva shrine is built in Chola style architecture.

Dwara Ganesha and Dwara Murugan, along with Durga, Dakshinamurti, Lingodhbavar, Brahma, Chandikeshwara, Nardhana Ganesha, and Nandi are kept around the Shiva shrine.

ANANTHAPADMANABHA OF THIRU-VANANDAPURUM: This deity represents Sri Vishnu in *yoga nidra* (sleep). With this installation, this form of Vishnu was represented outside India for the first time. The majesty and beauty of this form of Vishnu is a sight to behold. In this shrine, the Hindu Trinity is represented by the *Shivalinga* at the right hand of Vishnu and Brahma coming from the navel of Vishnu. In Sri Siva Vishnu Temple, Sri Venkateshwara is installed in a separate shrine built in Rayar style architecture. Sri Venkateshwara, the Power of Sustenance, also represents Lord Vishnu, one of the Hindu Trinity. He is regarded as *Kaliyuga Varada*: in the "degenerate" age of *Kaliyuga*, he is always close to the devotees and ever ready to bless and protect them. He is also called Balaji and Govinda.

NARASIMHA, VISHNU, AND LAKSHMI VARAHA SWAMI: This group is installed around the Venkateshwara shrine. Garuda

is installed in front of Venkateshwara. There is also a provision made in the ceiling, on the northern side, to see Vimana Venkateshwara. The crown on Venkateshwara's head signifies his supreme sovereignty. The lotus on which he stands represents Truth, which supports the Supreme Reality (*Brahman*). The lotus in his hands indicates the final goal of perfection; his conch signifies his call for the nobler life of man; his mace connotes his power to knock down one's desires; and the discus symbolizes the total annihilating power to destroy evil and lift one to a higher spiritual plane.

SHIVA AND VISHNU PARIVAR: In addition, the temple shrines include Shiva and Vishnu Parivar. Around the Shiva shrine, Sri Durga as the representation of Mata is in the form of Vishnu Durga standing on Mahisha's head. Next is Vighneshwara, or Ganesha, Remover of Obstacles. Then comes Sharada (Saraswati), Goddess of Learning, representing the presiding deity at Sringeri. The next shrine is occupied by Jaganmatha Parvati, consort of Sri Shiva, named Parvadavardhini, as in Rameswaram. Next to the Sri Shiva shrine facing the Lord is Sri Chandikeshwara.

SUBRAMANYA: By a fortuitous design by Dr. V. Ganapati Sthapati, Lord Subramanya (Karttikeya or Murugan), as son of Sri Shiva and nephew of Vishnu, along with his consorts Valli and Devasena, occupies the space in the middle of the temple, in front of the main entrance, between Shiva and Vishnu. This form is a representation of the deity in Vaithishwaran Koil, famous for curing many diseases. Navagrahas complete the Sri Shiva family groupings (*parivaras*). Many devotees conduct special *pujas* for one or more of the planetary gods and receive their blessings.

SRI AYYAPPAN, OR HARIHARAPUTRA: This deity, the son of Lord Shiva and Lord Vishnu in the form of Mohini, with eighteen holy steps, was built outside India for the first time at the Sri Siva Vishnu Temple. How appropriate that this temple has built a shrine for the son of *both* to complete the cycle started sixteen years ago! He is the symbol of unity among all sects of Hinduism. In addition, associated shrines

of Kannimula Ganapati, Nagaraja, and Maligaipurathu Amman are also present, as seen in Sabarimala in southeastern India.

OTHER DEITIES: Around Sri Vishnu the following deities are present: Sri Lakshmi, or Sri Devi, is the Goddess of Wealth. Many special functions are celebrated to the benefit of humanity and the congregation. Sri Krishna is a representation of the famous Udupi Temple deity. The next shrine is that of Sri Bhudevi. After being born as a human in the form of Andal, she married Sri Vishnu.

Then comes Hanumanji, who is well known to all Hindu devotees in the form of Bhakta Hanuman with folded hands, worshiping Lord Rama. The next shrine is that of Lord Rama with Sita and Lakshmana, as represented in Badrachalam on the banks of the Godavari in Andhra Pradesh. This is the only place where Sri Rama, to grant the wish of a famous devotee, appears in the

Vishnu Svarupa form with four hands and with Sita seated on his lap.

Temple Features

Sri Siva Vishnu Temple represents both classical and neoclassical art forms. The main entrance (*makara thorana vayil*) is like an arch. The artistic yet simple architecture surrounding the middle entrance door is drawn from an early style, almost 5000 B.C., inspired by Maya, considered to be the original temple architect. The Pallava style examples of these are seen in the Sri Siva Vishnu Temple in the Subramanya and Sharada shrines. The Subramanya shrine has a unique form, with the entire structure representing a decorated chariot drawn by elephants. In Chola style, highly stylized forms of the doorkeepers (*dvara-palakas*) stand at the entrance to the Shiva, Subramanya, and Ananthapadmanabha shrines.

In Vijayanagara style, the sanctum tower (*vimana*) can be seen from the outside, on top of the Ananthapadmanabha shrines. Inside the temple, the Rama and Hanuman shrines also have similarly ornamented *vimanas*. The pillars in the Sri Siva Vishnu Temple, although not as richly ornamented as in the original temples in India, are characteristic of that style. The Andal and Mahalakshmi shrines have ornamental superstructures inspired by the Vijayanagar style. The Ayyappan and Krishna shrines at the Sri Siva Vishnu Temple represent temple styles of Kerala and coastal Karnataka.

Some of the unique characteristics of the Sri Siva Vishnu Temple of Metropolitan Washington, D.C., are:

- In the early 1970s, the concept of unity in diversity was represented for the first time by combining Sri Shiva and Sri Vishnu in one temple.

PAGE 176, TOP: Andal on one of the *vimanas*.

PAGE 176, BOTTOM: Detailed work on the *vimana* and *gopura*.

PAGE 177: Top of the *gopura* with *kalashas* and detailed ornamentation.

- The concept of unity in diversity was taken to its zenith, again for the first time, by creating the *rajagopura* as one combined structure, emphasizing the oneness of God, or the Highest Reality, *Brahman*.

- It is the first temple to have Lord Vishnu (Ananthapadmanabha) in the *yoga nidra* form outside India.

- It is the first temple to have Lord Ayyappan with 18 consecrated steps outside India.

- Sri Siva Vishnu Temple optimizes the concept of a personal deity (*Ishta Devata*) by providing many deities, 46 in all.

- Sri Siva Vishnu Temple used fibers and special resins mixed with white cement for outside *vimanas* to reinforce the structure to survive through many winters. This method is now being used by many temples in their construction.

Down through the ages, temples and humans have had an influence on each other. There is a continuity of philosophical and social purpose in the successive changes in architectural style. The emotional commitment and desire to retain Hindu values of life persist in the Sri Siva Vishnu Temple. In addition, several interesting themes emerge in the construction of the temple, echoing general historical trends. Temple architecture has always been adapted to local environmental conditions; the immigrant-inspired Sri Siva Vishnu Temple follows this trend. Temples have always received patronage and support from kings, and later, from rich landlords; the Sri Siva Vishnu Temple receives its support from the members of its generous congregation.

Looking to the Future

The vision of the Sri Siva Vishnu Temple began with the concept of bringing Hindus together, but increasingly it has become a place that brings together Hindu customs and heritage with American values of community and volunteerism. In a new millennium, it will be a symbol of the Hindu community in America. Sri Siva Vishnu Temple's commitment to this future is already evident. From 1992, the temple has facilitated summer camps for children. Throughout the 1990s, the temple has facilitated Free Health Fairs conducted by physicians and other health professionals. In 1997, it launched the Children's Fund in an effort to develop youth and education programs and meet the needs of a fast-growing Hindu population in Washington. In 1998, Sri Siva Vishnu Temple developed a new initiative on community service and volunteerism, focusing on Hindu families as well as the broader community. In 2000, it started to work with the Mithra Mandala, an organization for destitute and old women.

ENTRANCE TO
TEMPLE
AUDITORIUM
SHOES & COAT
STAND →

PLEASE
NO SHOES
HERE

PLEASE NO SHOES
BEYOND
THIS POINT

AD
P

in th
on S

KAL
TEMP

Sri Maha Vallabha Ganapathi Devasthanam

Flushing, New York

The Hindu Temple Society of North America, formed on January 26, 1970, established a Hindu Religious Cultural Center Complex on Bowne Street in Flushing, New York. The street is named after a distinguished American who has a place in history for his contribution to religious freedom and to the antislavery movement in the United States. It is interesting to note that this project, which began on Indian Republic Day on January 26, 1970, was consecrated on July 4, 1977, America's Independence Day, stressing the role of the institution in strengthening and harmonizing the ideals that the two countries and cultures stand for.

The logo of the Society depicted on the outside wall of the temple is adapted from Sri Sathya Sai Baba's ecumenical symbol, a light surrounded by insignias of several religions with *Om* on top. It signifies the universality, catholicity, and spirit of tolerance of Hinduism. Stressing the supremacy of the Absolute and symbolizing the main aspects of major religions, the Center represents the fundamental unity at the core of all religions. The temple was designed by Barun Basu and Padmasri M. Muthiah Sthapathi of Chennai, India.

PAGES 178 and 179: Front view of the Ganesha Temple, Flushing, New York. The first temple to be built in the United States and one of the very few temples built right at the street front.

PAGE 180, RIGHT: A section of the *gopura* shows a gigantic *gopura thangi* (one who shoulders the *gopura*). The symbolic guardian of a Hindu temple, he forms part of the ornamentation of this *gopura*.

PAGE 180, LEFT: Line drawing of Lord Ganesha. *Line drawing courtesy of V. Ganapati Sthapati & Associates, Chennai, India.*

PAGE 181: Elaborately decorated *rajagopura* with five *kalashas*—the emblematic water vessels crowning the entrance tower of a temple.

Main Deities

Everything in Hinduism begins with the worships of Lord Ganesha, who is installed as the main deity in the New York temple. With an elephant head and human form, he represents the universality of creation. All creation is said to begin with sound, and he is that primal sound *Om*, or *Pranava*, out of which the universe has been manifested. When Shakti (energy) merges with Shiva (matter), both Ganesha (sound) and Lord Skanda (light) are born.

The temple flagpole (*dhvajastambha*) is located in the outer passage (*prakara*) in front of Sri Maha Vallabha Ganapati. The insignia (*lanchana*), made of brass and fixed on top of the pole, is the figure of Mushika (mouse), the vehicle (*vahana*) of Lord Ganesha. With brightly shining ritual vessels (*kalashas*) on top, the *dhvajastambha* reflects the rays of the rising sun, and the numerous bells ring the *Omkara* at the flowing of the early morning breeze, beckoning the devotees to their favorite deities.

The temple has five principal sanctums—for Sri Ganesha, Sri Shiva, Sri Venkateshwara, Sri Mahalakshmi, and Sri Shanmuka. In addition to the beautiful idols (*vigrahas*) of the deities sculpted in black granite stone, there are also *vigrahas* made of the alloy called *panchaloha*, which is fashioned from five metals: gold, silver, bronze, copper, and brass. These metal idols (*utsavamurtis*) are also worshiped, and are taken out of the sanctums on festival days for special worship and occasionally for procession, as they are accorded a main role during festivals (*utsavas*).

The temple has *panchaloha vigrahas* of Sri Rama, Sita, Lakshmana and Hanuman, Sri Krishna and Radha, Sri Satyanarayana and Ramadevi, Sri Sudarshana and Sri Narasimha, Sri Ranganatha, Sri Durga, Sri Saraswati, Sri Nataraja and Shivakama, Sri Ayyappan, Sage Agasthya (the patron saint of the temple and his consort, Lopamudra Devi, who also is the flowing holy river Cauvery), Saint Manikkavachaka, and Saint Aruna Giri Natha. Besides these, there are

granite *vigrahas* of Sri Brahma and Sri Nagendra, a silver *vigraha* of Devi Khodiar Matha and a marble *vigraha* of Sri Gayatri Matha. Sri Raghavendra Swamy Brinda-vana is located in a separate sanctum across the street from the main temple.

Wall Murals

The best of Indian art and tradition is depicted on the walls. The cosmic dance of Lord Shiva as Lord Nataraja adorns the wall behind the Ganesha sanctum. In another depiction next to the Lord Shiva sanctum, Lord Shiva appears in the form of Guru—Dakshinamurti seated under a banyan tree, imparting wisdom and knowledge to the Seven Sages.

On the wall in front of the Sri Lakshmi sanctum, we see Lord Vishnu reclining on the coiled serpent Adisesha, with Sri Mahalakshmi adorning his chest, Brahma the Creator sprouting from His navel, and Garuda, who has taken the form of an eagle, waiting to serve the Lord. The wandering Sage Narada with his *tambura*, from which divine music emanates, is also portrayed.

On the wall in front of the Sri Venkateshwara sanctum is a depiction of *Gitopa-desha*, or the scene in the *Bhagavad Gita* in which Lord Krishna teaches Arjuna on the Kurukshetra battlefield. The *Gita* is regarded by many scholars as allegory, in which the hero, Arjuna, is said to represent the

individual soul and Sri Krishna, the Supreme Soul. The blind King Dhrita-rashtra is the mind under the spell of ignorance, and his hundred sons represent the numerous evil tendencies in man. The Kurukshetra battle symbolizes the perennial conflict between the good and evil in man. The warrior who listens to the voice of the Lord speaking from within ultimately wins the battle. In the words of Mahatma Gandhi, "It is not a history of war between two families or two kings but the history of the spiritual struggle of man, the war between God and Satan, going on in the human heart."

On the wall adjacent to the Lord Shanmukha sanctum, there is a depiction of the scene in which the Divine Mother gives the spear (*vel*) to Sri Skanda when he is about to lead the gods in their war against the demonic forces. Sri Skanda uses the *vel* to annihilate all the *asuras* led by Surapadma and Taraka, and reestablishes righteousness.

On the four pillars are depicted Virabhadra, Narasimha, Gajasamharamurty, and Mahakali.

As in the Ganesha Temple in Flushing, the Navagrahas are generally installed in every Shaiva temple in South India. In many North Indian temples they are depicted on the lintels of doors, to protect the temple and all those who enter it from the evil effects of the planets.

PAGE 185, TOP: The logo of the Center, depicted on the outside front wall of the temple, is adapted from Sri Sathya Sai Baba's ecumenical symbol. It shows a lamp surrounded by the insignias of several religions, with *Om* at the top. The logo signifies the universality, catholicity, and spirit of tolerance of Hinduism. While stressing the supremacy of the Absolute and symbolizing the main aspects of the major religions, the Center represents the fundamental unity at the core of all religions.

PAGE 185, BOTTOM: *Vimana* with delicate decorations.

Hindu Temple of Atlanta
Riverdale, Georgia

The Hindu Temple of Atlanta is the culmination of deeply felt spiritual aspirations of the Hindus in the Atlanta area. The organization is a nonprofit entity founded in 1986. The temple opened on December 1, 1990, with *Sri Ganapati Pratishthapana*, installation of the deity. It became a full-fledged functional house of worship in 1992. Besides providing a congenial atmosphere for spiritual advancement, it also serves as a focal point for celebrating the cultural diversity of the Hindu community. Daily worship, grand festivals, exquisite cultural programs, and a variety of children's educational programs radiate the power of this spiritual sanctuary.

It was on June 22, 1986, that members of the community gathered on a vacant lot in Riverdale to perform the ground-breaking ceremony for the Hindu Temple of Atlanta. In March 1989, after assurances and pledges were received to fund the project, the actual construction of the structure began. The first phase of construction required about 21 months.

PAGES 186 and 187: A stunning view of the vast temple complex in Atlanta, Georgia—dedicated to Lord Venkateshwara. The grand *rajagopura* at the center rises magnificently over the structure.

PAGE 188: A special ceremony being held for the idol of Garudar prior to installation.
Photograph courtesy of Hindu Temple of Atlanta, Atlanta, Georgia.

PAGE 189, LEFT: Architectural ornaments on the *vimana*. Andal and other beautiful female figures are used to enhance the aesthetic value of the building and to act as symbols of fertility and prosperity.

PAGE 189, RIGHT: The main deity in the temple, Lord Venkateshwara.
Photograph courtesy of Hindu Temple of Atlanta, Atlanta, Georgia.

The first idol installed on these premises was that of Sri Maha Ganapati. Various religious services took place after three priests from India arrived to conduct them. Images (*murtis*) of Sri Venkateshwara (Balaji), Sri Devi (Lakshmi), Bhudevi, Durga, Navagrahas, and Anjaneya were installed by May 1993.

The Legacy of Tirupati

However, this bland masonry structure was yet to become a full-fledged Indian temple as designed by Padmasri M. Muthiah Sthapathi, master architect of temples (*sthapati*) from Chennai, India. He prepared a master plan that incorporated the styles reminiscent of those that flourished in the times of the Pallava and Chola dynasties of India more than a thousand years ago. According to Sri Muthiah, the plans are based on *Maricha Samhita* and *Vaikhanasa Agama* texts, which contain the principles of temple construction and provide instructions on temple building. The design is very similar to that of Sri Venkateshwara temple in Tirumala, Tirupati.

The town of Tirupati is one of the most ancient and spectacular places of pilgrimage in India. It is situated in Chittoor district in southern Andhra Pradesh. The town owes

its existence to the adjoining temple of Lord Sri Venkateshwara, which is situated on Tirumala Hill. With a history that dates back to more than twelve centuries, the temple is the jewel in the crown of ancient places of worship in southern India. Tirumala Hill is 3,200 ft. above sea level, and is about 10.33 sq. mi. in area. It comprises seven peaks, representing the seven hoods of Adisesha, thus earning the name, Seshachalam. The seven peaks are called Seshadri, Neeladri, Garudadri, Anjanadri, Vrishabhadri, Narayanadri, and Venkatadri. The sacred temple of Sri Venkateshwara is located on the seventh peak, Venkatadri (Venkata Hill), and lies on the southern banks of Sri Swami Pushkarini. There are several legends associated with the manifestation of the Lord in Tirumala. The name Tirupati, meaning "the Lord of Lakshmi," should have been appropriately applied to the village on Venkata Hill (abode of the Lord). However, it has been popularly assigned to the municipal town at the foot of the hill, while the village around the hill near the temple is called Tirumala (Sacred Hill).

The second phase of construction of the Atlanta temple could not start until specially trained sculptors (*shilpis*) arrived from India in November 1993. The completion of the project—that is, converting

the masonry structure into an ornately sculptured and architecturally attractive temple—was, at last, near. The temple complex incorporates many of the traditional elements of an authentic South Indian temple:

- Four shrines (*vimanas*), one each for Venkateshwara, Sri Devi, Bhudevi, and Durga. Each one has a sanctum (*garbhagriha*). The Venkateshwara sanctum has an entrance hall (*mukhamandapa*) structurally connected to the main assembly hall. The other three sanctums have entrance porticos (*arthamandapas*) connecting them to the main hall.

- Main assembly hall (*mahamandapa*) in which devotees gather.

- Front lobby (entrance *mandapa*).

- Gateway tower (*rajagopura*) over the entrance *mandapa*, rising above all other structures.

- Separate shrine for Ganesha inside the main hall.

- Altar for the Navagrahas, the nine planet deities.

- Altar for Navagrahas, the nine planet deities.

- Separate shrine for Anjaneya in front of the main structure.

- Chariot-shaped temple for Garuda.

- Flagpole (*dhvajastambha*).

- *Balipitha,* pedestal of offering in the form of a flat lotus in bloom.

- *Yajnashala,* a place for performing sacrificial ceremonies (*havanas*) and other oblations.

- Front entrance *mandapa*.

The walls inside and outside, the *vimanas,* the *gopura,* and the entrances are decorated with ornate sculptures based on *Maricha Samhita* and *Vaikhanasa Agama*.

Transformation

The transformation of the building into a magnificent temple started with drawings on paper by the *sthapati*. All the necessary measurements and details were incorporated into the drawings. These were transfered onto 4 ft. by 8 ft. plywood planks so

that an actual working-size design of the various sections of the entire structure was available for the *shilpis* to follow.

Depending upon the weather and the season, the *shilpis* worked either inside or outside of the building complex. Every phase of the work was carefully scrutinized and approved for quality by the *sthapati* before the *shilpis* could go on to the next stage.

To start the brickwork on the *gopura* and *vimanas,* a grid (*pramana sutra*) was laid on the floor incorporating every intricate detail and containing all the precise measurements. It was vital that this grid be accurate

because it guided the *shilpis* in the construction, starting from the bottom of the towers all the way up to the top. Even a small error made at the bottom is magnified into a major flaw at the top.

THE *RAJAGOPURA:* The flat ceiling that covers all the halls and the sanctums is about 20 ft. above ground level. The four *vimanas* and the *gopura* rise above the ceiling of the building complex. The *rajagopura* rises approximately 40 ft. above ceiling level, rising tier upon tier (up to five tiers) and tapering into a pinnacle (*shikhara*) with a fanlike motif (*mahanasi*) on either side. Each story has four corners called

karnakutas, with each story holding seventy-six pillars. The *gopura* is 22 ft. by 14 ft. at the base and has four faces. On the east face and the west face, the area with door-keepers (*dvarapalakas*) is called *mukhashala*.

The south face of the *rajagopura* is decorated by a *mahanasi* on top, followed by Lord Narasimha at the top level and by Sri Mahavishnu in various poses on the next three levels. The lowermost level is again decorated with Sri Narasimha images. On the north face, Mahavishnu is on the top and lower levels and Narasimha on the three middle levels.

The sculpturing of the ornamental work is a very intricate and tedious process. It took nearly seven months to complete the work on the *rajagopura*. One has to watch the work in progress to comprehend its complexity.

SRI VENKATESHWARA (BALAJI) SHRINE: This shrine is designed in Chola architectural style with extensively detailed work on the outside. The top of this shrine is known as *Vishnukantha Vimana*. It is octagonal in shape with Garuda statues at the four corners. The *vimana* is divided into three parts—a pillared platform (*vedika*),

the "neck" (*kantha*), and *shikhara*. Facing east is a statue of Balaji, facing south is Dakshinamurti, facing west is Narasimha, and facing north is Adi Varaha. This *vimana* is 36 ft. tall and 17 ft. wide.

DURGA, LAKSHMI, BHUDEVI SHRINES: These three shrines are of similar dimensions, 27 ft. tall and 12.8 ft. wide. Statues on the *vimana* for Lakshmi are of Mahalakshmi in different poses and for Bhudevi shrine are those of Bhudevi. For the Durga shrine the architecture is slightly different. It is in the Pallava style and is a four-sided *Brahmakantha Vimana*, with Durga depicted in different forms. These three shrines have 112 pillars in addition to other decorative sculptures.

SRI ANJANEYA SHRINE: This shrine, 20.6 ft. high and 10.8 ft. wide, is located at the front entrance of the temple complex. The *vimana* has four different statues of Anjaneya.

SRI GANESHA SHRINE: The Ganesha shrine, 11.3 ft. high and 5.2 ft. wide, is the smallest shrine in the temple and is located in the *mahamandapa*.

THE NAVAGRAHAS: These nine planet

deities are installed on an open *vedika* inside the *mahamandapa*.

The doorways connecting the sanctums to the *mahamandapa* are decorated with sculptured details. There are three of them in addition to the one connecting the entrance *mandapa*. Starting from the bottom layer (*adhishtana*), elaborate carvings reach up to the ceiling ending in arched and decorative mythological motifs.

Padmasri M. Muthiah Sthapathi designed a unique interior incorporating statues of deities from various Indian temples. In niches flanked by carved pillars (*stambhas*) adorning the side walls are sixteen statues. Facing Lord Venkateshwara, by the right wall are the statues of Adi Varaha, Narasimha, Satyanarayana, Venkateshwara, Rama, Krishna, Dakshinamurti, and Chandrashekhara. At the left wall are Saraswati, Lakshini, Meenakshi, Kamakshi, Rajarajeshwari, Kamakoti Shakti, Durga, Subramanya Swami, and Ganesha. Most of the work on the statues was done on site. There are some repetitive forms such as the pillars and small lion-heads and small plaques.

After almost ten years from the start date,

on May 20 to 27, 1996, the *Maha Kumbhabhisheka* and *Sahasra Kalashabhisheka* were held. *Abhisheka* (literally, "bathing") denotes the ritual bathing of the image of a deity or sacred object. For the *Kumbhabhisheka*, a golden pot (*kalasha* or *kumbha*) with consecrated water was kept on the top of the temple.

What is the significance of having the idol inside the temple and a *kalasha* above it? The idol—such as Ganesha, Shiva, or Vishnu—has a particular form: it signifies the presence of *Brahman*, the Supreme Reality. The *kalasha* on top of the temple is not in the shape of any person or other image, and it thus represents the formless (*nirguna*, "without form") aspect of the Supreme Reality. A person approaching the temple from a distance is able to see the *kalasha* on top, but he or she enters the temple to worship the personal form of the Lord inside. Subjectively, this means that from a distance we see the highest goal we want to attain—the formless, *nirguna Brahman*—but in order to reach there, we must first go through the practice of worshiping the Supreme Reality with form (the *saguna* aspect of *Brahman*). Through worship of the Divine with attributes, we reach the highest—formless *Brahman*.

193

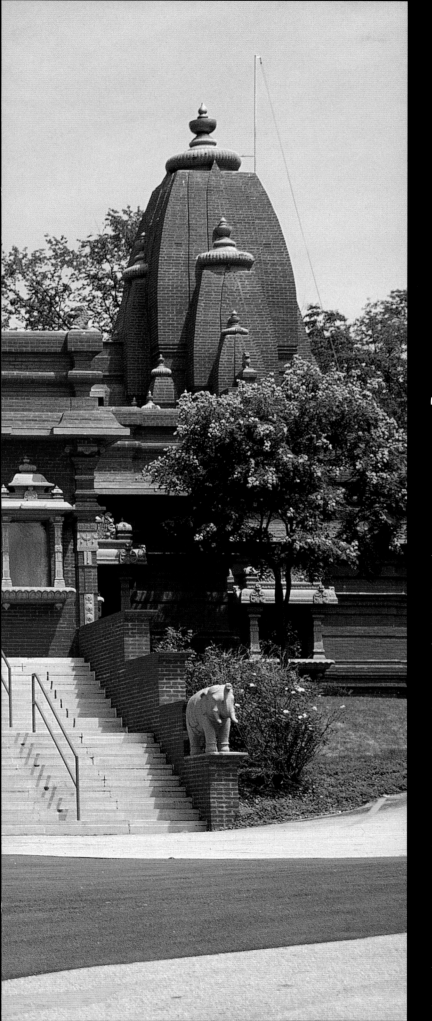

Hindu Jain Temple

Monroeville, Pennsylvania

The Hindu Temple in Pittsburgh, Pennsylvania, had its modest beginnings in the basement of an Indian store in Squirrel Hill, Pittsburgh, in late 1971. It arose as an offshoot of the then very active India Association of Pittsburgh. The need was felt that the growing immigrant Indian population required a permanent place of worship. Immediately plans were initiated to collect funds and establish a permanent location. In 1973, with the help of a few founding trustees, the current temple site in Monroeville was purchased—a 7-acre tract of land atop a picturesque hill, with a modern one-story church building. The Hindu Temple Society of North America, Pittsburgh, was incorporated in the state of Pennsylvania as a nonprofit organization. During the period 1973 to June 1984, this converted church building served as a unique religious center, where Hindus, Jains, Aryasamajis, and Sikhs worshiped under one roof as true Indian brethren.

Vision of Unity

From its very inception, the primary objective of the Hindu Temple (original name) has been not only to provide a nonsectarian united center of worship, but also to serve the cultural, social, and humanitarian needs of the Indian community and the community at large. An underlying objective has been to acquaint and foster among the children, the second generation born and raised in the United States, the great religious, philosophical, and cultural traditions of India; to instill in them such intrinsic values as truth, nonviolence, tolerance, and peace.

The structure was quickly embraced by the small community of Indians in the metropolitan Pittsburgh area, and the "temple" became a focal point and base for communal and religious activities. As the community expanded and grew, the need for a larger facility as well as a structure with stronger ethnic identity became apparent. Although the converted church-temple served the temporary needs of the community, it was felt that a truly authentic temple depicting Indian architectural style and in keeping

with the Hindu scriptures (*shastras*) should be built. In the debate that ensued, many divergent opinions arose, culminating in not one but three great temples of India, making Pittsburgh and its *Triveni* (three rivers), a holy center in the United States. First we envisioned building a beautiful temple dedicated to Sri Venkateshwara. The proponents of the universal approach continued to hold on to their lofty ideal. They reaffirmed, "The Hindu faith is essentially universal, catholic, permissive, and nondogmatic in its way of worship. The Hindu Temple of Pittsburgh is and shall remain nonsectarian and broad-based so as to meet the religious, spiritual, cultural, humanitarian, educational, and social needs of all its members."

The next few years, from 1976 to 1979, were indeed the lean years in the history of the Hindu Temple. Not only the very idea of building a new temple was questioned, but the very survival of the Hindu Temple was threatened. It took a great deal of courage and commitment to cast aside the doubts and move forward.

There is no other temple complex in the

world like this. When a devotee shared this vision with the late Sri G. D. Birla of India, Sri Birla was amazed at the daring concept and unorthodox approach. Although this concept of building a unique nonsectarian temple complex appealed to Sri Birla and he decided to help with this mission, he did point out that it will be an uphill task to hold such a diverse group together. The vision of a common place of worship and the cumbersome democratic process made the task formidable. In 1979, the Sikh group decided to build a *gurudwara* at a separate location.

Just at a time when the idea of a new temple was catching fire, the Monroeville borough unjustly refused the temple planners permission to build. Although many in the community saw this as an attack (by a few members of the Monroeville council) on the fundamental right to worship, the temple planners were hesitant to take the borough to court because of the costs involved. It was an act of divine providence that a devotee, a member of the Hindu Temple and associate of a large law office, volunteered to fight for the temple's legal rights at no cost. A court order to build the present

temple, overriding Monroeville's decision, was achieved.

The decision of the founding fathers of the Hindu Temple Society of North America, Pittsburgh, to build a cluster of Hindu, Jain, and Sikh temples around a central hall was an unprecedented and challenging idea. The committee members believed that various deities under one structure would bring new meaning to the basic Indian philosophy of unity among diversity. However, creating such a structure (that is itself rooted in traditional and ancient concepts) in a modern society caused a number of obstacles for all those involved in the project. First, for an architect trained in contemporary design to approach an ancient and alien subject such as an Indian temple was simply bizarre. Second, the community itself was divided on the design that their temple should take. One segment of the community expected a classical style, while the other segment wanted to capitalize on a unique modern design.

Initially the temple plan seemed to be doomed to failure since one simple design could not be decided upon. Fortunately,

PAGE 198, TOP: Decorative elephant used at the bottom of the staircase to welcome worshipers.

PAGE 198, BOTTOM: Finely decorated pillars line the interior of the temple.

PAGE 199: View from the *mahamandapa*. Natural light illuminates the entire temple interior.

the community's sense of unity and their dedication to their temple overcame the differences. As the prominent architect historian Percy Brown once wrote, "...like many medieval masterpieces, the Solanki Temples were not the produce of one mind, or even a group of minds, but were the spontaneous expression of the entire community, every individual, from the highest to the lowest being moved to take a personal interest in their construction." Thus, the Indian community of Pittsburgh was able to work together on a structure that they would all be proud of.

Turning Point

The year 1980 marked a turning point in the history of the new Hindu Temple. Seven patron families pledged an initial sum of money for the construction of the temple, so that the first phase, consisting of the foundation for the entire temple and walls of the three temples up to the roof level, could be completed.

Padmasri S. M. Ganapati Sthapati and the government of Andhra Pradesh provided the basic plans of the new temple at no cost, as the temple could afford none. The plans were drawn and redrawn by Shashi Patel to adapt them for local conditions. A devotee established contact with Sri G. D. Birla, and interested him in providing the architectural services and necessary deity images (*murtis*). In May 1981, Som Pura, representative of the late Sri Birla, arrived in Pittsburgh. After long discussions between the committee members and the architect, a decision was made for a simplified traditional form, known as Nagradi style, for the temple. This style of temple architecture is presently popular in northeast and central India. The architectural plan received universal approval. It was decided to build a temple housing the major deities of the Hindu pantheon, Jain Mahavirji, and a *havan kund* (or *homakunda*, fire pit for fire rituals).

After the outer design was decided upon, the inner plan was tackled. Initially an octagonal plan was considered. However, because of various functional limitations, this form had to be dismissed from serious consideration. As a result, a plan in the form of a cross evolved, based on a central hall and five temples surrounding it. On the main axis would be a Sri Lakshmi-Narayana temple with two subordinate temples of Sri Radha-Krishna and Sri Rama Parivar in the foreground. On the cross axis would be the Jain temple facing the Shiva temple.

PAGE 200: Entrance ornamentation shows Lord Venkateshwara flanked by Sri Devi and Bhudevi.

PAGE 201: Back view of the temple.

Amid renewed enthusiasm and after long and hard planning, the ground-breaking ceremony took place in October 1981 (*Dasserah* Day). It was an act of divine providence that Swami Sadanand Saraswatiji and Shri Sant Narayan Muniji of Parmartha Niketan, Rishikesh, happened to be visiting the United States at that time. On request, they obliged to visit Pittsburgh and lay the foundation stone for the new temple. The contacts thus established between the Hindu Temple and Parmartha Niketan proved to be of a great significance.

The shell structure started in the fall of 1980. The construction was to be in various phases depending on the availability of funds. The first phase of construction of building the foundation and the shells of the three major temples progressed rapidly with large-scale donations by the seven patrons and support from two hundred other families.

On February 6, 1983, the temple was vandalized, shocking the temple community. This act of wanton vandalism forged a new sense of unity and firm resolve to preserve, at any cost, the freedom and the right of worship. It produced a new sense of urgency, and the construction effort was stepped up with renewed zeal and firm resolve. After a bank loan was obtained, the four walls were raised and the roof was completed. Authentic and functional sanctum sanctorums were built, thanks to the generosity of a few dedicated families. Beautifully hand-carved marble *murtis* donated by benefactors arrived from India toward the end of 1983.

Since the ground-breaking ceremonies in 1981, the temple leadership had maintained close contact with Sri Sadanand Saraswati of Parmartha Niketan, culminating in the arrival of Sant Narayan Muniji in July 1983. With the arrival of Muniji in Pittsburgh, the temple came alive and became a vibrant place of worship, with daily prayers, *bhajans,* and *satsang.*

After the temple structure was constructed, it was decided to concentrate on completing the interior in preparation for the consecration ceremony for the deities. Dev Nagar designed the interior of the *mahamandapa* and five shrines. He drew inspiration from the details of the Nagara Style temples of the Mount Abu and Udaipur areas of Rajasthan, where he grew up. To keep the cost of the interior within a limited budget, he decided to simplify the construction process, concentrating on the essence of the decorative details and using locally available materials and craftsmen. All decorative work of the *mahamandapa* was constructed using a limited number of decorative shapes that were created in wood and installed by local carpenters. The flooring and pedestals for the deities were constructed with synthetic surface material resembling marble, which could be carved by carpenter's tools at less than half the cost of real marble.

The consecration ceremony (*Pranapratishtha*) was held in the summer of 1984. May 13, 1984, was a day of pure celebration for the Indian community of Pittsburgh. The consecration of the Hindu Temple became the fulfillment of a long-time dream, an idea that had been given form, shape, and content. For the children and the generations to come, the temple is more than a place of worship. It is a link to their roots, a symbol of their great Indian heritage, and a source of their identity and unity.

The *Pranapratishtha* ceremonies held on May 13 were conducted according to true Vedic tradition. This historical event marked the beginnings of another era during which the towers (*shikharas*) of the temple would be built, the *shikharas* that would proclaim to the whole world the essence of the Indian spirit. The consecration of the *murtis* in the new temple heralded the end of the beginning. There was no longer a question if the new Hindu temple would be built. Instead, the question had become: When it will be completed?

Final Phase

After the completion of the first phase, a second booster action became imperative to sustain the momentum. The trustees decided to take a loan from the bank to complete five functional temples. The bank demanded the loan to be guaranteed by personal assets of as many members as possible. Members willingly mortgaged their homes to obtain the loan, without which the *murtis* could not have been installed.

The basic structure of the temple was complete by the time the temple artisans (*shilpis*) arrived from India by late summer of 1988 to complete the job. The *shilpis* were responsible for the exterior intricate masonry work and ornate cement moldings. Hand-carving of individual bricks is an old art form. The *shilpis* have taken this art form and applied modern technology and their craftsmanship to it and created *shikharas* of elegance and grandeur. The entrance portico with a grand stone staircase is another unique feature of the temple. The team of *shilpis*, under the leadership of Padmasri M. Muthiah Sthapathi, created this outstanding temple and monument. Although the *shilpis* were the main artists behind most of the artistic work on the temple, local carpenters were also involved in making interior temple walls, arches, and brackets.

What we see in this temple complex is unity in diversity. Five temples under the same roof, including the Jain temple and one *yajna kund* (fire pit for fire rituals), which is symbolic of Arya Samaj. Given that *arya* means "noble," Arya Samaj consists of noble people dedicated to the principles of the Vedas.

On the occasion of the grand inauguration of this unique Hindu-Jain Temple of Pittsburgh, His Holiness Swami Chidananda Saraswati (Muniji) said: "The temple is a link between man and God, between the earthly life and the divine life, between the actual and the ideal. The temple is a means for crossing the ocean of *samsara*. Divine souls! Please remember this. Without overcoming the ego, one cannot expect the materialization of spiritual enlightenment. As soon as a man forgets his ego-self, he perceives every form as One. When everything becomes ours, there will not be deceit, fraud, anger, ego, or the feeling of vengeance against anyone. All are our kindred souls. In this evolution of the soul alone, one attains real happiness (*ananda*) and true contentment. Having attained this stage, life becomes purposeful and glorious."

Hindu Temple Society
Loudonville, New York

The origins of the Hindu Temple Society may be traced to the summer and fall of 1975. Frequent expressions of opinion in favor of such a society were evident at this time. A questionnaire specifically sought to explore the feelings of the community concerning the need for a temple and willingness to financially support it. The response was unexpectedly large and overwhelmingly favorable. A general meeting of interested people in the fall of 1975 led to a decision to form the Hindu Temple Society and an ad hoc committee to suggest a comprehensive plan.

The first landmark event was a meeting in January 1976, during which the Society was formally established and the first trustees elected and authorized to acquire property suitable for a temple. In April 1976, the Hindu Temple Society was incorporated as a nonprofit organization.

The next major event was the purchase of the property in Loudonville, New York, in April 1976. The financial risks were considerable: a loan was needed even for the down payment. But the decision—completely justified in hindsight—was made to go ahead.

The house on the 8-acre property had to be converted into a prayer hall. Thus was launched the renovation project of the summer of 1976, guided by able civil engineers and aided by active volunteers. The temple has seldom witnessed an outpouring of energy such as we saw that summer. The temple was inaugurated in grand style on August 28, 1976.

Consolidation

The years 1977-1985 were years of consolidation. Sunday services, celebration of major festivals, especially *Diwali*, activities aimed at children all became regular features. A kitchen, restrooms, and a parking lot were added. Elections to trustee positions were well contested, and the Temple Society grew in numbers. January 1985 marked another truly transforming event: the recruitment of Kurnaswamy Dikshitar as full-time priest. The stature of the temple as a place of sanctity, piety, and inspiring ritual grew immeasurably with his presence.

In 1987, once again the members of the Society rethought their future. Gradually, and not without controversy and debate, the idea grew and was endorsed that a larger, more aesthetic, more authentic, and more inspirational structure was needed. Now the members moved more slowly than in the early years but on a grander scale. Baran Basu of the United States was hired to design the temple, and Indianization was done by Selvaraja Stapathi. Plans were repeatedly made and scaled back, but finally on September 12, 1990, the Society contracted to build the new temple. As in 1976, the community was once again brave, and forged ahead with the construction phase despite having only one third of the required resources in hand.

The new temple was completed on November 1, 1991, and the grand *Diwali* celebrations between November 3 and November 7 attracted record attendance of more than 1,500 persons. The first formal idol installation ceremony at the new temple was the installation of Lord Ganesha

on January 23 to 26, 1992. Since January 26, 1992, all regular services of the temple have been conducted at the new facility.

End of the Beginning

The final event signifying what was truly characterized as the end of the beginning of the Hindu Temple Society was the idol installation ceremonies of Sri Mahalakshmi, Sri Narayana, Sri Shiva (Somanathji), and Sri Parvati (Prasannambika). The grand *Kumbhabhisheka* was held on June 17 to 21, 1992. These celebrations were performed under the direction of Sri Kurnaswamy Dikshitar according to the *Agama Shastra* by a renowned priest, Dr. Shamba Murthy Shivacharya from India, and others from various temples in the United States.

The project to construct entranceway towers (*gopuras*) was approved in 1993. After extensive research and discussion with various groups, a group headed by chief temple artisan (*shilpi*) Rajamanickam Selvaraj, a native

of Kumbakonam, Tamil Nadu, India, was selected. The crew of *shilpis* arrived from India in March 1995, and the work was started in April. The *shilpis* transformed a plain four-walled flat structure into a beautiful, authentic, and artistic temple.

Balasthapana ceremonies—the transfer of divine powers from the main deities to the ritual vessels (*kalashas*) and the metal idols (*utsavamurtis*)—were performed in May 1995, when the sanctum was closed for the construction to start. The *Pranapratishthapana* and *Kumbhabhisheka*—the transfer of divine powers and attributes back to the main deities—were performed on June 21 to 23, 1996. The initial *Kumbhabhisheka* and *Pratishthapana* for Sri Lakshmi Narayana and Sri Shiva Parvati had been performed on June 21, 1992. It so happened that exactly four years later on the same day, June 21, 1996, *Kumbhabhisheka* for the *gopura* began.

A unique feature of this temple is that the interior and all architectural details are

painted in the brightest colors to represent the ecstasy of the divine world. The temple also represents a blend of the modern and the traditional, the new and the old, preserving the time-tested traditional ways and values, and at the same time moving forward in the new world, adapting to the new ways of life. Several religious faiths, various forms of worship, and diverse kinds of rituals and customs have found their place in the Hindu religion. The Albany Hindu Temple reflects this unifying vision by providing deities that represent various branches of Hinduism.

Sri Ganesha Temple of Nashville
Nashville, Tennessee

Those of us who arrived in Nashville, Tennessee, in the late 1960s and early 1970s were of the notion that eventually we would go home to settle down. But soon we realized that home is here in America, thousands of miles away from Mother India. In a sense, as pioneers, we were confronted with the reality of raising a new generation, born on this soil, without the emotional and spiritual support provided by our great religious institutions. The need for a strong religious and cultural center to foster our rich heritage was strongly felt here and in a number of other communities around the United States of America.

Informal discussions were held in 1978 and 1979, and a committee was formed in 1980 to provide an organizational structure for a temple and cultural center. There was considerable discussion regarding the name of the organization as well as its long-term goals. Finally in October 1980, the Hindu Cultural Center of Tennessee was officially incorporated in the state of Tennessee.

Under the auspices of the Hindu Cultural Center, the members began meeting at various homes to observe religious functions and festivals. As the number of participants steadily increased, they found it necessary to locate to a larger meeting place. While continuing to meet this way, they began their search for a suitable place as their permanent home. They did not have to wait long, for an ideal 13-acre site was located in the Bellevue area with gently sloping hills and a magnificent view. On *Ganesha Chaturthi* day, August 22, 1982, the ground-breaking ceremony for the Hindu Temple was performed at the temple site by the chief priest from the Pittsburgh Venkateswara Temple. This grand event was witnessed by several hundred devotees from Middle Tennessee, and a group of members from the local community took a pledge to support the cause.

The temple planners were fortunate to have one of the leading temple architects from India, Padmasri M. Muthiah Sthapathi, visit them in 1983. A survey of the membership revealed that the overwhelming majority of the people wanted three deities installed in the temple, Ganesha, Shiva, and Vishnu, and it was decided to have Lord Ganesha as the main deity in accordance with the wishes of the community. Muthiah Sthapathi incorporated these wishes in his plans. In January 1984 it was decided to have the temple project completed in several phases. On *Ganesha Chaturthi* day in 1984 construction began for the first phase of the project.

A Blend of the Traditional and Modern

The Sri Ganesha Temple complex is a product both of traditional design and modern innovation, a combination of the old and the new. Thus, in order to better appreciate it, it is important to look at the history of Hindu architecture and traditions and to note the variations that make this temple appropriate to time and place.

The design of the Sri Ganesha Temple of the Hindu Cultural Center is based on the temple architecture of the Chola Dynasty (900 A.D. - 1150 A.D.), which was at its height during the reign of Rajaraja and Rajendra Chola. The temples at Tanjore (Thanjavur), which was originally known as Rajarajaeshwaram and Gangaikonda Cholapuram in Tamil Nadu, attest to the architectural excellence achieved during this period.

PAGES 210 and 211: Nestled against the rolling hills of Nashville, Tennessee, and set in wooded surroundings, the Sri Ganesha Temple is an architectural wonder.

PAGE 212: Entrance to the main sanctum sanctorum (*mulasthana* entrance).

PAGE 213: Entrance stairway elegantly designed with elephant, lion, and other motifs. The temple flagpole can be seen in the background.

PAGE 214, TOP: Decorative *vimana*.

PAGE 214, BOTTOM: Detailed work above the entrance door.

PAGE 215, BOTTOM: Worshipers at the *homa kunda*.

PAGE 215, TOP: Line drawing of Lord Ganesha. *Line drawing courtesy of M. Muthiah Sthapathi, Chennai, India.*

As surviving examples show, it was not until 600 A.D. that temples took on an elaborate form. The earlier ones were quite simple in plan, with a small sanctum (*garbhagriha*) enclosed on three sides and opening to the east onto a columned hall (*mandapa*). The *garbhagriha* and *mandapas* were flat-roofed. The surfaces of the outer sanctum walls and the *mandapas* were ornate, covered with figures of deities and mythical beings. Examples of such early temples can be found among the ruins at Aihole in the Dharwar and Dhapwad district of Karnataka and at Tigawa in the Jabbulpore district, both of which are from the fifth century A.D. It is interesting to note that the walls of the inner sanctum were left quite plain, a tradition that is continued to this day.

This simple model of a temple became much more elaborate over time. The biggest change was in the tower (*shikara*), which became highly ornate and significantly taller with multiple tiers (*karnakutas*). The Chola temple of Tanjore is an example of this trend, having a very elaborate, 190-ft. tall sanctum tower (*vimana*), making it one of the tallest temple structures to this day. Also, later temples were enclosed by a series of courtyards called *pradakshina patha* or *prakara*, which were used during festivals for processions of the deities.

At the Nashville temple, all of the images in the *garbhagriha* are made of granite, following a tradition established by many temples all over India: Kedhareshwar at Kedharinath, Kashi Vishwanath at Kashi, Badhrinarayana at Badhrinath, Ragunath at Devaprayag, Lingaraja at Bubaneshwar, and Omkareshwar on the banks of the river Narmada, to name a few. In fact the naturally formed (*svayambhu*) *Shivalinga* of the Sri Ganesha Temple is from the Narmada near Omkareshwar, a place that is additionally sanctified by Adi Shankara, who received his *sannyasa* from Guru Govind Bagavadpada there.

The design of the Sri Ganesha Temple follows the basic Chola pattern in shape, decoration, and proportion; however, there are some variations. The main *prakara* is indoors, fused into the *mahamandapa*; this modification allows for climate-controlled comfort during worship. The main *vimana* has five tiers, rising 48 ft. into the air. This temple has sixteen forms of Ganesha in the niches (*garbhakoshtas*) on the outer walls of the Ganesha sanctum—a feature of no other temple in North America to date. And, of course, it was built using modern construction methods and materials and includes modern conveniences; however, the artwork has all been done by traditional Indian craftsmen.

The Sri Ganesha Temple thus combines the old with the new, producing a structure that should serve this area for generations to come.

Inauguration

The inauguration of a temple is an elaborate affair, involving many rituals prescribed by the Vedas. Together these rituals are called *Pratishtha*, which literally means "the installation of a deity." The *Kumbhabhisheka* ceremony is central to the *Pratishtha*, marking the transfer of power into the idol. The idols thus prepared give a focus for the prayers of the common man.

The deities consecrated during the inaugu-

ration of the Nashville temple were:

GANESHA: The main deity of the temple is Lord Ganesha (Vighneshwara, Ganapati). Lord Ganesha represents *Om*, or the *Pranava*, chief mantra of the Hindus. Nothing can be done without uttering it. This explains the practice of invoking Ganesha before beginning any rite or undertaking any project.

Ganesha's various names and his very form hold rich symbolism. Ganesha is also called Vighneshwara, "the remover of obstacles (*vighna*)," and this power in him is invoked before any major undertaking. His two feet represent the power of knowledge and the power of action. Ganesha's

vehicle (*vahana*) is a mouse (*mushika*). The significance of riding on a mouse is the complete conquest over egoism, which the mouse represents. In his hand he holds an elephant prod (*ankusha*), which represents his rulership of the world. It is the emblem of divine royalty.

Ganesha's large ears and closed mouth beckon us to listen more and talk less. Elephants are very wise animals; this indicates that Lord Ganesha is an embodiment of wisdom. It also denotes the process of evolution: the mouse gradually evolves into an elephant and finally becomes a man. This is why Ganesha has a human body, an elephant's head, and a mouse as his vehicle. The elephant is wise and

strong, but gentle at the same time. Ganesha is also called Ganapati, "the Lord of *ganas*," or groups, such as, for instance, groups of elements or groups of senses. He is the head of the followers of Shiva, the celestial servants of Lord Shiva.

The Vaishnavas also worship Lord Ganesha. They have given him the name of Tumbikkai Alwar, which means "the divinity with the proboscis (the elephant's trunk)."

OTHER TEMPLE DEITIES: Also included in the temple are Sri Shiva, Sri Venkateshwara, Sri Parvati, Sri Subramanya, Sri Lakshmi, Sri Rama, Sri Krishna, Sri Jagannath, and Sri Durga.

Sri Shiva Vishnu Temple
Davie, Florida

The Shiva Vishnu Temple in Broward County in the sunshine state of South Florida is a Hindu temple based on the traditional principles outlined in the *Agama Shastras.* The concept of combining Shiva and Vishnu as main deities within the same temple was conceived of in 1993. The predecessor organizations to the temple were the Hindu Temple of South Florida and the Vedic Hindu Temple of South Florida. The original temple shrine consisting of pictures of deities was inaugurated in 1989. In May 1993, the temple was reorganized and registered as a nonprofit religious organization in the state of Florida.

Sri Ganesha Homa and ground-breaking ceremonies were performed in August 1996 to inaugurate the construction of a traditional temple, with Shiva (Ekambaranatheshwara) and Vishnu (Venkateshwara) as the main deities. Other deities planned for the temple included Ganesha, Parvati (Kamakshi), Murugan (Karttikeya), Saraswati, Ayyappan, Lakshmi (Sri Devi), Andal (Bhudevi), Ram Parivar, Anjaneya, Krishna, and the Navagrahas.

In 1996 Dr. V. Ganapati Sthapati of Mahabalipuram (near Chennai, India), was invited to advise the community on building a South Indian Dravidian-style temple based on the *Vastu Shastra*. The preliminary drawings for the temple and a separate community hall were drawn up and presented to the community in June 1997. On *Vijayadashami* day in October 1997, a new Balalaya shrine was created, with the consecration ceremony (*Pratishthapana*) performed of the movable images (*utsavamurtis*). These images, made of the five-metal alloy known as *panchaloha* and of wood (*athimara*), represented the deities to be installed in the new temple.

In 1997, the construction committee, consisting of experienced community architects and engineers, initiated the process of getting approvals and permits from Broward County. The site plan was approved in June 1998. On June 14, 1998, the ceremony for laying of the foundation stone (*shilanyasam*) was performed by H. H. Sri Sri Sri Tridandi Chinna Jeeyar Swamiji.

Fund-raising activities started at a fast pace with annual temple banquets and personal individual solicitation for sponsorship of *Ishta Devatas*. Additional adjacent land of more than one acre was donated to the temple for parking facilities.

The civil and building construction work began on April 19, 1999. Twelve temple artisans (*shilpis*) from Mahabalipuram, India, arrived on April 10, 2000, and started work on the temple soon thereafter. Under the supervision of Ganapati Sthapati, the images of the deities (*vigrahas*) were carved by noted stone sculptors from Mahabalipuram, using resonant black granite.

Temple Structure

The temple is a large structure with two entrance towers (*rajagopuras*) and two sanctum towers (*vimanas*) over each of the main shrines. The total area of the temple is more than 6,000 sq. ft. The architecture of the main Shiva shrine and his family grouping (*Parivar*) is built according to Chola and Pallava style (tenth century) architecture, and the main Venkateshwara (Balaji) shrine and the *Parivars* are built according

to Vijayanagara style (twelfth century). The Ayyappan shrine is built according to the style of Kerala. Elaborate decorations are carved over the shrines and the pillars.

Dr. V. Ganapati Sthapati, our chief *Vastu* architect, is a master temple designer and builder with an international reputation. His assistant, Sthapati Madhu Selvanathan, was instrumental in putting together a team of eleven *shilpis,* with Sthapati Nagaraj as the supervisor. All of them worked long hours for nineteen months to create an architectural masterpiece.

The layout of the Shiva Vishnu Temple complex accommodates Shiva on the south side and Vishnu on the north side. The two main shrines are designated as Shiva Vastu and Vishnu Vastu. Both of them are facing east and aligned along the north-south axis. The sanctums (*garbhagrihas*) occupy a square grid of 3 by 3 units, signifying 9 by 9 = 81 smaller units at the center called *Brahmasthana,* the nuclear energy field. The *garbhagriha* is annexed to an entrance hall (*mukhamandapa*) for performing various worship ceremonies. Around the *garbhagriha* of Shiva and Vishnu sufficient space is provided for free circumambulation (*pradakshina*).

Around the *garbhagriha,* along the peripheral wall, are minor shrines of *Parivara Devatas,* namely Ayyappan, Saraswati, and Karttikeya on the western side of Shiva's shrine, while Sri Devi and Bhudevi are installed behind the Vishnu shrine. On the southern side are the shrines of Ganapati and Kamakshi, while on the north, the shrines of Sita Rama, Radhakrishna, and Anjaneya. They are so dimensioned that they resonate with the main sanctums. The shrine areas include Garuda, Vishnu's vehicle (*vahana*), and an offering pedestal (*balipitha*); and Nandi, Shiva's *vahana,* and a *balipitha* for Shiva. The Navagrahas are installed in the northeast corner by the Shiva Vastu. Each of the two main shrines also has its own temple flagpole (*dhvajastambha*). Shiva Vastu and Vishnu Vastu each has a large front hall for the congregation of worshipers. These two *vastus* are also linked by a common passage with openings at the ends.

There are two towers, each with three stories, one for Shiva and the other for

Vishnu. The towers and *vimanas* are so designed as to resonate with each other, giving an effect of a structural symphony. All the structures and pillars are spatially harmonious so that a spirit of oneness prevails today and should continue to prevail for all days to come.

Consecration Ceremonies

For many months the community planned and prepared for the temple consecration ceremonies. The *Kumbhabhisheka* and *Pratishthapana* for the temple and all the deities took place over three days, starting on November 23 and culminating on November 25, 2001. The auspicious date was fixed by Vedic pundits and astrologers according to Hindu *shastras.*

Agama pundits from India arrived for this historic and auspicious function under the leadership of Sri Savya Sachi Swamigal of Karnataka, India, a well-known *Agama Shastra* pundit who has performed innumerable *Kumbhabhisheka* rituals in India and in the United States.

Sri Sri Radha Krishna Temple
Spanish Fork, Utah

Surrounded by majestic mountain peaks and azure skies, Utah's Sri Sri Radha Krishna Temple was founded by Caru Das (Christopher Warden) in 1996. The beginnings of the project can be traced back to 1992 with the purchase of a 5.5-acre plot in Spanish Fork, just south of Provo, Utah. An additional 9.5 acres were added later that year. Devotees constructed a 3,500 sq. ft. temple and ashram on that site, which was the focus of group activities until the ground-breaking for the current temple on November 10, 1996. Construction on the new temple began on February 16, 1998, after the plans were approved by the Utah County building inspectors.

Spacious Beauty

Situated on an elevated 15-acre plot in rural Utah, this 50-ft.-high temple was modeled after a famous devotional site in India called Kusum Sarovar, "temple on a lake of flowers." It features a main dome 25 ft. in diameter, surrounded by seventeen other domes.

The temple's building plan includes 108 arches and columns, sculptures, and murals, as well as open patios, colonnades, gardens, fountains, and an outdoor stage and amphitheater that can accommodate crowds of up to 5,000 at a time. The main temple shrine houses exquisite black teakwood and gold-leafed altars, and marble deities carved from quarries in Jaipur, India.

Designed by Vaibhavi Devi, the founder's wife, the temple incorporates the traditional architectural styles of ancient India. Part of the temple's beauty lies in its panoramic mountain surroundings and its expansive view of the South Utah Valley. The landscaping around the temple includes a beautiful lily pond stocked with multicolored koi. Inside a gazebo a gold-leafed statue of Krishna playing on his flute overlooks the scene, while peacocks wander about the area and sometimes mount the outdoor stage for an impromptu performance.

Vaibhavi Devi says, "With its lofty domes, elaborately designed arches and columns, and architectural style of traditional India, this will be one of the most beautiful buildings in all of America." Caru Das adds, "Half of the beauty of the building will lie in the magnificence of its setting, high on a hilltop, with a commanding view of South Utah Valley, panoramic vistas on all sides, and yet clearly visible from Interstate 15."

Visitors are greeted by wandering llamas and a 200,000-gallon freshwater pond and waterfall outside the temple. Ascending a wide stairway to the second story, hand-carved teakwood doors open into the main dome area, which features arched windows and a white marble floor. Centered under the 33,000 lb. dome is a 9 ft. lotus flower, constructed of green and pink marble.

The deities housed in the temple include Radha Krishna, Sita Rama, Lakshmana, Hanuman, Chaitanya, Nityananda, Ganesha, and Shiva. The main alcove features a teakwood throne. Eight 40-in.-high marble deities, which were hand-carved in India

PAGES 226 and 227: Front view of the Sri Sri Radha Krishna Temple, set amid the rolling hills of Spanish Fork, Utah.

PAGE 228: Main entrance to the temple.

PAGE 229: View from the reflecting pool.

by Krishna artisans, also adorn the dome area. Two of them—Krishna carved from black stone and Radha, from white—occupy the throne opposite the large entry doors. They embody the divine couple, representing the ultimate in sacred worship of Krishna.

The building can hold nearly 500 people indoors, in addition to its outdoor accommodations. Its first floor also features teakwood doors, an ice-white quartz floor, and a large lobby that contains a variety of Hindu statuary. A large gift shop is also housed on this level near the lobby, featuring literature, clothing, jewelry, beads,

pictures, and altar paraphernalia.

A Temple for All

In addition to providing a place for worship, the temple is open to the public from just before midday until closing at night. Construction of the temple was partly funded by a donation by the Church of Latter Day Saints, and it is the sincere hope of the temple's founders that this facility will become a meeting and congregation area for all community groups, not just the followers of Krishna Consciousness. Services are well attended by the residents of the greater Salt Lake City area, and Brigham

Young University students and those from local schools are frequent guests.

To the 3,500 Asian-Indian Americans residing in Utah the significance of this achievement cannot be understated. The first Indians arrived in Utah more than one hundred years ago as share-croppers in the region. This is the first temple to have been built there since their arrival a century ago.

The beauty of this temple stands as a testament to the dedication of its devotees, and is a shining example of Utah's growing Asian-Indian community.

A local newspaper wrote about the emerging temple: "Caru Das, who along with his wife Vaibhavi Devi, made his vision of building the 1,500 sq. ft. building come to fruition, said the temple's location is a testament to pluralism in America. . . . Indeed, Das and his wife are unmatched nationwide in creating a Krishna temple that captures the exquisite details of true Indian architecture. And that it exists here in this rustic Utah County setting, where 90 percent of the population are members of the Church of Jesus Christ of Latter Day Saints, makes it all the more remarkable."

PAGE 232, TOP: View of the massive domes and ornamentation of the temple.

PAGE 232, BOTTOM: The *mahamandapa* with the main sanctum at the far end.

PAGE 233, TOP: Exterior wall ornamented with pillars and fine work.

PAGE 233, BOTTOM: Intricate work on an archway that forms a series of archways that encircle the temple.

Sri Venkateswara Temple Pittsburgh
Penn Hills, Pennsylvania

Sri Venkateswara Temple, situated in Penn Hills, an eastern suburb of Pittsburgh, has become the illustrious abode of Sri Venkateshwara (Venkateswara). It is one of the first Hindu temples of North America, and has come to be known as the Tirumala of the Western Hemisphere. The temple architecture is modeled after the famous Venkateswara Temple in Tirupati, India.

The temple was established as a nonprofit religious organization in August 1975. The idols (*vigrahas*) were a gift from Tirumala Tirupati Devasthanams of Andhra Pradesh. Since then the temple has cherished a number of important milestones, celebrating them with memorable religious and cultural functions.

The First of Its Kind

The Sri Venkateswara Temple follows the *Pancharatra Agama*, an ancient text comprising 108 *samhitas* (collections). The deity in the main sanctum sanctorum (*garbhagriha*) in the main hall (*mahamandapa*) is Sri Venkateshwara (Lord of Venkata, a representation of Vishnu).

PAGES 234 and 235: Front view of the famous Sri Venkateswara Temple near Pittsburgh. Set high on the Penn Hills, this is one of the first temples to be built in the United States.

PAGE 236: Side view of the temple complex, with the entrance to the community hall in the foreground. The temple can be seen in the background behind the community hall.

PAGE 237: The interior of temple, showing the pillars and ornamentation.

The ground-breaking ceremony took place on June 30, 1976, amid great excitement in the whole country, as this was the first temple to be built in the United States and designed like the great temple of Andhra Pradesh, dedicated to Lord Venkateshwara. The blueprint for the temple was drawn up by Sri Dev Nagar, a local architect, and very soon thereafter construction began. The construction progressed and the consecration ceremony (*Pratishthapana*) was held on November 17, 1976, with devotees traveling from all over the United States to witness this great event.

After this auspicious event, plans were set in motion to celebrate the *Kumbhabhisheka*, which took place on June 8, 1977. Thereafter, the main tower (*rajagopura*) was built and consecrated on October 22, 1978. The water tank used for festivals, also known as *pushkarini*, was inaugurated on May 28, 1979. The main auditorium (*kalyana mandapa*) was completed on November 23, 1990. The final *prakara* (veranda or passage around the sanctum sanctorum) was completed on September 1, 2001.

Access to the temple is through a side entrance; the main *rajagopura* entrance is open during special occasions and in summer. Upon ascending the steps of the *rajagopura*, one sees a life-size mural depicting the *Gitopadesha*, the renowned "Divine Song" (*Bhagavad Gita*) of Lord Krishna (the ninth incarnation of Vishnu), as he reveals his divine nature to Arjuna on the eve of the Mahabharata War. To the left of the mural is the sanctum (*sannidhi*) of Sri Ganesha (the Lord of the Ganas, the troops of Lord Shiva).

It is customary to proceed to the left of the flagpole (*dhvajastambha*) and the offering pedestal (*balipitha*) when entering the *mahamandapa*, and exit from the right. The *dhvajastambha* is the flagpole on which is hoisted the flag of the main deity, Sri Venkateshwara, to announce special festivals at the temple. During festivals, offerings are placed on the *balipitha*.

The *prakara* surrounding the *mahamandapa* adds spaciousness to the temple. The *vahanas* (divine mounts) are kept there.

These are used for carrying the metal idols (*utsavamurtis*) in procession during special occasions. The three *vahanas* are Garuda Vahana (the divine kite, a vehicle of Vishnu), Gaja Vahana (elephant), and Sesha Vahana (Adisesha, the Divine Serpent).

Satyanarayana Puja is performed at the western end of the *prakara*. This popular *puja* is attended by a large number of devotees, particularly on weekends and full-moon days.

The *mahamandapa* has four pillars in the center, which form a gateway to the sanctum sanctorum. The main shrine (*garba-gudi*), guarded by two *dvarapalakas* (guards), Jaya and Vijaya, belongs to Sri Venkateshwara. To the left is the *sannidhi* of Padmavati, seated on a lotus of eight petals. She is worshiped as the Goddess of Wealth, both spiritual and material. On the right is the *sannidhi* of Bhudevi (Goddess of Earth), who is also known as Andal. She is sculpted standing on a lotus platform (*padmapitha*) holding blue lilies (*nilorpalas*) in her hands.

Her right hand holds a parrot.

Sri Venkateshwara is represented here with four arms and in a standing position (*sthanakamurti*) on a *padmapitha*. His rear right hand carries the discus (*sudarshana chakra*), symbolizing the original and indestructible thought of the Supreme Being. The rear left hand grasps the conch (*sanka*), representing knowledge and wisdom. The front right hand is in the *varadahasta* position of affording protection, and the front left hand is resting on the hip (in the *katyavalambita hasta* pose).

Facing the main shrine of Sri Venkateshwara is the *sannidhi* of Garuda, who is the *vahana* of Vishnu. Garuda is in a standing position with his hands folded in prayer. This *sannidhi* also has the metal idol (*utsavamurti*) of Sri Anjaneya, son of Vayu and a great devotee of Sri Rama, the eighth incarnation of Vishnu.

Pilgrimage Center

The temple has grown in the past 25 years,

PAGE 238: Elegantly decorated *ratha* (chariot), which is used to take the *utsavamurtis* around the temple in ceremonial procession.

PAGE 239: Main entrance to the temple.

PAGE 240, TOP: A depiction of *Gitopadesham*—Sri Krishna giving Arjuna the teachings of the *Bhagavad Gita*.

PAGE 240, BOTTOM: Passageway around the temple for *pradakshina*.

PAGE 241, Top: Temple *vimanas*.

PAGE 241, BOTTOM LEFT: *Rajagopura* with *kalashas* on the top.

PAGE 241, BOTTOM RIGHT: Decorative mural in the interior of the temple.

serving 125,000 devotees a year from all over the United States and the world. Since the inauguration of the temple, a kitchen, large auditorium, and dining hall facilities have been added to facilitate the needs of the many visitors.

The Silver Jubilee celebrations commemorating the establishing of the temple began on Vijaya Dasami in 2001, and continued for one year.

Sri Venkateswara Temple has become a major pilgrimage center in the United States. This is perhaps the only temple in the world where, annually, more than 20,000 *pujas* are performed on behalf of

devotees who request those services by mail, phone, fax, and e-mail. A sacramental offering called *kumkuma prasada* is mailed to these devotee families after the *pujas* have been performed.

The temple truly belongs to its multitude of devotees, because the contributions come from literally thousands of donors. This fact enables all visitors to be treated with equal deference.

The temple encourages and supports the rich heritage of India's performing arts by organizing many cultural events. There is no eminent musician who has not performed in this abode of the Lord of Shrinivasa. ⚱

Hindu Society of Nevada
Las Vegas, Nevada

The Hindu Society of Nevada, also know as the Hindu Temple and Cultural Center of Las Vegas, was formed in 1995 to provide a permanent venue for engaging in the religious and cultural traditions of Hindus. A common gathering ground is not only important for the current purposes but also for those of future generations. The Hindu Temple and Cultural Center of Las Vegas began as a vision, and after its completion, it will provide a physical space for Indians throughout the Las Vegas valley to maintain their traditions and share them with their families.

For years, community members had opened their own homes or rented out community halls all over Las Vegas as gathering places for religious and cultural events. These temporary spaces were transformed for an afternoon or evening into Indian cultural halls. Now, the community has established a venue for its activities, which is no longer a traveling stage but a permanent site. It is a testimony to the importance of religion and Indian culture in the lives of the members of the Hindu community and the desire to share those values with the greater Las Vegas population.

The Hindu Society of Nevada was formally established in 1995 with by-laws and constitution formed and tax-exempt status acquired. The first fund-raiser held in June 1995 was a great success, demonstrating that the small but dynamic Indian community was committed to supporting a project of this size. With this type of enthusiasm, devotion, and dedication, the stage was set to build the first Hindu temple in the gambling capital of the world, Las Vegas.

The search for the temple site took almost two years. During the search process, the temple planners considered empty lots and existing buildings from the northwest to the southeast. The empty lots would have required a rezoning process for a religious building. The planners also toured existing churches with the idea of buying one and converting it into a temple. Despite these various options, they chose a site that was pre-zoned for a religious building. Not only is the site easily accessible from all parts of the valley, but its slightly elevated position also offers an exquisite view of the valley and the surrounding mountain peaks. The 5-acre parcel of land is located next to a neighborhood park and an elementary school.

A temple planning and design committee was established. The noted Shashi Patel, chief architect from Pittsburgh, who has extensive experience in designing Hindu temples in America and Europe, was hired by Hindu Society of Nevada to design the Hindu Temple of Las Vegas.

Construction and Consecration

During 1999, engineers and consultants worked on infrastructure plans. The grand ground-breaking ceremony was held on April 21, 1999, after the date was chosen by Sri Krishnamacharyulu, an Indian priest from Los Angeles, who had identified that date as auspicious according to the Hindu scriptures. Another ground-breaking ceremony, performed by Bhanu Joshi, a local priest, was held on May 6, with great excitement among the community members. The building permit was issued by the City of Las Vegas on May 26, and construction work began.

PAGES 242 and 243: Nestled away in a residential suburb of Las Vegas is the Hindu Temple of Las Vegas. Restricted by local ordinances to shape and color, this temple still stands out among other buildings as a Hindu temple.

PAGE 244: Masterfully carved wooden Ganesha figure.

PAGE 245, LEFT: Sanctum for Lord Ganesha prior to the *Pranapratishthana* ceremony for the sacred installation of the idol.

PAGE 245, RIGHT: Line drawing of the discus (*chakra*), the weapon held by Lord Vishnu in his upper right hand.
Line drawing courtesy of V. Ganapati Sthapati & Associates, Chennai, India.

Early in 2001, images of deities (*murtis*) were ordered to be carved out of marble by temple artisans from North India. An ordained Hindu priest, Sri Gopal Krishnamacharyulu, was hired from India as a permanent priest for the temple.

The preparations for the opening ceremonies for consecration of the temple started in earnest. Various committees were formed to celebrate this wonderful occasion. The temple was consecrated during ceremonies spanning April 27, 28, and 29, 2001. Visitors from all over the United States arrived to witness this gala event. Las Vegas was transformed from a gambling capital into a spiritual haven.

The committee is very grateful to the Indian community of Las Vegas for their generous donations for the first phase of this two-phased project. The first phase, completed at the end of January 2001, covers approximately 5,000 sq. ft. of built-up floor space, including the main temple building, which is more than 3,000 sq. ft. It has a capacity to hold close to 500 people, and can accommodate classrooms, priest's quarters, and an outdoor patio. The second phase,

which will consist of a two-story cultural hall with an auditorium and a full commercial kitchen, will provide 7,000 sq. ft. of space on each floor. This much space is necessary to accommodate not only the current requirements of our community, but also the expanding needs of the coming years.

The temple complex will be a gathering place for attendees of both religious and cultural activities. The temple itself serves as a religious center, and a priest is available for *pujas* and other ceremonies. The outdoor patio is intended for holding cultural events. Classes are held for both children and adults on meditation, yoga, the *Bhagavad Gita*, as well as for learning computer skills.

A milestone was reached when the consecration ceremony, *Maha Pranapratishtha Mahotsav*, was held on October 26 through 28, 2001, for all the deities, except for the Jain *Pratishtha*, which took place on November 3 to 4, 2001. Grand religious celebrations were held and rituals performed by priests from all over the country. The event was very well attended by the local community and visitors from all over the country.

The Installed Deities

The temple has the following idols installed:

KRISHNA PARIVAR (KRISHNA, RADHA): Because of his great power, Lord Krishna is one of the most commonly worshiped deities in the Hindu faith. He is considered to be the eighth *avatara* of Lord Vishnu. Sri Krishna delivered the teachings that constitute the *Bhagavad Gita* to Arjuna, the warrior prince, on the battlefield of Kurukshetra. He, like Lord Rama, is also known for his bravery in destroying evil throughout his life. Lord Krishna is usually depicted as playing the flute, and often together with Radha. The pair symbolizes the eternal love between a human being and God.

SHIVA PARIVAR (SHIVA, PARVATI): Lord Shiva appears in a blissfully meditative posture. He has matted hair, which holds the flowing Ganges River and a crescent moon, a serpent coiled around his neck, a trident in one hand, and ashes smeared all over his body. Lord Shiva's attributes represent his victory over demonic activity. His vehicle is a bull named Nandi, symbol of happiness and strength. Lord Shiva is often worshiped in the form of *Shivalinga*, the formless form of the Divine.

BALAJI AND PADMAVATI: Venkateshwara (Venkateshwer or Venkatachalapathi) is another form of Lord Vishnu. He is also known as Balaji or Bithala.

RAMA PARIVAR (RAMA, SITA, LAKSHMANA, HANUMAN): Lord Rama, hero of the *Ramayana* epic and epitome of a virtuous man, is one of the most adored deities of the Hindu pantheon. He holds a bow and arrow, indicating his readiness to destroy evil. He is commonly pictured in a family setting, with his wife Sita, brother Lakshmana, and devotee Hanuman, who sits near his feet. Hanuman, the monkey general, helped Rama fight evil King Ravana, who had captured Sita. During his battle against Ravana, Lakshmana, Rama's brother, was wounded and Rama sent Hanuman to get a healing herb from the Himalayan mountains. Hanuman was very strong but not very smart. He couldn't remember which herb he was supposed to bring, so he brought back the whole mountain. Hanuman is the patron deity of fighters and represents the ideal devotee. His devotion to Rama is shown by Rama's image on his chest and by the sign of Vishnu on his forehead.

GANESHA: Ganesha, also known as Ganapati, Vighneshwara, and Vighnaharta, is an extremely popular Hindu deity. He is called the Lord and Destroyer of Obstacles. People mostly worship him to ask for success in undertakings and for intelligence. He is worshiped before any venture is started. He is also the deity of education, knowledge, wisdom, literature, and the fine arts.

DEVIS—DURGA, GAYATRI, SARASWATI, AND LAKSHMI: Goddess Durga, also known as Parvati or Lalita, is the consort of Lord Shiva and exists in various divine forms, both friendly and fearful. Two of her fierce but very powerful forms are Durga (Goddess Beyond Reach) and Kali (Goddess of Destruction). Both have eight hands and great power and energy (*shakti*). Durga rides on a lion and Kali rides on the corpse of a demon. The family of Lord Shiva—wife Parvati and sons Ganesha and Karttikeya—is an ideal example of family unity and love. Parvati has a charming personality and is worshiped by married women wishing for a happy married life.

The consort of Lord Vishnu, Lakshmi, is the goddess of prosperity, purity, chastity, and generosity. Her four hands represent four spiritual virtues. She sits on a fully

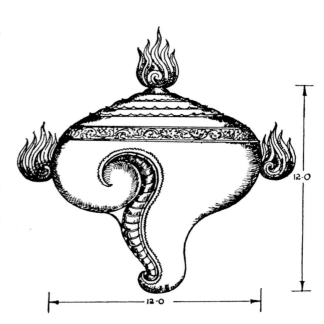

HINDU TEMPLE & INDIAN CULTURE CENTER

blossomed lotus, the seat of divine truth. Her personal charm is considered par excellence. An aura of divine happiness, mental and spiritual satisfaction, and prosperity always exists around her. One palm is extended to bless the people.

The Goddess of Knowledge, Saraswati is the consort of Lord Brahma and possesses the powers of speech, wisdom, and learning. She has four hands representing the four aspects of the human personality engaged in learning: mind, intellect, alertness, and ego. She holds the sacred scriptures in one hand and a lotus, symbolizing true knowledge, in the second. With her other two hands she plays the music of love and life on the *vina*. She is dressed in white, a sign of purity, and rides on a white swan. In one hand she carries a spear called *shakti*, which symbolizes the destruction of negative tendencies in a human being.

JAIN PARIVAR (MAHAVIRJI AND PARSH-VANATHJI): The life of Bhagavan Mahavira, the 24th *Tirthankara* (Jain master), is not merely an apotheosis or a deified ideal; his teachings epitomize the quintessence of the culture of compassion, nonviolence, equanimity, and understanding the viewpoint of others. The concepts of "many-sidedness" (*anekant*) and "probability" (*syadvad*), on which he laid great stress, reinforced the intellectual and philosophical foundation of relativism, mutual understanding, and tolerance.

Bhagavan Parshvanath was born about 380 years before the enlightenment (*nirvana*) of Bhagavan Mahavira, or in the tenth century B.C. Like other *Tirthankaras*, important events of earlier incarnations of the being that became Bhagavan Parshvanath are available in Jain scriptures. Study of these incidents reveals that amnesty and compassion played a major part in his life. In every incarnation, his rival, Kamath, continued to torture him, yet, he continued to forgive and forget.

A Celebration of Life

Sri Venkateshwara Swami Temple of Greater Chicago

Aurora, Illinois

Thousands of devotees from the Midwestern states, especially from the Chicago area, used to travel to Pittsburgh to have *darshana* of Sri Venkateshwara Swami. While the experience was spiritually rewarding, the time and effort required to make the trip were making it difficult for many to have his *darshana* as often as their hearts desired. The state of affairs continued until 1985. As a result of the philanthropy of nine families who donated 20 acres of land in Aurora (a far west suburb of Chicago) for the proposed Balaji temple, a beginning was made to realizing a dream that many had held.

Construction of the Sri Venakteswara Swami (Balaji) Temple was originally conceived by a staunch devotee who was the prime mover behind the project. It was the devotee's intention to build a temple in the fashion of the famous Tirumala temple in India, which would follow all worship and rituals in the true tradition of Tirumala. A group of devotees registered the institution on October 4, 1983, with the devotees serving as trustees. They then started looking for people who had a similar interest in this project. In March 1984, when another meeting was held, only four more members attended, but they decided to build a temple for Balaji. They proposed to raise the money among their friends and others who were interested in seeing a temple built. The effort to seek out more supporters continued. Three more supporters attended the next meeting, held on June 24, 1984.

In May 1984 two devotees attended the *Maha Kumbhabhisheka* of the Malibu Temple in California and met master temple architect Padmasri M. Muthiah Sthapathi of Chennai. He was invited to Chicago for consultation. Sri Subhash Nadkarni, a reputed architect of Chicago, was also contacted, and he graciously agreed to help. With the help of both these architects, work started on the design of the temple. The resulting design is an excellent blend of the ancient *Shilpa Shastra* and modern architectural technology. A unique feature of the temple is a provision for circumambulation (*pradakshina*) inside the temple, not only around the presiding deity, but also around all the major shrines inside the temple.

Beginning Phases

Search for a suitable site for the temple started in April 1984, and in June 1984 the contract was signed for purchase of a 70-acre farm. The temple did not require 70 acres, but since the seller was not willing to sell a smaller parcel, a group of devotees agreed to buy the entire parcel of land and donate 20 acres out of it to the temple. On October 12, 1984, the final contract was signed, and the first *puja* was performed in the farmhouse on the newly acquired land on October 13, 1984.

The first fund-raising banquet for the temple was held on May 24, 1985, with the goal of raising sufficient sums to construct a temple without borrowing any money. Cash and pledges were received at that event to make progress possible. Pledges were to be made good before the end of 1986 in order for the donor to be recognized as a sponsor of a shrine or a deity. The board of trustees was expanded to fifteen members. In June 1985 the ground-breaking ceremony (*Bhumi Puja*) was performed by the late Morarji Desai, former Prime Minister of India.

When the plans were drawn and Shiva shrines were added to the original plans and the basement was changed into an auditorium, the estimates surpassed the original anticipated cost. To meet the start-up expenses, an amount was borrowed against the 50 acres of land owned by the land partners. The actual construction of the temple began in November 1985.

Inauguration and Consecration

In April 1986 eighteen temple artisans (*shilpis*) arrived from India to do the traditional architectural and sculptural work on the temple. Sri Tirumala Tirupati Devasthanams of Andhra Pradesh graciously agreed to give an interest-free loan to cover

the expenses of the idols (*vigrahas*) and the artisans.

Kumbhabhisheka ceremonies were performed on June 20, 21, and 22, 1986. The then mayor of Aurora, Mr. Pierce, and Swami Chinmayananda of Chinmaya Mission participated in the inauguration ceremonies. A total of 6,000 devotees witnessed the ceremonies. Sri Sampathkumar Bhattacharya of Bangalore was the head priest who performed the rituals, along with a host of other priests who came with him from India. The temple priests Sri Vedala Rangachari and Sri Vedala Srinivasachari assisted them.

A major event of 1996 was the *Pratishthapana* installation ceremony for Dasavatharams, Swami Ayyappan, *dvarapalakas* (door-keepers), the Navagrahas, Nandi, Mushika, and Peacock. The event was a grand success and very well attended.

In addition to the Lord Venkateshwara Swami (Balaji) shrine, there are other shrines in the temple to different deities. On either side of the main shrine are shrines for Sri Devi (Lakshmi) and Bhudevi (Andal). In the two corners in front of the main shrine are shrines for Sri Kanyaka Parameshwari and Sri Ayyappan. In the two corners further away are shrines for Sri Anjaneya and Sri Satyanarayana. Closer to the entrance are shrines to Ganapati, Subramanya, Shiva, and Parvati.

PAGE 254, RIGHT: Minor shrine of Lord Shiva.

PAGE 254, LEFT: Line drawing of Lord Vishnu. *Line drawing courtesy of V. Ganapati Sthapati & Associates, Chennai, India..*

PAGE 255: Detailed and intricate work on the pillars that line the *mahamandapa.*

PAGE 256, TOP: Detailed work on the *vimana*.

PAGE 256, LEFT: Minor shrine along the inner wall of the temple.

PAGE 256, RIGHT: Silver elephant used in ceremonial processions.

PAGE 257, TOP: View of two *vimanas*.

PAGE 257, BOTTOM: Intricate ornamentation adorns the capitals of pillars.

SRIRAMAVATHARA

On the image, signs read:

PLEASE LEAVE YOUR SHOES HERE

NO SHOES BEYOND THIS POINT PLEASE

Hindu Temple Society of Southern California
Calabasa, California

A spiritual inheritance and a physical landmark on the Metropolitan Los Angeles horizon stands as what is commonly known as the Malibu Temple, located amid the rolling hills of the Santa Monica mountain range, in Calabasa, California. This temple is a legacy that will be left behind to the children of today's Hindu community, so that they can cherish their ancient cultural heritage and pass it on to their own children.

The temple is built for Lord Venkateshwara, the main deity, and has several shrines for other deities. The temple is built according to *Shilpa Shastra* in Chola style of temple architecture. The temple architect (*sthapati*) of the Malibu Temple was none other than the famous Padmasri M. Muthiah Sthapathi of Chennai, India, who has designed temples all over the world. This temple is one of the largest and most authentic Hindu temples in the Western Hemisphere. A humble beginning in 1977 has blossomed into this remarkable achievement.

Fulfilling Spiritual and Cultural Needs

In April 1977, a group of dedicated men and women of the Indian community in Los Angeles convened a meeting to discuss building a temple and a cultural center to fulfill the spiritual and cultural needs of the community. They realized that those who made this country their new home could easily lose their sociocultural identity in the course of time, thus rendering themselves rootless and insecure. Such a state may not endanger the lives of the first generation, but is bound to affect the lives of the second and succeeding generations if a sense of direction is not made available at the right time. The ideals and values of Hindu philosophy and India's rich cultural heritage and high moral traditions have helped Indians living outside India to maintain peace and harmony in their lives.

As a result of that meeting of the minds, efforts were made to create an organization to accomplish this task. These efforts led to the formalized founding of the Hindu Temple Society of Southern California on July 10, 1977, with a status of a nonprofit organization. The new organization created an interim board with representation from different local associations to underscore the goal of achieving cultural unity and integrity.

To this end, the Hindu Temple Society extensively explored contemporary opinions, thoughts, convictions, and approaches, and analyzed the potential impact of the project on future generations and lifestyles. The members decided to build a main temple to enshrine Lord Venkateshwara (Venkateswara, Balaji), with the main temple to be glorified with additional

shrines for other deities. The temple was planned to include a cultural center with all facilities for a congregation of at least 500 persons. An intensive drive was made to raise funds and to enroll members.

In April 1978, the General Body of the Society elected a board of organizers. Obviously, the main and immediate task of this board was to select an appropriate site for the construction of the temple. The board nominated a site-selection committee, which scanned southern California for a suitable site for a reasonable price. After investigating many sites, the committee selected a site of 4.5 acres located in Malibu as most suitable owing to its pristine environment, proximity to all utilities, and easy accessibility by road. The Temple Society did not have sufficient funds to purchase this land, so a group of 30 devoted members bought the land in June 1978 and donated it to the Society a year later.

In October 1978, Padmasri S. M. Ganapati Sthapati, the *Asthana Sthapati* of Andhra Pradesh and Purushottam Naidu, Commissioner of Religious Endowment of Andhra Pradesh, were invited to Los Angeles to design the temple. All necessary plans and architectural documents were prepared by Ravi Varma, a local architect and member of the Temple Society. A conditional use permit from the Los Angeles County Regional Planning Commission and a coastal permit from the California Coastal Commission were obtained after a very lengthy process and several public hearings in June 1979 and January 1980, respectively.

Construction and Installation

The ground-breaking ceremony for the construction of Lord Ganesha's temple was celebrated in January 1981, with Sant Keshavadas of the Temple of Cosmic Religion performing the *Bhumi Puja*. The construction work started in 1981, and the dedication of the temple with the installation of Lord Ganesha took place on May 24, 1981. In December 1982 seven temple artisans (*shilpis*) arrived from India to take charge of the sculptural work. They completed all the sculptural decorations for the Ganesha temple in April 1983, paving the way for the celebration of the *Kalasha Kumbhabhisheka* of the Ganesha Temple on

PAGES 262 and 263: Side view of the Vishnu Complex with *rajagopura* and minor shrines. Flagpole and main sanctum are toward the left. A wall (*prakara*) encloses this magnificent structure set in the foothills near Santa Monica, in Calabasa, California.

April 24, 1983. Sri Thanga Bhattar, Chief Priest at the Madurai Meenakshi Temple, performed the ceremony with great devotion and dignity.

On April 18, 1982, the ground-breaking ceremony for the Lord Venkateshwara (Balaji) Temple was performed. With God's grace, the Hindu Temple Society of Southern California celebrated the *Maha Kumbhabhisheka* of Lord Venkateshwara Temple on May 13, 1984. The construction work on the main temple commenced on

November 15, 1982. A construction loan was arranged with the State Bank of India, on the strength of the securities provided by 30 members. The idols of Lord Venkateshwara, Padmavati, Andal, Garudalvar, and Lord Ganesha arrived in Los Angeles on January 14, 1984. These idols, carved out of black granite, were prepared and organized by Tirumala Tirupati Devasthanams of Andhra Pradesh.

Padmasri S. M. Ganapati Sthapati and

three *shilpis* arrived in Los Angeles in March 1984 and did the initial work on the temple; however, Ganapati Sthapati had to return to India, along with his crew. A second crew of *shilpis* then undertook the sculptural work on the main temple, this time under the supervision of Padmasri M. Muthiah Sthapathi.

The installation of the idols and the *Maha Kumbhabhisheka* of the main temple were completed on May 13, 1984. The *Maha Kumbhabhisheka* ceremony was celebrated with all the traditional Vedic rites on May 7 and concluded on May 13, 1984. The ceremonies were performed by priests invited from India, Pittsburgh, and New York. During the *Maha Kumbhabhisheka*, the idols of Padmavati, Andal, Garudalvar, Lord Ganesha, Lord Shiva, and Lord Murugan were installed.

The next phase of construction involved the completion of the shrines for Lord Krishna, Lord Rama, the final shaping of the main tower (*rajagopura*), and creation

of residential facilities at the temple site for the priests and a manager.

April 1987 was a turning point in the history of the temple with the *Maha Kumbhabhisheka* of the *rajagopura*. The event was marked with great emotion and celebration. The shrines for Sri Rama and Sri Krishna as well as the cultural hall had also been completed at the same time.

A completely separate temple was built on the site to house Lord Shiva and was named the Shiva Complex. Shrines for Lord Ganesha, Lord Shiva, Lord Subramanya, and Goddess Jyothi were completed, and the complex was enclosed with a 5-ft.-high compound wall. In 1995 the board decided to increase the area of the complex and add shrines for Lord Ayyappan and goddess Durga; enlarge the shrine for Goddess Jyothi; and install the Navagrahas. The whole complex would be roofed with a *rajagopura* at the entrance of the complex. The construction started in 1996, and it is anticipated that the complex will be completed by the end of 2002, at which point this temple complex will be among the most impressive Hindu temple sites in the United States.

PAGE 264, TOP: Back view of the temple with the main sanctum in the foreground. Also within view are the *arthamandapa* and *mahamandapa*, with the *rajagopura* in the background.

PAGE 264: Detailed work showing an elephant and other design elements on the side of the staircase to the entrance of the main sanctum.

PAGE 265: Ornate *prakara* in the foreground with main temple building in the background.

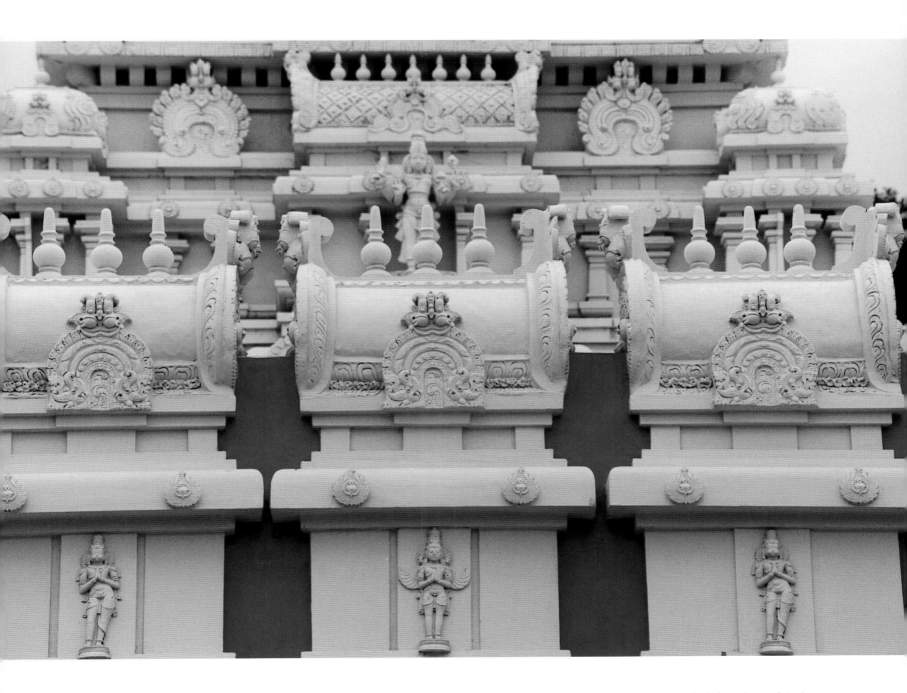

Hindu Samaj Temple
Wappingers Falls, New York

The origin of the Hindu Samaj can be traced back to 1969, when several hundred Indian professionals had settled in the Mid-Hudson Valley in the state of New York. In 1970, a friendly gathering was hosted for discussing the spiritual and cultural activities for the Indian community. At that time most of the young families thought they would be going back to India within a few years, and they saw no compelling reason to get involved in religious activities. A few families, however, did not give up on their vision and pursued their spiritual activities by hosting *Bhagavad Gita* study, fire rituals (*homas*), and *pujas* at their homes on a rotating basis. Occasionally these activities were also combined with those of the Sikh community.

A survey conducted in late 1972 revealed that community interest was growing in establishing a venue for religious and cultural activities. Community activities continued on a regular basis, under the informal name of Hindu Samaj, until the organization was officially incorporated in 1973 as a spiritual, philosophical, charitable, and cultural institution with a formal constitution.

Vision Realized

In 1975, a 5.2-acre site with a barn-like structure was bought for the Samaj in Wappingers Falls, New York. For the renovation of the barn and the associated property, a loan from a local bank was arranged. During this time period, an Indian architectural firm, Barun Basu Associates, developed plans for a temple and its surroundings. The architect also created a scale model for the future Hindu Samaj temple.

Two life-size granite idols (*murtis*) of Lord Vishnu (Venkateshwara, Shrinivasa, or Balaji) and Lakshmi (Padmavati) were sculpted for the temple by the Tirumala Tirupati Devasthanams (TTD) in India. As part of the wide array of cultural and educational activities sponsored by TTD, the Sri Venkateswara Institute of Traditional Sculpture and Architecture was founded there to preserve and promote the age-old cultural heritage of India in the areas of traditional sculpture and architecture. The institution was started to train students in the traditional arts of stone carving, *sudai* (cement work), metal and wood sculpture, traditional painting, and temple architecture. Most temples get their idols from the

production unit of this institute, which creates stone sculpture according to traditional Hindu mythology and the *Shilpa Shastra*. The institute sculpts stone idols based on specifications given by various temples in India and abroad. Idols of Sri Venkateshwara and Sri Padmavati are supplied and installed, free of cost, at different temples around the world, on request.

The *murtis* were graciously hosted for the community by a devotee at his residence, and they received daily worship until they were moved to the renovated building that would serve as the temple (*mandir*). The *mandir* was inaugurated in 1976 on the auspicious morning of Thanksgiving Day and the Fifty-first birthday of Bhagavan Sri Sathya Sai Baba. Both the Thanksgiving and birthday celebrations took place in the building that same afternoon of November 23, 1976.

Besides the daily worship of the deities by the dedicated devotees in the community, major Samaj activities included organizing spiritual programs and *pujas*, classes on spiritual topics, several language classes, discourses, music lessons, and yoga classes for children and adults.

While all this wonderful work was carried on, the search for a site that was more suitable for

the permanent home of the society was in progress. In 1993, a fitting piece of land, 9 acres in size, was purchased in Wappingers Falls for construction of the temple, which created a new sense of pride and urgency among the congregation.

The installation of the first brick (*Shankushthapana*) for the new temple and cultural center was performed in May 1995. With newfound excitement, the community supported the construction of the building with generous donations.

The community selected the architect previously engaged for building the basic structure of the temple. The grand opening ceremony for the new building was celebrated on March 23, 1997. The *Pranapratishtha* of the Jain *murtis* was celebrated in the summer of 1997.

The traditional temple construction and sculpting work was overseen by Padmasri M. Muthiah Sthapathi from Chennai, India. Muthiah Sthapathi provided the designs and overall supervision for the construction of the entranceway towers (*gopuras*) of the temple. Construction of the *gopuras* started on November 6, 1999. A group of temple artisans (*shilpis*) arrived from India and proceeded to do an excellent job of transforming the shell of the

buildings into architectural wonders of delicate craftsmanship.

During this period, preparations for the grand *Pranapratishtha* and *Kumbhabhisheka* ceremonies were getting under way and became the culmination of the dreams, designs, planning, execution, and hard work of a number of community members. The *Pranapratishtha* and *Kumbhabhisheka* ceremonies were celebrated in a fitting manner.

Remarkable Idea

A remarkable idea supported the establishing of this temple, and of many others that have been built in areas where the community is not large enough to facilitate building temples for a single deity. This temple is a multi-deity temple and also includes a sanctum sanctorum for Jain worshipers. This seems to be a growing trend in the United States after the first such temple was built in Pittsburgh.

Situated in Wappingers Falls, New York, this temple has another unusual feature. All the sanctums are standalone units. They house Sri Durga, Sri Parvati, Sri Radha Krishna, Sri Rama Parivar, Sri Shivalinga, Sri Ganesha, Sri Venkateshwara, and Sri Shrinathji. The main hall has access to each shrine, and the entire area is roofed so that the complete temple area and the architecture are completely protected from the elements.

The outstanding quality of Hindu temple architecture is its spiritual content. The fundamental purpose of temple-building art was to represent in concrete form the prevailing religious consciousness of the people. It is mind materialized in terms of rock, brick, or stone. This characteristic of Hindu architecture is emphasized by the treatment of its wall surfaces. The scheme of sculpture that often covers the whole of the exterior of the temple is notable not only for the richness of its decorative effect, but also for the deep significance of its subject matter. Carved in high or low relief are all the glorious gods of the age-old mythology of the country, engaged in their well-known ceremonials, an unending array of imagery steeped in symbolism, thus producing a never-ending story of absorbing interest. The Hindu Samaj Temple at Wappingers Falls, New York, continues this rich legacy of Indian art and architecture.

PAGE 272: Such intricate designs can be seen on all pillars throughout the temple. Minor shrines appear in the background.

PAGE 272: Concept line drawings of the temple. *Line drawing courtesy of Baran Basu, Connecticut.*

PAGE 273: In the foreground, left to right, Shiva's *vahana,* Nandi the bull; *dvarapalaka;* and *utsavamurtis.*

So, too, knowledge does not lessen when shared with or imparted to others. On the contrary, it increases in clarity and conviction on giving. It benefits both the receiver and the giver.

Why do we do pradakshina?

When we visit a temple, after offering prayers, we circumambulate the sanctum santorum, that is, we do *pradakshina*.

We cannot draw a circle without a center point. The Lord is the center, source, and essence of our lives. Recognizing him as the focal point in our lives, we go about doing our daily chores. We do *pradakshina* to remind us that the Lord is at the center of our lives. Also, every point on the circumference of a circle is equidistant from the center. This means that wherever or whoever we may he, we are equally close to the Lord. His grace flows toward us without partiality.

Why is pradakshina *done only in a clockwise manner?*

As we do *pradakshina*, the Lord is always on our right. In India the right side symbolizes auspiciousness. It is a telling fact that even in the English language it is called the "right" side and not the wrong one! So as we circumambulate the sanctum sanctorum, we remind ourselves to lead an auspicious life of righteousness, with the Lord, who is the indispensable source of help and strength, as our guide—the "right hand," the *dharma* aspect of our lives. We thereby overcome our wrong tendencies and avoid repeating the sins of the past.

Indian scriptures enjoin: "*matrudevo bhava, pitrudevo bhava, acharyadevo bhava*"—"may you consider your parents and teachers as you would the Lord." With this in mind, we also do *pradakshina* around our parents and divine personages.

After the completion of traditional worship (*puja*), we customarily do *pradakshina* around ourselves. In this way we recognize and remember the Supreme Divinity within us, which is idolized in the form of the Lord we worship outside.

Why do we ring the bell in a temple?

In most temples there are one or more bells hung from the top, near the entrance. The devotee rings the bell as soon as he enters, thereafter proceeding to do *darshana* of the Lord and to pray. Children love jumping up or being carried high in order to reach the bell.

Is it to wake up the Lord? But the Lord never sleeps. Is it to let the Lord know we have come? He does not need to be told, as he is all-knowing. Is it a form of seeking permission to enter his precinct? It is a homecoming, and therefore entry needs no permission. The Lord welcomes us at all times. Then why do we ring the bell?

The ringing of the bell produces what is regarded as an auspicious sound. It produces the sound *Om*, the universal name of the Lord. There should be auspiciousness within and without in order to gain the vision of the Lord, who is all-auspiciousness.

Even while doing *arati*, we ring the bell. It is sometimes accompanied by the auspicious sounds of the conch and other musical instruments. An added significance of ringing the bell, conch, and other instruments is that they help drown out any inauspicious or irrelevant noise that might disturb or distract the worshipers in their devotional ardor, concentration, and inner peace.

Why do we offer food to the Lord before eating it?

In Western tradition food is taken after a prayer of thanksgiving—grace. Indians make an offering of food to the Lord and later partake of it as *prasada*, a holy gift from the Lord. In temples and in many homes, the cooked food is first offered to the Lord.

The offered food is mixed with the rest of the food and then served as *prasada*. In our daily *puja*, we, too, we offer food (*naivedyam*) to the Lord. Why do we do so? The Lord is omnipotent and omniscient. Man is a part, while the Lord is the totality. All that we do is by his strength and knowledge alone. Hence, what we receive in life as a result of our actions is really his alone. We acknowledge this through the act of offering food to him. This is exemplified by the Hindi words in the *arati* prayer: *Jai Jagadisha Hare*—"I offer what is yours to you." Thereafter, what we have offered to the Lord is akin to his gift to us, graced by his divine touch.

Knowing this, our entire attitude to food and the act of eating changes. The food offered will naturally be pure and of the best quality. We share what we get with others before consuming it. We do not demand, complain, or criticize the quality of the food we receive. We do not waste or reject it. We eat it with cheerful acceptance (*prasada buddhi*). When we become established in this attitude, it goes beyond the purview of food and pervades our entire lives. We are then able to cheerfully accept all we get in life as the Lord's *prasada*.

Before we partake of our daily meals, we first sprinkle water around the plate as an act of purification. Five morsels of food are placed on the side of the plate, acknowledging the debt owed by us to the divine forces (*devata runa*) for their benign grace and protection; our ancestors (*pitru runa*) for giving us their lineage and a family culture; the sages (*rishi runa*) for realizing, maintaining, and handing down to us the divine Knowledge; our fellow beings (*manushya runa*), who constitute society, without the support of which we could not live as we do; and other living beings (*bhuta runa*) for serving us selflessly.

Thereafter the Lord, the life force, who is also within us as the five life-giving physiological functions, is offered the food. This is done with the chant (referring to the five physiological functions: respiratory (*prana*), excretory (*apana*), circulatory (*vyana*), digestive (*samana*), and faculty of thinking (*udana*). After offering the food thus, it is eaten as *prasada*, blessed food.

A *kalasha* is a brass, mud, or copper pot filled with water. Mango leaves are placed in the mouth of the pot and a coconut is placed over it. A red or white thread is tied around its neck or sometimes all around it in an intricate diamond-shaped pattern. The pot may be decorated with designs. When the pot is filled with water or rice, it is known as *purnakumbha*, which represents the inert body, which when filled with the divine life force, gains the power to do all the wonderful things that makes life what it is.

On all-important occasions such as a house-warming or wedding, a *kalasha* is placed near the entrance as a sign of welcome, accompanied by rituals. It is also used in a traditional manner when receiving holy personages. Spiritually evolved beings are full and complete, for they identify with the infinite Truth (*purnatvam*). They are filled with joy and love, and represent all that is auspicious. We greet them with a *purnakumbba* (full pot), acknowledging their greatness and offering them a reverential welcome with a full heart.

Before the creation came into being, Lord Vishnu was reclining on His snake-bed in the milky ocean. From His navel emerged a lotus from which appeared Lord Brahma, the Creator, who thereafter created this world. The water in the *kalasha* symbolizes the primordial water from which the entire creation emerged. It is the giver of life to all and has the potential of creating innumerable names and forms, the inert objects and the sentient beings and all that is auspicious in the world. The leaves and coconut placed in the *kalasha* represent creation. The thread represents the love that "binds" all in creation. The *kalasha* is therefore considered auspicious and is worshiped.

When the *asuras* and the *devas* churned the milky ocean, the Lord appeared bearing the pot of nectar, which blessed one with everlasting life. Thus, the *kalasha* also symbolizes immortality. The waters from all the holy rivers, knowledge of all the Vedas, and the blessings of all the deities are invoked in the *kalasha*, and its water is thereafter used for all the rituals, including the consecration ceremony, *abhisheka. Kumbha-abhisheka,* or *Kumbh-abhisheka,* of a temple is done in a grand manner with elaborate rituals, including the pouring of one or more *kalashas* of holy water on top of the consecrated entity.

Offenses Against the Divine Name

The *Narada Bhaki Sutra* celebrates love of the Lord. It tells us that the glory of the Names of the Lord is indescribable and that a devotee should try to avoid offenses against the Divine Name (*namaparadha*). The offenses to be avoided are:

- To look upon God merely as a deity or a principle.

- To look upon the Vedas as a book or as having an author.

- To discriminate between *bhaktas* on the ground of their caste.

- To look upon one's preceptor as an ordinary human being.

- To regard an image or picture of God as wood, stone, metal, paper, or clay.

- To treat *prasada* (food offered to the Lord) as ordinary food.

- To treat *charanamrita* (water in which the sacred feet of the Lord have been washed) as ordinary water.

- To regard *tulsi* (the basil plant) as an ordinary plant.

- To regard the cow as an ordinary beast.

- To regard the *Bhagavad Gita* or the *Bhagavata* as ordinary books.

- To regard the divine sports as human activities.

- To compare the sports of the Lord with earthly love or sex-pleasure.

- To regard the *gopis* as others' wives (in relation to the Lord).

- To regard the *rasa* dance of Sri Krishna as an amorous sport.

- To discriminate (between touchables and untouchables) in festivities connected with the Lord.

- To have no faith in God and the *shastras* and to turn into an unbeliever.

- To practice *dharma* with a doubting mind.

- To be slothful in discharging one's religious duties.

- To judge devotees by external things.

- To comment on the merits and demerits of saints.

- To have a high opinion about one's own self.

- To revile a particular God or scripture.

- To turn one's back on an image of God

- To approach an image of God with shoes on.
- To wear a garland in the presence of an image of God.

- To approach an image of God with stick in hand.

- To approach an image of God in a blue garment.

- To approach an image of God without washing one's mouth and cleaning one's teeth.

- To enter a temple of God without changing one's clothes after evacuating one's bowels or after sexual intercourse.

- To stretch one's arms or legs before an image of God.

- To chew betel leaves before an image of God.

- To laugh loudly before an image of God.

- To make an undesirable gesture.

- To hover about women.

- To lose one's temper.

- To salute anyone else in the presence of an image of God.

- To visit a temple immediately after eating something that gives a foul odor.

- To insult or assault anyone.

- To make gestures expressive of lust or anger.

- To fail in one's duty to a stranger or a holy man.

- To regard oneself as a devotee, a pious soul, a learned person, or a virtuous person.

- To associate with unbelievers, profligates, sanguinary persons, greedy people, and liars.

- To blame God in adversity.

- To practice virtue with a sinful motive.

- To regard oneself as pious even though oppressing others, even slightly.

- To refuse to maintain one's wife, children, family dependents, the needy, and holy individuals.

- To offer something to God, treating it as enjoyable by oneself or to enjoy it without offering it to God beforehand.

- To swear by the name of one's *Ishta Devata*.

- To sell *dharma* in the name of God.

- To expect anything from anyone other than one's chosen deity.

- To violate the injunctions of the scriptures (*shastras*).

- To behave as a knower of *Brahman*, even though lacking such knowledge.

- To discriminate between Vaishnavas belonging to different sects.

- To behave as God.

- To revile particular *avataras* by discriminating between their respective *lilas*.

- To call anyone God, even by mistake.

- To believe, even by mistake, that God is dependent on anyone else.

- To give *prasada* or *charanamrita* of the Lord to anyone through greed.

- To insult a picture, image, or name of God.

- To oppress, intimidate, or wrong anyone.

- To renounce faith on losing in a controversy or on one's failure to establish a proposition.

- To regard the birth and activities of various *avataras* as commonplace.

- To regard the pair forms of the deities such as Sri Radha and Sri Krishna as distinct or separate.

- As an overzealous disciple, to act against the spirit of the guru's behest.

BUDDHIST-JAIN-SIKH TEMPLES

One Land, Many Faiths

India is world-renowned for its incomparable spiritual legacy. We associate the country largely with Hinduism, but several other now global religious movements have had their beginnings there, including Buddhism, Jainism, and Sikhism, each of which has left its mark on the landscape of sacred architecture on the Indian subcontinent. The New World, where the followers of these faiths have immigrated, has likewise provided rich soil for nurturing a diversity of faiths and establishing their houses or worship. Especially the past twenty-five years have witnessed a radical change in the religious landscape of North America. Houses of worship for various faiths can be found in virtually every major American city, as well as in the larger cities of Canada. Among them are Jain, Sikh, and Buddhist temples, a small sampling of which is presented on the following pages.

Wat Florida Dhammaram, Kissimmee, Florida

Both Jainism and Buddhism arose about the sixth century B.C. Jainism can be considered both a philosophy and a religion. It was founded by Vardhamana Mahavira (599-527 B.C.), called *Jina* (spiritual conqueror), a contemporary of Buddha. Similarly to Buddhists, the Jains deny the divine origin and authority of the Veda and revere the saints of Jain doctrine whom they call *Tirthankaras* (prophets or founders of the path). Mahavira is believed to have been the twenty-fourth *Tirthankara*. In India, Jainism is largely concentrated in Gujarat and Rajasthan, Karnataka, and the larger cities on the Indian subcontinent. Although most Jains live in India, they have also emigrated to other countries, including the United States and Canada. There are more Jain

temples and groups in the United States than in any other country outside India. Many of these houses of worship are shared Hindu-Jain temples.

Like Jainism, Buddhism had its roots in North India around the sixth century B.C., when a warrior prince called Siddhartha Gautama left behind his royal home to search for spiritual enlightenment. Sitting under the now legendary Bodhi tree at Bodh Gaya, Buddha attained enlightenment. Although initially intent on remaining where he was, "seeing all things as they really are," the Hindu god Brahma persuaded Buddha to teach others the truths that even the gods did not know. He thus became the Buddha, the "the enlightened one," a spiritual teacher who taught others

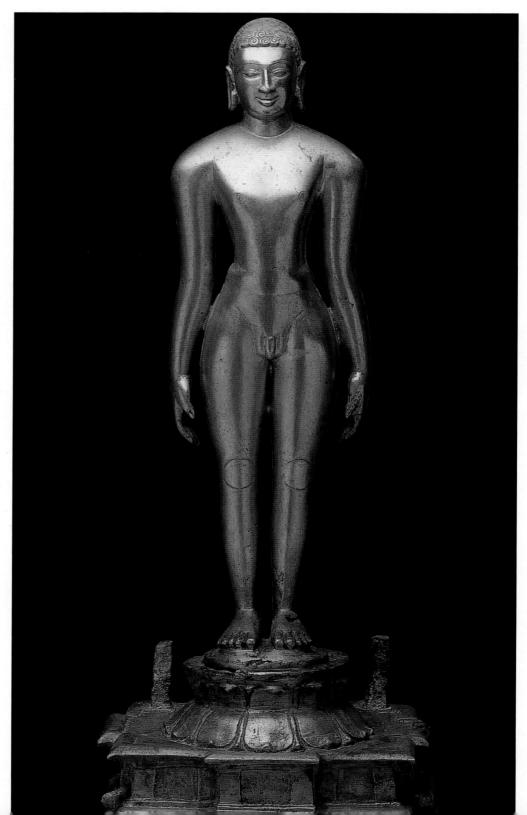

the way to escape from suffering and the endless cycle of birth, death, and rebirth. These teachings have won widespread acclaim among Western seekers representing a broad variety of professional and national groups. A combination of Asian immigrants and new converts from the West have established many and diverse places of worship, reflective both of Buddhism's Asian roots as well as its more recent emergence in the West.

The Sikh religion developed around the late fifteenth century in what is now Pakistan and the Punjab region of India. The word *Sikh* is derived from the Pali *sikkha* or Sanskrit *shishya*, meaning "disciple." Sikhs are disciples of their ten Gurus (religious teachers), beginning with Nanak (b. 1469) and ending with Gobind Singh (d. 1708). Guru Nanak was born into a family of Hindu merchants in the village of Talvandi, near the city of Lahore, Pakistan. Nanak's teachings were collected in the holy book of the Sikhs known as the *Guru Granth Sahib*. Influenced by the Hindu Sant tradition of northern India, Guru Nanak's teaching developed with an emphasis on monotheism, social equality, and the central role of the *satguru,* or true teacher. The Sikh house of worship is a *gurudwara,* which means "gateway to the guru," and such gateways have now become many in all parts of the United States and Canada.

Wat Florida Dhammaram
Kissimmee, Florida

Wat Florida Dhammaram is a Buddhist monastery. The founder of this monastery is the Venerable Chaokhun Phra Tepvaraporn (Im Arindamo). He is an assistant to the abbot of Wat Sommanusviharn in Bangkok, Thailand. On a visit to Florida, the Venerable Chaokhun Phra Depvaraporn saw the need of having a Buddhist monastery for Buddhist people who live in Florida. With approval from the late abbot of Wat Sommanudviharn, the Venerable Chaokhun Somdej Phra Wannarat began fund-raising in Thailand. Due to the similarity in climate between Florida and Thailand, and the availability of wonderful piece of property in Kissimmee on the doorstep of Walt Disney World, an agreement was made on July 25, 1992, to purchase the property with the money raised in Thailand. The property was approximately two acres in size.

The Venerable Chaokbun Phra Depvaraporn asked devotees in Florida to seek permission to have a Buddhist monastery in Kissimmee. He named the monastery "Wat Florida Dhammaram." The main Buddha image was donated by a devotee, who also donated 268 Buddha images, a set of *Tripitaka* (Buddhist canon) written in both Thai and Pali, and many other items.

The ground-breaking ceremony for the monastery was held on April 15, 1993. Ten monks from Thailand joined many Florida residents in witnessing the traditional ceremony.

Monastery and More

The monastery is a place for holding religious functions, studying Buddhism, and practicing meditation. It is also a spiritual shelter and a learning center for youngsters who wish to learn the Thai language and culture.

Several structures have been built since the initial ground-breaking. They include Kuti Samucky, dedicated in April 1996 and used as the monks' residence. Ubosot, dedicated in May 1997, is used to conduct religious functions. This building holds a statue of the Buddha and has many historical murals inside. Thai House, Sala Talay, was dedicated in 1997 and is used to display the daily Buddha statues. The Memorial Cultural Center, dedicated in February 1998, serves as a school. A separate structure, dedicated in 1999, serves as a kitchen and dining room. The Sirimahamaya Vihara (The Temple of the Queen Sirimahamaya, the Buddha's mother) was dedicated in June 11, 2000. The bell tower was dedicated in September 2000. According to Thai custom, the bell is struck to announce special events at the monastery and temple complex.

The monastery has purchased an additional 5.6 acres of adjacent land for further development.

West Meets East

The *Orlando Sentinel* from the nearby city of Orlando ran a story about Wat Florida Dhammaram in September 1998. A few quotes from the article reveal the appreciation of a Western observer:

"Gold-colored spires bend upward on each of three triangular rooftops, stacked one on another. Above the entrance is a mosaic of tiny mirrors and shiny red, green, and blue metal pieces. 'Wat Florida Dhammaram,' is spelled with these sparkly pieces in English and in Thai.

"A concrete path leads visitors past rose bushes, around a fountain and through a perimeter of stone tablets shaped like head-stones. The tablets and everything beyond them are stamped with religious symbols and art: gems, which Buddhists say protect them from temptation, and flowers with eight petals representing the religion's eight precepts."

PAGES 282 and 283: Front view of the Buddhist monastery, with temple and guards in the foreground, in Kissimmee, Florida. These guards are similar to the *dvarapalakas* found in Hindu temples.

PAGE 284: Guard watching over the temple.

PAGE 285: The inner sanctum and prayer hall.

The journalist goes on to describe the temple interior: "Inside the temple, only a few chairs are set up along the walls. The rest of the floor space is saved for kneeling, bowing, and praying to another golden Buddha icon. . . . There's a throne to the right, where a monk sits when leading prayer or chants. On the other side, a jewel-encrusted container holds a tiny bit of the ashes from the bones of the Buddha. The ashes were a gift from high-ranking monks and government officials in India, where Buddhism began. . . . Fourteen paintings, imported from Thailand, cover the walls. Ten depict the last incarnations of the man who began as a mortal, but meditated his way to his holy status, became known as the Buddha, and shared his sermons with followers. Pictures of the first Buddhist temples hang in each of four corners."

Growth of Buddhism in the West

In many Western countries Buddhism is today the fastest-growing religion. In North America many Buddhist centers have sprung up almost overnight, offering teachings and meditation retreats even in remote regions. Today Buddhism is espoused not only by those in the alternative culture, as was the case in the 1960s, but also by businessmen, physicists, computer programmers, housewives, real-estate agents, and even by sports stars, movie actors, and rock musicians.

What is characteristic of Western Buddhism in its present phase of development is the focus on Buddhist practice, especially the practice of meditation. In this phase it is not the academic study of Buddhist texts and doctrines that dominates, or the attempt to interpret the *Dhamma* (Buddhist teaching) through the prism of Western thought, but the appropriation of Buddhism as a practice that can bring deep transformations in one's innermost being as well as in the conduct of everyday life. This does not necessarily mean that Buddhist practice is being taken up in accordance with canonical or traditional Asian models. Adaptations of the *Dhamma* to Western culture and ways of thinking are commonplace, but Buddhism is viewed principally as a path to awakening, a way that brings deep understanding of the mind and makes accessible new dimensions of being.

PAGE 288, TOP: Line drawing of Buddha. *Line drawing courtesy of V. Ganapati Sthapati & Associates, Chennai, India.*

PAGE 288, LEFT: The Sirimahamaya Vihara (Temple of the Queen Sirimahamaya, the Buddha's mother). A lovely statue of Mother and child are housed there.

PAGE 288, RIGHT: Goddess of the Land housed in the gardens of the monastery.

PAGE 289: The entire wall inside the main shrine is beautifully adorned with paintings depicting the life of Buddha.

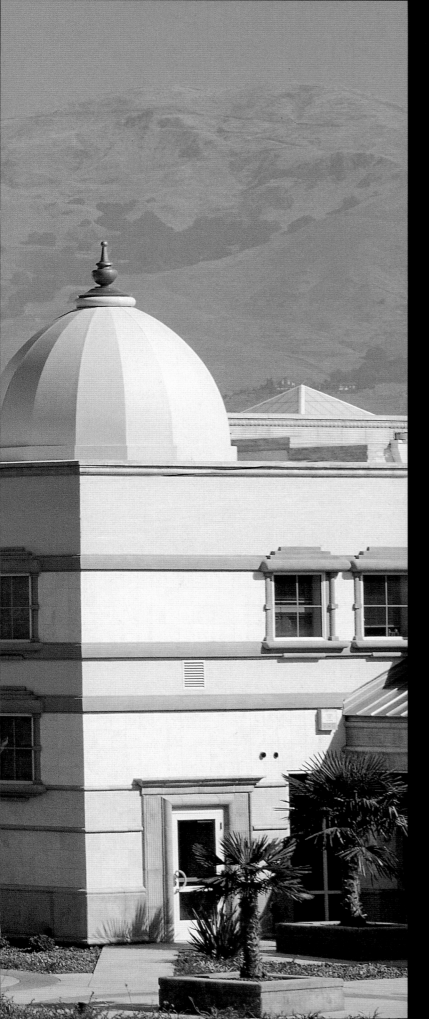

Jain Center of Northern California
Milpitas, California

A temple is a place where we develop a feeling of unity irrespective of where we come from. It allows us to forget our differences, whether we are rich or poor, educated or uneducated. We get a feeling that we all are created equal, helping to strengthen our faith in religion and in people. A temple is a place not only to worship but also to seek peace of mind, to increase our spiritual and internal mental energy, to gain knowledge, to build a stronger character, and to live a better life from day to day. A temple is the place where we learn to respect all living beings equally, appreciate and adopt the positive attributes of others, and strengthen our faith in Jainism. Jain Bhawan is the place to worship those who attained liberation (*moksha*) and showed us the path for attaining that liberation ourselves.

It must first be acknowledged that the art and architecture of Hindu, Buddhist, and Jain temples share common Indian motifs that are elegantly portrayed in human, animal, and floral forms. Beyond these generic features, Jain temples stand uniquely by themselves, because of the distinctive myths, doctrines, and concepts that have inspired their artistic forms.

More characteristic of the sacred orientation of Jain art and architecture are the images of *Jinas* or *Tirthankaras* (Jain spiritual masters). Unlike other religious sects of those times, the Jainas invariably selected secluded picturesque sites for their temples, and cave-temples for meditation and related rituals. According to Jaina religious inscriptions, a devotee is just like a pilgrim who is journeying through life as a stranger in this world. He is required to perform the journey on the path of truth, knowledge, and perfect conduct.

Under One Roof

From the day the Jain Bhawan was formed in 1995, the members were determined to build a Jain temple that would be unique. Every member of the community wanted to build Jain Bhawan by keeping in mind Bhagavan Mahavir's fundamental teachings. With this broad goal in mind, they derived a set of objectives that had everyone's whole-hearted consent.

With land purchased on April 11, 1997, the Bhawan design was started. Standing on approximately 1.75 acres of land, the Jain Bhawan is a 24,000-sq.-ft., two-story building with parking spaces for 135 cars.

The initial team of architects consisted of a local architectural firm, supported by Shashi Patel, an architect from Pittsburgh who specializes in temple design and has worked on more than 20 Indian temple projects in the United States. Later development was headed by Kartik Patel. The first floor houses the community center with an auditorium, kitchen, dining hall, classrooms, and restrooms. The second floor consists of a temple, a *bhakti sthanak* (singing room) and two meditation rooms reserved exclusively for religious activities.

The religious area on the second floor houses the main sanctum (*garbha graha-gabhara*) and *bhakti sthanak*. Temple builders (*sompuras*) in India authentically designed the sanctum in accordance with the *Vastu Shastra*. It has many detailed carvings and houses seven statues of Jain masters (*Tirthankara pratimas*), including Mulnayak. A total of 37 well-crafted niches (*gokhalas*) surround the sanctum and the main hall in front of the sanctum (*rang mandapa*). Three pictures (*chitrapats*) and a white marble plaque inscribed with a mantra (*navkar maha mantra shila*) add beauty to the *bhakti sthanak*. The *rang mandapa*, between the *gabhara* and the *bhakti*

sthanak, is surrounded by eight beautifully carved marble columns adorned with *ashthmangals*—attributes of enlightened masters, the *Tirthankaras*—and other traditional designs, all of which enhance the beauty of the temple. Provision has been made for separating the *rang mandapa* and sanctum area from the *bhakti sthanak* by a motorized vertical partition that can be dropped down when the *bhakti sthanak* is in use for devotional or study sessions or other religious activities. There are two meditation rooms (*upasray*) that can also be used by the monks and nuns (*sadhu* and *sadhvi*).

The Jain Center of Northern California had very grand consecration ceremonies, *Pratishtha Mahotsav*, from August 4 through 7, 2000, in Milpitas, California. Despite the beauty and grandeur of the consecrated center, the biggest achievements of Jain Bhawan are unity, mutual respect and love, teamwork, professionalism, and dedication. The backbone of all of the efforts to build the temple has been a team of untiring volunteers.

Jain Bhawan houses the first Jain temple in North America to have consecrated *pratimas* that represent all Jain traditions under one roof—Shwetambar, Digambar, Sthanakwasi, Terapanthi, and those inspired by Shrimad Rajchandraji.

The top floor of the temple complex is the temple itself, and the bottom floor houses a community center. The temple structure and all the *pratimas* are made from marble, and every detail has been executed according to the traditional prescriptions for sacred architecture. A private company located near Ahmedabad, India, made all the carvings of pillars and temple along with all the *pratimas*. They were shipped from India, and an American contractor assembled them at the Jain temple site. We held the first ever *Pratishtha Mahotsav* consecration festival in modern times with no *ghee boli* (auction-bidding to perform *puja*) and with widespread community participation.

Essence of Jainism

For spiritual evolution Jaina aspirants are required to observe the following five vows (*vratas*): nonviolence, truthfulness, non-stealing, celibacy, and nonpossession. Observance of these *vratas* by monks and nuns is done rigorously and perfectly, and hence their vows are called *mahavrata*. On the

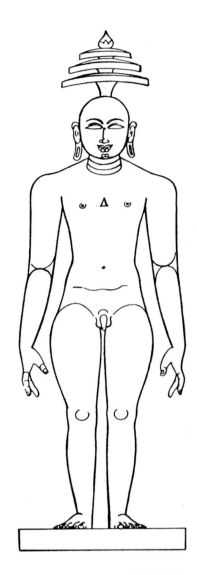

PAGE 294: Bhagavan Chandraprabh (left), Bhagavan Mahavirswami (center), and Bhagavan Shantinath (right).

PAGE 295, TOP: Bhagavan Aadinath (also known as Bhagavan Rishabhdev, the first *Tirthankara*).

PAGE 295, BOTTOM: Bhagavan Vasupujayswami (left), Bhagavan Parshavnath (center), and Bhagavan Munisuvratswami (right).

other hand, observance by householders being partial, their vows are called *anuvrata*. In addition to these five *anuvratas*, householders practice seven supporting vows as well. The five primary vows are:

1. Abstinence from injury to life (*pranatipata-viramana*): This is the fundamental vow from which all other vows stem. Ascetics abstain from all killing, while householders abstain from intentional killing. For food the destruction of the higher forms of life from two-sensed beings upward is strictly forbidden to all Jainas, so they are strict vegetarians.

2. Abstinence from falsehood (*mrushavada-viramana*): Ascetics abstain from all falsehood, gross and subtle. Householders abstain from five gross falsehoods relating to persons, animals, immovable property, deposits left with them, and evidence either in or out of court. Truthfulness is not speaking what is only factually true, but speaking what is factually true as well as good, pleasant, and wholesome.

3. Abstinence from stealing (*asatta-adana-viramana*): This vow consists in not taking what is not given by the owner. Monks and nuns may accept a thing given by its owner only if it is in accord with monastic rules.

4. Abstinence from sexual activities (*maithuna-viramana*): Ascetics abstain from all sexual activities. For householders this vow means refraining from all illicit extramarital sexual activities.

5. Abstinence from possessions or attachment (*aparigraha*): Monks and nuns have renounced all possessions. Whatever things they use for the sustenance of their body and for the performance of religious activities (in strict accordance with monastic rules) are not owned by them, nor do they have any attachment for them. For householders, this vow means limiting their desire for possessing, and hence actual possessing.

PAGE 296, TOP: Bhagavan Parshavnath (the twenty-third *Tirthankara*).

PAGE 296, BOTTOM: View from the *bhakti* hall of the main sanctum and *rang mandapa,* carved out of marble in India and assembled in the United States. All architectural details were fashioned according to the *Shilpa Shashra Anusar.*

PAGE 297: The majestic main entrance on the ground-floor of Jain Bhavan.

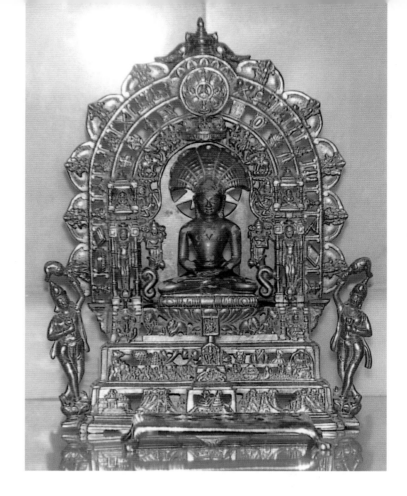

Gurudwara Sahib El Sobrante
El Sobrante, California

About twenty-five miles north of San Francisco, a hilltop of the El Sobrante Valley hills is the home of the Gurudwara Sahib El Sobrante, serving the Sikh community in the San Francisco Bay Area. The *gurudwara* came into existence in the late 1970s. Before then, local Sikhs used to carry out their religious ceremonies in private homes; however, as more and more Sikhs immigrated to the Bay Area, the Sikh community decided that a Sikh temple was necessary to serve local Sikhs, providing a place not only for worship but also for conducting ceremonies such as weddings, Akhand Path ceremonies, and others.

The Beginnings

It was around the mid-1960s that a few Sikhs in the San Francisco Bay Area started discussing their vision of establishing a *gurudwara* in their area, a vision that gave birth to an organization called The Sikh Center of San Francisco Bay Area, with its headquarters in Berkeley.

PAGES 298 and 299: Front view of *gurudwara* in El Sabrante, California. This building is perched on a beautiful hilltop near San Francisco.

PAGE 300: The main hall, whose main feature is the *palki*, the palanquin in which the holy scripture, the *Guru Granth Sahib*, is ceremonially installed. It may be fashioned of wood, gold, or marble.

PAGE 301: This decorated palanquin houses the *Guru Granth Sahib* and other symbols. The *Guru Granth Sahib* is the nucleus of the Sikh way of life. Anyone may enter this place and worship, providing they take off their shoes, cover the head, and bow in front of the *Granth Sahib* to show respect.

The efforts were spearheaded by the students and graduates of the University of California Berkeley, with the help of other Sikh community members living in and around Berkeley. The efforts began with monthly gatherings in the homes or apartments to celebrate *Sangrand*, the beginning of the lunar month. The gatherings began with prayer services using a photograph of Guru Nanak Dev Ji and a *Gutka Sahib*, a small version of the *Guru Granth Sahib*, the holy scripture of the Sikhs; the worship service was followed by tea, coffee, and cookies. It was just a matter of time before the *Guru Granth Sahib* replaced the *Gutka Sahib*, Guru Ka Langar (full meals) replaced tea and cookies, and rented halls

replaced the private homes for the gatherings of the worshipers.

A serious search began for a site on which to build the Gurudwara Sahib. A dream of the few was to build a replica of the Golden Temple at Amritsar, India, which has been a model and an inspiration to builders of many Sikh shrines. Others in the community were happy to build a simple place for worship, as long as they had a temple of their own. While the search was on for a piece of vacant land or a building, fund-raising efforts were underway locally, statewide, nationwide, and even in Canada. In the year 1976, approximately 5 acres of a hillside in El Sobrante,

California, were purchased to house the envisioned *gurudwara*.

The setting on a hillside in El Sobrante was reminiscent of the holy Sikh city of Anandpur in Punjab, India—Anandpur meaning "the City of Bliss" in Sanskrit. After Amritsar, Anandpur is the second most important center of the Sikh religion. One of the *gurudwaras* of Anandpur, the Kesgarh Sahib, became the model for the first design of the El Sobrante temple.

The access road and the parking lots were completed in 1977, marked with a *Nishan Sahib* (Sikh flag) installation. This event was used to raise funds for the first phase

of building construction, which would include a dining hall, lobby, kitchen, and bathrooms. The first phase of the building was completed in May 1979. The dining hall was used for prayer services and the lobby, for serving meals.

The foundation of the building was laid by representatives of four religions (Hindu, Muslim, Christian, and Sikh) and five initiated (*amritdhari*) Sikhs—"five beloved ones" (*panj pyaras*). During the time span between the purchase of the land and completion of the building, weather permitting, the monthly meetings were held outside on the grounds, and food (*langar*) was cooked on an open fire built at the site.

PAGE 302: View of the decorated domes of the *gurudwara*. The architecture shows influence from both the Hindu and Muslim traditions.

PAGE 303: Side view of the *gurudwara,* which stands high on a hilltop in northern California.

Soon after the opening of the center, the Sikh Council of North America held its first annual meeting there. The White House also sent a representative to that session—President Jimmy Carter's mother, Lillian Carter.

Golden-Domed Building

Very soon the congregation outgrew the initial building at the site. Architectural and engineering planning and fund-raising began for the *gurudwara* as we know it today. The original very traditional design, which replicated the Kesgarh Sahib Gurudwara, was replaced by a blend of Sikh and modern architecture, providing more usable space within the footprint of the building. The new building was completed in June 1992, becoming one of most magnificent *gurudwaras* in the North America. The Gurudwara Sahib is equipped to accommodate 700 to 800 people.

Situated as it is on a hilltop and given its unique architecture, the Gurudwara Sahib El Sobrante attracts many visitors. At the northeast wing of the second floor, a huge deck offers a breathtaking view of the El Sobrante Valley and San Pablo Bay.

The building has now become a landmark in Contra Costa County, with its image appearing in calendars published by the public agencies of the county. A caption from one of the pictures appearing in a local calendar reads: "The golden-domed Sikh Temple in Richmond, constructed with contributions from the East Bay Sikh Community, and the Hillcrest Baptist Church on the hillside above San Pablo Dam Road, reflect the religious and ethnic diversity of the West Contra Costa."

Past Legacy, Future Plans

The congregation has outgrown the current complex also, and now plans are underway for expansion of the lobby and building of a new dining hall as well as classrooms. Whatever expansion is still planned, the Gurudwara Sahib El Sobrante stands as a remarkable representative of the Sikh legacy, steeped in the traditions of its faith. As all *gurudwaras,* the El Sobrante temple is open to all communities. In the House of the Lord, all are equal, irrespective of their status in the world outside. With entrances from all sides, the *gurudwara* signifies that it is open to all without any distinction, and that God is omnipresent. On a visit to the temple, the head is kept covered as a mark of respect to the *Granth Sahib,* and shoes are not allowed inside. Like all other *gurudwaras,*

the El Sobrante temple has a *langar* hall, a community kitchen where food is served to all devotees with no distinction of caste, creed, or status. The *darbar* is the main hall of the *gurudwara,* where all ceremonies are performed. Inside the *darbar* is a platform on which the *Guru Granth Sahib* is placed, covered by a sheet of cloth known as an *romalla.* A canopy rises above the scripture. During the night, the holy scripture is housed in a room called the *sachkand.*

In this picturesque California setting, the Sikh community members continue to practice their faith, adhering to their belief in one God, abstaining from idol worship, and practicing tolerance and love of others, with a deep dedication to the ideal of hospitality and generosity. It is, indeed, a "House of God" or "House of Guru," as its very name, *gurudwara,* suggests.

PAGE 304, TOP: *Khanda* is the insignia of the Sikhs, and Sikh places of worship include a pole bearing a yellow flag with the *khanda* image.

PAGE 304, BOTTOM: Four symbols are housed in the *palki* (canopy), where the *Guru Granth Sahib* is installed. The one to the left and the two to the right represent *Omkar*, which stands for God as the Primal Being and for God's unity. The second symbol from the left is called *Miri-and-Piri* and represents the balance between spiritual and worldly matters. Sikhs are expected to maintain this balance, an idea introduced by Guru Hargobind and represented by two stylized swords.

PAGE 305, TOP: Decorative detail on the dome.

PAGE 305, BOTTOM: Ornamentation on the *palki*.

Architects of Featured Temples

Dr. V. GANAPATI STHAPATI

Born in the year 1927 at Pillayarpatti, a village near Karaikudi in Tamil Nadu, Dr. V. Ganapati Sthapati hails from an illustrious family of traditional temple architects and sculptors who have an unbroken lineage of a hundred decades. Among others, the family has built the great Brihadeeswara Temple of Tanjore (Thanjavur), the treasurehouse of Indian art and architecture. Son of Sri Vaidyanatha Sthapati, a renowned architect, sculptor, and Sanskrit scholar, V. Ganapati Sthapati has made a remarkable contribution to the field of Indian art and architecture.

As the doyen of the Hindu architectural treatise, the *Vastu Shastra*, he has been doing research in the field of *Vastu* science and technology for the past 40 to 45 years. A graduate in mathematics and Sanskrit, Ganapati Sthapati is propagating this supreme science both in India and abroad. He is solely responsible for the resurrection of the works of the great Brahmarishi Mayan, who was the progenitor of Indian science and technology.

As the Principal of the Government College of Architecture and Sculpture, Mamallapuram, near Chennai, India (the only institute of this kind in the entire world), for a continuous period of 27 years, from 1961 to 1988, Dr. Ganapati Sthapati worked hard to restore and elevate the status of India's sacred art and architecture. By affiliating with the University of Madras, he could offer degree courses, thereby bringing academic status to age-old traditional learning and also initiating many youngsters into this traditional technology.

After retirement from government service, he established the Vaastu Vedic Trust, as well as a research institution called Vaastu Vedic Research Foundation, of which he is the Founder Director, aimed at research, development, and globalization of the *Vastu Shastra*. He is also the proprietor of a professional guild named V. Ganapati Sthapati & Associates, dealing with design and construction of temples and sculptural works. He has a number of temples and other projects to his credit, both in India and abroad.

At present, he is active in reviving sacred building architecture along scientific lines and has established the firm Vaastu Vedic Designers & Builders to accomplish that goal. His contribution to architecture of buildings other than temples is also significant. The library and administrative block for Tamil University in Tanjore and the Muthiah Mandram in Madurai are palatial buildings that speak of his capacity for designing and executing works of grandiose nature. He has also Indianized modern buildings such as Muthiah Mandram, Rani Seethai Mandram, Kalaignar Arangam, and Anna Arivalayam in Chennai. They are appreciated as visual musical forms, a quality attributed to

Indian architecture. To crown it all, he is the master architect and builder of the world-famous statue of Ayyan Thiruvalluvar, the 133-ft. wonder in stone that has been erected off the shore in mid-sea at Kanya Kumari, at the southern tip of India. This colossal marvel has taken him to the pinnacle of his life's achievement as a traditional architect and builder.

Dr. Ganapati has authored a number of books on the science and technology of *Vastu* and has conducted two international seminars entitled "International Seminar on Mayonic Science and Technology" (the science so termed after its originator Mayan). He has also participated in as many as 80 seminars in India and abroad and presented research papers on Indian science and technology. In order to cater to the needs of aspirants in *Vastu* learning from India and abroad, Ganapati Sthapati has also given form to a teaching institution called the International Institute of Mayonic Science and Technology, which conducts workshops and discourses on *Vastu*. Under the aegis of this institution, he has conducted workshops in India and abroad, evincing the interest and attention of contemporary engineers, architects, and scholars. A workshop entitled "Workshop on Scientific *Vaastu* with Special Reference to Building Architecture" was successfully conducted in Salem, Pondicherry, and in Rajapalayam in Tamil Nadu, with about 150 architects and engineers participating.

Sri Ganapati conducted a three-day workshop in Washington, D.C., on June 15, 2001, exposing the intelligentsia and the engineering community of the West to the age-old scientific culture of *Vastu*. He found a receptive community eager to learn more of this supreme science. More than 40 architects and engineers of the Western world attended the workshop. The engineering fraternity of the West was deeply impressed when Ganapati Sthapati drew a parallel between the Einsteinian equation of $E = mc^2$ and the *Vastu* formula of *Vastu* = *Vāstu*, where *Vastu* is the energy containing matter, and *Vāstu* is matter containing energy. The architects and engineers both of India and abroad who have attended the *Vastu* workshops have now taken to practicing *Vastu*-based design and execution of buildings in India and across the globe.

Among the notable books he has authored are *Sirpachennool (Iconometry)*, *Temples of Space Science*, *What Is a Temple?*, *Some Glimpses of the Science and Technology of Vaastu Shastra—Redefined, Reinterpreted and Illustrated*, *Commentary on Mayan's "Aintiram,"* *Who Created God*, *Vaastu Shastra—A Scientific Treatise, Not a Religious Document*, and *Vaastu Purusha Mandalam*. He has also formed a publishing house named Dakshinaa Publishing House, to undertake the publishing of his research works to popularize and also to preserve sacred architecture science for generation to come. One of the recent publications, entitled *Building Architecture of Sthapatya Veda*, authored by Dr. Ganapati Sthapati, has won the attention of scholars, architects, and engineers of both India and abroad. This valuable work, which is a compendium of talks delivered by Ganapati Sthapati at various forums, has brought out in full the science and technology of *Vastu Shastra* to convince beyond doubt that it enjoyed the independent and unique status of a Veda, known among the temple artisan (*shilpi*) community as *Sthapatya Veda* or *Vastu Veda*.

Dr. Ganapati has also earned a number of titles and awards

offered by prestigious institutions and universities, including a Doctorate degree conferred by the Maharishi Mahesh Yogi Vedic University in Holland, in 1995; an Honorary Fellowship by the Indian Institute of Architects in 1993; and the National Award for Master Craftsmanship from the President of India in 1973, among others.

Dr. Ganapati Sthapati has visited United States of America, United Kingdom, Australia, France, Fiji Islands, Hawaii, Germany, Holland, Singapore, Malaysia, and Mexico for professional and research purposes.

The pulsating and vibrant researcher and sculptor in the man called Dr. Ganapati Sthapati has given forth many startling research discoveries on the intricacies of the traditional art and architecture of India. He is quite optimistic that one day *Vastu* will rule the world not only of architecture, but more. He has identified theories about the origin of the Universe and its life forms through his research on the works of Mayan, scaling heights far beyond the mundane world of modern science and technology.

PADMASRI
"Shilpa Kalamani"
M. MUTHIAH STHAPATHI

Born December 14, 1941, at Eluvankottai, a village near Ramnad District in Tamil Nadu, Padmasri M. Muthiah Sthapathi hails from an illustrious family of traditional architects and sculptors known as *Vishwakarma*, with an ancient lineage of masters skilled in constructing temples and carving granite idols. His father as well as his grandfather traditionally constructed many temples and carved numerous granite stone idols in India. The family has made a remarkable contribution to the field of Indian art and architecture.

After his basic education in Devakottai, Tamil Nadu, he joined the Mamallapuram Sculpture School, studying there from 1957 to 1961. Under the guidance of his illustrious guru, Sri Vaidyanatha Sthapathi, he learned the art of temple architecture and sculpting, as well as Sanskrit. On completion of his training at the college, he started constructing many temples and also carved numerous deity images (*vigrahas*).

Muthiah Sthapathi is a specialist in preparation of plans for temples, execution of temple projects, and carving of granite stone idols according to the *Shilpa Shastras*. He has been working as Advisor Sthapathi in the H.R. and C.E. (Hindu Religious and Charitable Endowments) Department, Government of Tamil Nadu in the Cadre of S.E. (Superintending Engineers).

Some of his current projects in India include the construction of the Arupadai Veedu Temple complex in granite stone at Besant Nagar, Chennai; carving of a Sri Vishnu granite *vigraha*, which is 110 ft. in height; construction of the Sri Kalabhyraveswara Swamy Temple in granite at Adichunchanagiri, Bangalore; and construction of a stone *Alankara Mandapa* at Tiruvannamalai.

Major projects completed in India include carving a 60-ft. Sri Adi Shankara in granite for Kanchi Kamakoti Peetam and carving a 60-ft. Sri Krishna idol out of granite for Sri B. K. Birla. Another recent project was a 32-ft. granite *vigraha* of Sri Anjaneya at Nangainallur. The Vishvarupa Anjaneya on a lotus pedestal was carved out of a granite hill in Tamil Nadu and was transported to Mumbai in a trailer and installed by the Shankaracharya of Kanchi on February 9, 2000. With its pedestal, the idol stands 40 ft. tall. Weighing 55 tons, it took one year to complete. A new construction of a 175-ft. entrance tower (*rajagopura*) at Tenkasi has brought him the title "Shilpa Kalai Semmal," conferred by Srimati Soundara Kailasam at the Tenkasi *Kumbhabhisheka* in the presence of Sri Krupananda Variar and 100 poets. Other construction and sculpting work includes a list of projects that is unending; among the projects are:

- Construction of Sri Meenakshi Sundareswara Temple in Uttaraswami Malai, New Delhi.

- Construction of Satguru Sri Gnanananda Aalayam at Tennangur.

- Carving a 60-ft. single-stone granite statue of Lord Krishna that was installed at the Birla Museum, Calcutta.

- Renovating the sanctum towers (*vimanas*) and main entrance towers (*rajagopuras*) of the Kamakshi Temple and the 130-ft. high *rajagopura* of Sri Varadharajaperumal Temple.

- Renovations and new construction of Kumarakottam Temple, all at Kanchipuram, Tamil Nadu.

- Construction of the Sri Utthara Chidambara Nataraja Temple at Satara in Maharashtra. This temple is like the Chidambaram Nataraja Temple, with four side *rajagopuras* sponsored by four state governments. Stone-carved *vigrahas* of 108 Shiva Karanas are installed there.

Some of the projects that Muthiah Sthapathi has worked on in the United States include Sri Ganesha Temple in New York; Sri Meenakshi Temple in Houston, Texas; Sri Venkateswara Temple (Malibu Temple) in Los Angeles, California; Sri Shiva-Vishnu Temple in Livermore, California; Sri Ganesha Temple in Nashville, Tennessee; Sri Venketeswara Temple in Chicago, Illinois; Sri Venkateswara Temple in Atlanta, Georgia; Sri Lakshmi Temple in Boston, Massachusetts; Sri Murugan Temple in Washington, D.C.; Sri Venkateswara Temple in Memphis, Tennessee; Sri Radha Rani Temple in Austin, Texas; Hindu Temple of Kentucky in Louisville, Kentucky; Sri Bharatiya Temple in Lansing, Michigan; and Sri Karuniariamman Temple in Detroit, Michigan. In London, he worked on the Sri Murugan Temple, and in Bangkok, the Sri Maha Mariamman Temple.

Muthiah Sthapathi is the *Asthana Sthapathi* of the Sri Kanchi Kamakoti Sri Sankara Mutt, Kanchipuram. He is the recipient of India's prestigious award of the "Padmasri" title, conferred by the President of India in 1992; the "Shilpa Kalamani" title, conferred by His Holiness, the Sankaracharya Swamigal of Kanchi Kamakoti Peetam in 1976 on the occasion of the *Kumbhabhisheka* of Sri Kamakshi Amman Temple, Kanchi; the "Shilpa Kala Rathnakara" title, conferred by the Raja of Kashi on the occasion of the *Kumbhabhisheka* of Tribhuvana Temple at Allahabad, Uttar Pradhesh; the "Mahonnatha Shilpa Kala Shiromani" title, conferred by the Adhyayana Universal Mission of New York; the "Shilpa Shastra Simham" title, conferred by Sri Bhuvaneshwari Swamigal at Madhya Kailash *Kumbhabhisheka* in the presence of Dr. M. A. M. Ramasamy, Pro-Chancellor of Annamalai University and the Raja of Chettinad; the "Shilpa Shastra Vidya Saraswathi" title, conferred by Tamil Nadu Anmiga Peravai; the "Shilpa Kalai Arasar" title on a gold plaque, conferred by Thavathiru Kundrakudi Adigaklar of Tiruvannamalai Aathinam; and the "Kalai Vendar" title, conferred by the Tamil people at Myanmar (Burma).

SHASHI D. PATEL

Born in Kenya and educated in India, Shashi D. Patel graduated in Architecture in 1968 from the School of Architecture, Ahmedabad, India. He attended the Graduate School at Carnegie Mellon University in 1973.

In the United States since 1971 and now a U.S. citizen, Shashi Patel did his early architectural work in India and Kenya. His 29 years of architectural practice—15 years at Celli-Flynn and Associates and 14 years with other registered architects in various countries—gave him valuable experience. Some of his work included being part of the Design Team for the Addition to State Capitol Building project in Harrisburg, Pennsylvania. His work as Project Architect on that project yielded him the "Arthur Ross Award, Classical America" in 1989. As Project Architect, he designed several Safari Lodges in Kenya, Uganda, and Tanzania. He also designed the Victoria Redevelopment and Barbarons Hotel at Seychelles Islands in the Indian Ocean and served as Project Architect for miscellaneous projects in Nairobi, Kenya.

He serves on many boards, including the following: member of the Board of Hindu Heritage Research Foundation; trustee and member of the Executive and Building Committee, Hindu Temple of North America, Pittsburgh; President, Gujarati Samaj of Greater Pittsburgh (1991); Vice President of Boca International, Pittsburgh Chapter 2002. In 1998 he was honored as a Paul Harris Fellow of Rotary International. He also received the Golden Arch Award for excellence in the field of Architecture from NRI Institute, New Delhi, India, in 1992, and received the Gold Star Award from Mussoorie International School for Architectural Design and Project Management in 2000.

Shashi Patel has been responsible for designing more than 24 temples in the United States. Some of those projects are featured in this publication, including: the Hindu Jain Temple in Pittsburgh, Pennsylvania; the Sri Venkateswara Temple in Pittsburgh, Pennsylvania; the Temple of Understanding in New Vrindaban, West Virginia; the Ganesha Temple in Flushing, New York; the Ganesha Temple in Nashville, Tennessee; the Shiva Vishnu Temple in Aurora, Illinois; the Shiva Vishnu Temple in Cleveland, Ohio; and the Hindu Temple in Atlanta, Georgia. The projects were undertaken in association with Padmasri M. Muthiah Sthapathi, temple architect from Chennai, India.

Shashi D. Patel and Associates, Architects and Planners, in Pittsburgh, Pennsylvania, is a young firm now in its fifteenth year. The firm has been privileged to design and oversee large and small construction projects, ranging over the entire United States and including consulting assignments outside the United States (Canada, India, Portugal, Kenya, United Kingdom, and Australia). Expertise extends not only to institutional buildings such as schools and community buildings, but also hotels, motels, office buildings of all sizes and types, commercial development, residential buildings, shopping centers, and urban complexes of various sizes.

BARUN K. BASU

Barun Basu has more than 30 years of experience in planning, design, and construction administration of a wide range of projects, both nationally and internationally. Educated at the University of Bombay, he received a Bachelor's degree in Architecture in 1962; he earned his Master of Architecture degree in 1967 at the University of California, Berkeley. As the founding Principal of Barun Basu Associates, he is responsible for the overall performance of a team of designers and consultants. Barun Basu has served as Project Architect for various municipal, educational and institutional facilities, specializing in rehabilitation work, as well as institutional facilities requiring special attention to patients with behavioral problems in confined spaces.

Mr. Basu is involved in a number of professional and community organizations, which include the Board of Directors of the American Institute of Architects/CT; Chairman, Committee on the Environment, AIA/CT; Trustee, Connecticut Trust for Historic Preservation; Trustee, Connecticut Valley Hindu Temple Society; former President, Rotary Club of Montville; and Director, New London Main Street.

Barun Basu has been responsible for designing many churches, temples, community centers, and commercial buildings. He has worked with many temple architects (*sthapatis*) from India on the Connecticut Valley Hindu Temple Society and Community Hall in Middletown, Conneticut; the Poughkeepsie Temple in Poughkeepsie, New York; the Hindu Temple and Cultural Center in Albany, New York; the Hindu Temple Society and Community Hall in Flushing, New York; and the Ved Mandir in New Brunswick, New Jersey. All of the above projects, excluding the Ved Mandir, are included in this book.

He was also involved in coordinating two years of sculpting work in Hyderabad under Padmasri S. M. Ganapati Sthapati and Department of Endowments for the New York Ganesha Temple. In addition, he has been involved in supervising the sculptural work in Bangalore by sculptor Vankatraman Bhatt.

SUBHASH A. NADKARNI

Subhash Anant Nadkarni is an architect from Mumbai (Bombay), India, who graduated in 1964 from the Academy of Architecture in Mumbai. In addition, he has done postgraduate work at the Architectural Association in London, England.

He serves as President of Archiform, Inc., Architects, in Winfield, Illinois, a firm established in 1985. He has designed various buildings such as banks, corporate offices, industrial buildings, and clinics. At present, he specializes in hospitals and medical office buildings, having designed sixteen cancer centers throughout the United States.

Among the many temples designed by Subhash Nadkarni are the Sri Venkateswara Swami (Balaji) Temple of Greater Chicago in Aurora, Illinois (1986). This temple was designed in traditional South Indian architectural style, with exterior decorations designed and overseen by Padmasri M. Muthiah Sthapathi. Subhash Nadkarni also designed the following temples and Hindu cultural structures: the Hindu Temple of Atlanta (also known as Sri Venkateshwara Swami Temple) in Atlanta, Georgia; the Bharatiya Mandir in Chicago, Illinois; and the Jain Temple in Chicago, Illinois, working together with temple architect Sri Sutaria from India for exterior decorations that followed the traditional Jain temple architecture style. In addition, he worked with Swami Chinmayananda on the initial plans for Chinmaya Mission Chicago buildings.

Some of the temples Subhash Nadkarni is working on in the year 2002 are the Shirdi Sai Baba Temple in Woodridge, Illinois; the Vaishnav Samaj Temple in Addison, Illinois; the Hindu Temple of Central Florida, Orlando, Florida, working with Mr. Kishor Pathare, architect, and Padmasri M. Muthiah Sthapathi of India; and the Vipassana Meditation Center in Chicago, Illinois.

Subhash Nadkarni is a voluntary architect/consultant for the Hindu Temple in Lemont, Illinois, working on the Swami Vivekananda Hill improvements project. He also serves as consultant for various other temples in the Midwest region of the United States.

ARUN PRADHAN

Arun Pradhan, born in 1940 in Lakhanode, Madhya Pradesh, India, graduated from the Sir J. J. College of Architecture, Mumbai, India, in 1964. After immigrating to Canada in 1967, he pursued further studies in the field of architecture.

Arun Pradhan's membership in professional organizations includes: A.I.I.A.

(Associate of the Indian Institute of Architects); A.R.I.B.A. (Charter Member of the Royal Institute of British Architects); M.R.A.I.C (Member, Royal Architectural Institute of Canada); and N.C.A.R.B. (Registered in the states of Texas and Michigan, USA). He has served as member of various architectural committees of the city of Scarborough, the Ontario Association of Architects (OAA), and of municipal planning departments.

The first temple Sri Pradhan designed was the Hindu Sabha Temple in the city of Brampton in Ontario. Because of the unusal, innovative design of the three temple towers (*shikharas*), the temple has become one of the landmarks in the city. A new construction material, fiber-reinforced plastic, was used in combination with glass blocks, admitting an abundance of light into the main deity area. The design was a successful marrying of the past and the present with a futuristic view—while maintaining the principles of traditional Hindu temple architectural design.

He also designed a Ganesha Temple for the Hindu Temple Society of Canada in Richmond Hill, Ontario. This temple was designed according to the temple architecture style of South India, with a 16-column hall (*mandapa*) and two main towers (*rajagopuras*) and *vimanas*. A new material, glass-reinforced cement, was tested in Toronto for application in the harsh Canadian winter climate with its freeze-thaw cycles. A recent new design project was completed for the Sri Swaminarayan Hindu Mandir in Toronto, which includes a Cultural Complex and a Sant Nivas (priest residence). Costruction of this mega-project will started in May 2002.

The architectural frm of Papadopoulos & Pradhan Architects Inc. has served as Prime Consultants for large-scale projects such as Bell Cellular Communition Centre in Toronto, JVC Canada Ofifices, a multimedia showroom and warehouse, and Hindu Sabha Temple in Brampton, as well as medium-scale projects such as upgrading of existing facilities, including interior design, space planning for Parkway Place Complex, Concord Place Complex, IBM, Bell Canada, and Insurance Bureau of Canada, and renovation work for the Bank of Nova Scotia branch offices and shopping center facilities, to name a few.

The firm has extensive experience with design, contract administration, municipal compliance, and upgrading of existing facilities. The scope of work includes: building design, site plan development, condition survey and feasibility studies, hard landscaping, space planning, interior design and rehabilitation work for corporations, institutions, and religious organizations.

The firm is involved in design, field review, and interior design services for Sri Swaminarayan Hindu Mandir Sanstha in Detroit, Michigan, Chicago, Illinois, and Houston, Texas. Architectural work for religious institutions also includes Vishnu Mandir in Richmond Hill and a new temple complex in Hamilton, Ontario. The firm also has parciticipated on a volunteer basis to provide design and construction document review for the Armenian Orthodox Church and Greek Orhodox Church in Toronto.

Arun Pradhan is President of the firm and George Papadopoulos is a principal partner conducting research on new material and providing contract management of all project construction.

MAP OF FEATURED TEMPLES

Gurdwara Sahib El Sobrante - El Sobrante, California
Hindu Community and Cultural Center - Livermore, California
Hindu Temple Society of Southern California - Calabasa, California
Jain Center of Northern California - Milpitas, California
Connecticut Valley Hindu Temple Society - Middletown, Connecticut
Sri Shiva Vishnu Temple - Davie, Florida
Wat Florida Dhammaram - Kissimmee, Florida
Hindu Temple of Atlanta - Riverdale, Georgia
Hindu Temple of Greater Chicago - Lemont, Illinois
Sri Venkateswara Swami Temple of Greater Chicago - Aurora, Illinois
Sri Siva Vishnu Temple - Lanham, Maryland
New England Hindu Temple - Ashland, Massachusetts
Paschima Kasi Sri Viswanatha Temple - Flint, Michigan
Hindu Temple of St. Louis - Ballwin, Missouri
Hindu Society of Nevada - Las Vegas, Nevada
Sri Maha Vallabha Ganapathi Devasthanam, Flushing, New York
Hindu Temple Society - Loudonville, New York
Sri Ranganatha Temple - Pomona, New York
Hindu Samaj Temple - Wappingers Falls, New York
Hindu Temple and Cultural Society of USA - Bridgewater, New Jersey
Hindu Community Organization Dayton - Fairborn, Ohio
Hindu Sabha - Brampton, Ontario
Hindu Temple Society of Canada - Richmond Hill, Ontario
Hindu Jain Temple - Monroeville, Pennsylvania
Sri Venkateswara Temple Pittsburgh - Penn Hills, Pennsylvania
Shri Ganesha Temple of Nashville - Nashville, Tennessee
International Society of Divine Love - Austin, Texas
Sri Meenakshi Temple Society - Pearland, Texas
Sri Sri Radha Krishna Temple - Spanish Fork, Utah
New Mathura Vrindavan and Golden Palace - Moundsville, West Virginia

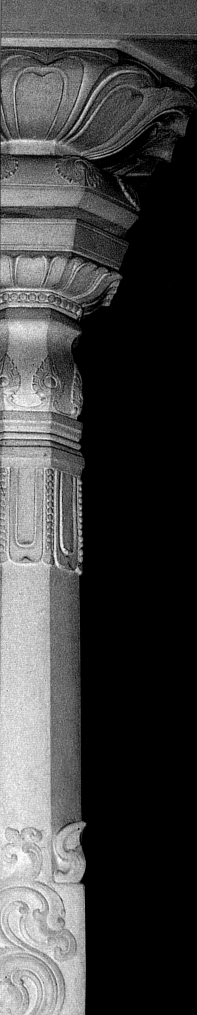

Hindu Univesity of America

It is well known that Hinduism is a highly philosophical religious tradition with a universal outlook, appeal, and values. It is the "Religion of Man" to borrow a term from Nobel Laureate Rabindranath Tagore. The Hindu tradition is grounded in Vedic thought (from the Sanskrit *veda*, meaning "knowledge"), making it a truly knowledge-based philosophical system.

Hinduism is the repository of a large mass of knowledge based in secular and sacred disciplines of human knowledge—language, literature, grammar, sciences, health sciences, mathematics, humanities, social sciences, political thought, statecraft, philosophy, and religion. This system has the unique privilege of building perfect harmony between apparently conflicting things—between the secular and the sacred, between science and religion.

Although Hindu traditions, in their origin, are identified with India, Hindu interactions with and influences over other societies and traditions in the world can be seen throughout human history. There have been universities in ancient India—Takshila, Nalanda, and others—that were the seats of highest learning and research. These universities produced world scholars like Panini, Kautilya, and Varah Mihir, whose works are highly respected and have attracted students from all over the world. In the present phase, Hindus are spread all over the world. In United States, the Hindu population includes academics, researchers, doctors, industrialists, businessmen, engineers, IT professionals, venture capitalists, and other professionals. Many Hindu ashrams and traditions such yoga are well known to people all over the world. Hinduism is a living religion in North America, with its own distinctive features and contributions.

Brief History

Hindu University of America was incorporated in the state of Florida in 1989 and started teaching activity in October 1993. It provides formal education in subjects related to Hindu philosophies, religion, and culture. The University currently offers Master's and Doctoral degrees in seven disciplines of Hindu Studies: Hinduism, Hindu philosophies, yoga education, yoga philosophy and meditation, Vedic astrology, Ayurvedic sciences, and Divine Music. Future plans include expansion into other areas.

Initially, the University operated from temporary offices in Orlando and then from Tarpon Springs. In year 2000, the University acquired property, now measuring more than 12 acres, in Orlando, Florida.

Hindu University has been imparting instruction through correspondence courses all these years. Steps to appoint full-time faculty began in October 2001, after inauguration of its permanent campus on September 8, 2001. The University has offered appointments to world-class academics and scholars. A resident teaching program and on-campus research program began in Spring 2002 with resident faculty.

Hindu University – Its Nature and Purpose

Hindu University is an American university and is to be viewed as a direct service to America—its people, society, and educational system. It is a broad-based institution encompassing all aspects of Hindu thought, life, traditions, religion, and culture. The word *Hindu* is an all-encompassing term with which people adhering to the age-old tradition of Bharat, i.e., India, no matter where they are settled in the world, can associate with. It is not the intent of the University to promote any one aspect or one view or one practice over others, but to present all that is authentically available under many terms—Hinduism, Vedic thought, *Sanatana Dharma*, and other similar terms; or under specific terminology such as Shaivism, Vaishnavism, Buddhism, Jainism, Sikhism. The words *Hindu* and *Hinduism*, as used in Hindu University of America's name and in its various documents, have the broadest possible connotation.

The primary purpose of Hindu University of America is to fulfill the demand in the West to learn about Hinduism and systems originating in India in a rigorous and authentic fashion. A need existed for such a learning center to meet the pent-up demand of many who wanted to study Hindu thought and traditions for different reasons. The University is meant to provide to the Western world a place to look for guidance in matters relating to Hinduism, Indian languages, yoga and meditation, Ayurveda, Vedic ideas, and spiritual upliftment.

The doors of Hindu University are open to all qualified students seeking to learn about Hindu-based knowledge. For persons of Hindu heritage from India, the Caribbean, and other parts of the world, the University provides much-needed opportunity to study and understand their heritage.

Students not seeking to pursue degree programs at the University can earn credits elsewhere by doing courses in Indian languages and culture. It is meant to be an institution for developing and articulating Hindu viewpoints on national and international affairs. American universities with departments of Indian/South Asian studies shall find Hindu University a rich resource of both man and material for research.

The University is guided by its mission to provide each student with a liberal education that helps unfold the unlimited potential within him or her. Students of Hindu University become citizens of the world, shaped in universal values and oriented toward a holistic life.

Graduate Programs

Currently the University is authorized by the Florida State Department of Education and the State Board of Independent Colleges and Universities to award Master's and Doctoral degrees in the area of Hindu Studies. At this writing, in early 2002, degree programs are offered in the following: Hinduism, Hindu Philosophies, Yoga Philosophy and Meditation, Yoga Education (only Master's degree), Ayurvedic Science (only Master's degree), Hindu/Vedic Astrology, Divine Music. There are plans to add additional courses to this list.

Eligibility for Admission to Graduate and Post-Graduate Programs

Students with a minimum of a Bachelor's degree in any area are eligible to register for a resident-full-time or correspondence (Master's/Doctoral) degree program. For instructions by correspondence, one can join any time of the year; regular programs are offered during Fall and Spring semesters. Intensives are arranged during the Summer semester.

Persons not interested in a degree program may audit courses. Students of other institutions can offer these courses for credit transfer. Non-degree students may *not* already have earned a Bachelor's degree.

University Campus

The University campus is located at 113 N. Econlockhatchee Trail, Orlando, Forida 32825. A building construction plan is in place, in keeping with modern needs of a growing university with a grand vision. The long-range plan envisages construction in stages. It is a multi-block plan comprised of an administrative block, academic blocks, classrooms, student facility, library block, Ayurveda lab, auditoriums and residences for faculty and students.

Individual persons and charitable organizations are welcome to finance the building of rooms, wings, schools, or residential units in the name of their loved ones or organizations. All donations are tax deductible, as Hindu University of America is a 501C(3) tax-exempt, not-for-profit corporation.

Students

The University has students registered in both Master's and Doctoral programs. Currently, most of the students are registered in correspondence programs and are located far and wide in countries like Malaysia and the Netherlands. A good number of them are enrolled in Yoga Education and Vedic Astrology. There are several students registered for Doctoral programs, mainly in the areas of Hinduism and Hindu Philosophies. Campus teaching has begun, and from Fall 2002 onward, the University will be registering students for on-campus classes.

University Extension Centers and Collaborations

The demand for Hindu University courses prompts opening its Extension Centers at places other than Orlando. A center has already been functioning in Colorado. Some interested persons have approached the University from Houston and other locations. The University welcomes such invitations and is prepared to open Extension Centers. The main considerations are quality education, given by highly qualified faculty. Two such collaborative efforts are:

An Extension Center at VYASA in Bangalore, India, for Yoga Philosophy and Meditation and Yoga Education Collaboration with American Council of Vedic Astrology in Sedona, Arizona, for programs in Vedic Astrology.

There shall naturally be more such centers and arrangements, as time goes on.

Research and Development

Research is an integral part of the University's activities. Research is not limited to Doctoral programs. To promote scholarship and research in selected and general areas, the University funds proposals received from academics anywhere in the world.

It is basically through research and publications that the university will become a center of excellence on Hindu Studies and other Indic subjects. Not in the too-distant future, one can visualize that there will be schools in major study areas, such as a School of Indic languages for Sanskrit and other Indian languages. Also we can envision a School of Ayurveda, School of Vedas, School of Hindu Philosophy, and so on.

Professional Courses in the Future

At some stage the University shall provide for programs in modern and professional areas such as Computer Science, Engineering, Health Sciences, Management, and Commerce. While imparting instruction in these areas and conducting research, the students will also be exposed to Hindu religion, languages, and culture by a University requirement to study such courses, thereby providing the benefit of receiving instruction that molds the students into holistic personalities, no matter what their chosen profession.

Faculty

A university is basically what its faculty makes it. Working on this principle, highly qualified persons have been offered appointments at Hindu University of America. These are the world's very best scholars in their areas of specialty. Currently we have faculty who have at a minimum a Ph.D. degree, extensive teaching experience, a history of successfully sponsoring Ph.D. students, and an outstanding publication record.

The Board of Directors is keen to have endowed chairs instituted by organizations and philanthropists.

Non-Degree and Service Courses

Apart from formal degree programs, the University is taking initiative in other directions. Other programs include: Certificate Program in Hindu Priesthood, Certificate Program in Yoga, Certificate Program in Panchkarma. Also initiated are other activities such as Hindu Youth and Heritage Camps, extension lectures, seminars, conferences, Hindu senior citizen meetings, and interfaith seminars. The University's social and community services will include Family Counseling, Religious Consulting, Astrological Consulting, and the like.

The vision of Hindu University is to promote openness in religious understanding, deeper philosophical research, spiritual growth, and propagation of peace in the light of the Hindu tradition.

Information on the University

For more information on the University and its programs, please contact the President of the University or Chairman of the Board of Directors at the University address:

113 N. Econlockhatchee Trail
Orlando
FL 32825
USA
Telephone: 407-275-0013
Email: admin@hindu-university.edu

The Council of Hindu Temples of North America

The Council of Hindu Temples of North America represents a group of autonomous Hindu Temples across the United States.

The objectives of the Council are:

1. To actively promote the development of temples, through the sharing of technical and managerial information, as well as providing resources through which architects, builders, sculptors, priests, artists, performers, and other related services may be sourced.

2. To promote the teaching of Indian languages and of Hindu culture, especially among Hindu youth.

3. To publish a newsletter through which all members may be kept abreast of issues affecting the temples and the general Hindu community.

4. To promote interfaith dialogue so as to foster an understanding of all peoples living in the United States.

5. To provide assistance and relief to the underprivileged, disadvantaged, and victims of natural disasters in local member communities.

Board of Directors:

Sri Venkateswara Temple, Penn Hill, Pennsylvania
Sri Maha Vallabha Ganapati Devasthanam, Flushing, New York
Sri Meenakshi Temple of Houston, Pearland, Texas
Sri Siva Vishnu Temple, Lanham, Maryland
Sri Paschima Kasi Viswanatha Temple, Flint, Michigan
Sri Ganesha Temple, Nashville, Tennessee
The Hindu Temple of Greater Chicago, Lemont, Illinois
The Hindu Temple Society of Southern California, Calabasa, California
The Hindu Temple of St. Louis, Ballwin, Missouri

Contact Info:

The Secretary
Council of Hindu Temples of North America
c/o Sri Maha Vallabha Ganapati Devasthanam, Flushing
45-57 Bowne Street, Flushing, NY 11355
Tel: (718) 460-8484
Fax: (718) 461-8055
www.indianet.com/ganesh

Acknowledgments

During the years that led up to this book, I have drawn often and long upon the time, advice, wisdom, and goodwill of many people. To them I owe a depth of gratitude — without them this would be a lesser volume. I am likewise grateful to those friends, colleagues, and associates who opened to me their insights and told me their stories, who opened doors, responded to inquiries, or commented on some portion of the project. Among the many people I would like to thank are:

Dr. V. Ganapati Sthapati, Chennai, India
- *for text, line drawings, and various assistance and guidance*

Padmasri M. Muthiah Sthapathi, Chennai, India
- *for text, line drawings, and various assistance and guidance*

His Holiness Sri Swami Sahajananda
    Divine Life Society of South Africa
    - *for text assistance and guidance*

His Holiness Sri Swami Saradananda
    Ramakrishna Mission South Africa
    - *for text assistance and guidance*

His Holiness Sri Swami Tejomayananda
    Chinmaya Mission, India
    -*for text assistance and guidance*

His Holiness Sri Swami Chidananda
    Chinmaya Mission, India
    - *for text assistance and guidance*

The management staff of all temples featured in this book
    - *for all their assistance in making this book a reality*

Hindu University of America
    - *for jointly publishing this project*

Council of Hindu Temples of North America
    -*for being an associate publisher for this project*

Management staff of www.culturopedia.com, Hyderabad, India
    - *for text assistance*

Rudite Emir, San Francisco, California
    - *for editing the text and providing guidance*

Hal Belmont, San Francisco, California
    - *for printing and other assistance*

Dr. G. V. Naidu, St. Louis, Missouri

Dr. K. V. Siva Subramanian, Washington, D.C.

Finally, for all kinds of support having to do less directly, but no less essentially, with this book's completion, my fondest appreciation goes to my parents, Narian and Neelavathy Kolapen, my wife Satyabhama, and my son Sañjay. In addition to my appreciation for Sañjay's contribution as photographer, I also thank him for the personal support he has given me in seeing this project through to completion.

Mahalingum Kolapen
Orlando, Florida
July 2002

Contact Information

Connecticut Valley Hindu Temple Society
11 Training Hill Rd, Middletown, CT 06457
Phone: (860) 346-8675   Fax: (860) 346-6772
www.cvhts.org

Gurudwara Sahib El Sobrante
3550 Hill Crest Road, El Sobrante, CA 94803
Phone: (510) 223-9987
www.geocities.com/gurdwaraworld/gurd9.html

Hindu Jain Temple
615 Illini Drive, Monroeville, PA 15146
Phone: (724) 325-2073   Fax: (724) 733-7475
www.hindujaintemple.org

Hindu Sabha
9225 The Gore Road, Brampton, Ontario L67 3Y7, Canada
Phone: (905) 794-4638   Fax: (905) 794-3294
www.hindusabha.com

Hindu Samaj Temple
3 Brown Road, Wappingers Falls, NY 12590
Phone: (845) 297-9061   Fax: (845) 297-9061
www.hindusamajtemple.org

Hindu Community and Cultural Center
1232 Arrowhead Ave., Livermore, CA 94550
Phone: (925) 449-6255   Fax: (925) 455-0404
www.livermoretemple.org

Hindu Community Organization Dayton
2615 Lillian Lane, Fairborn, OH 45424
Phone: (937) 429-4455

Hindu Temple and Cultural Society of USA, Inc. - Sri Venkateswara
Temple
7890 Old Farm Road, Bridgewater, NJ 08807
Phone: (908) 725-4477
www.venkateswara.org

Hindu Temple of Atlanta, Inc.
5851 GA Hwy 85, Riverdale, GA 30274
Phone: (770) 907-7102   Fax: (770) 907-6080
www.hindutempleofatlanta.org

Hindu Temple of Greater Chicago
10915 Lemont Road, Lemont, IL 60439
(630) 972-0300   Fax: (630) 972-9111
www.ramatemple.org

Hindu Temple Society
450 Albany Shaker Road, Loudonville, NY 12211
Phone: (518) 459-7272
www.albanyhindutemple.org

Hindu Temple Society of Canada
10865 Bayview Avenue, Richmond Hill, Ontario L4S 1M1, Canada
Phone: (905) 883-9109   Fax: (905) 883-9834

Hindu Society of Nevada
1701 Sageberry Drive, Las Vegas, NV 89144
Phone: (702) 304-9207
www.hindutempleoflasvegas.org

Hindu Temple Society of Southern California
1600 Las Virgenes Canyon Road, Calabasa, CA 91302
Phone: (818) 880-5552   Fax: (818) 880-5583
www.geocities.com/malibutemple

Hindu Temple of St. Louis
725 Weidman Road, Ballwin, MO 63011
Phone: (636) 230-330
www.hindutemplestlouis.org

International Society of Divine Love - Barsana Dham
400 Barsana Road, Austin, TX 78737-8705
Phone: (512) 288-7180   Fax: (512) 288-0447
www.isdl.org

Jain Center of Northern California
722 South Main Street, Milpitas, CA 95035
Phone: (408) 262-6242
www.jcnc.org

New England Hindu Temple, Inc. - Sri Lakshmi Temple
117 Waverly Street, Ashland, MA 01721
Phone: (508) 881-5775   Fax: (508) 881-6690
www.srilakshmitemple.org

New Mathura Vrindavan and Golden Palace
Rd 1 Box 318 A, Moundsville, WV 26041
Phone: (304) 843-1600
www.newvrindaban.com

Paschima Kasi Sri Viswanatha Temple
147 South Elms Road, Flint, MI 48532
Phone: (810) 732-1760
www.kashitemple.org

Sri Ganesha Temple of Nashville
521 Old Hickory Boulavard, Nashville, TN 37209
Phone: (615) 356-7207   Fax: (615) 353-9346
www.ganeshatemple.org

Sri Maha Vallabha Ganapathi Devasthanam, Flushing, NY
45-57 Bowne Street, Flushing, NY 11355
Phone: (718) 460-8484
www.indianet.com/ganesh

Sri Meenakshi Temple Society
17130 McLean Road (C.R.104), Pearland, TX 77584-4630
Phone: (281) 489-0358
www.meenakshi.org

Sri Ranganatha Temple
25 Old Route 202, Pomona, NY 10970
Phone: (845) 364-9790
www.ranganatha.org

Sri Shiva Vishnu Temple
5661 Dykes Road, Davie, FL 33331
Phone: (954) 680-8571
www.shivavishnu.org

Sri Siva Vishnu Temple
6905 Cipriano Road, Lanham, MD 20706
Tel: (301) 552-3335   Fax: (301) 552-1204
www.ssvtemple.html

Sri Sri Radha Krishna Temple
8628 South Main Street, Spanish Fork, UT 84660
Phone: (801) 798-3559
www.iskcon.net/utah

Sri Venkateshwara Swami Temple of Greater Chicago
1145 West Sullivan Road, Aurora, IL 60507
Phone: (630) 844-2252   Fax: (630) 844-2254
www.balaji.org.

Sri Venkateswara Temple Pittsburgh
1230 South McCully Drive, Penn Hills, PA 15235
Phone: (412) 373-3380   Fax: (412) 373-7650
www.svtemple.org

Wat Florida Dhammaram
2421 Old Vineland Road, Kissimmee, FL 34746
Phone: (407) 397-9552   Fax: (407) 397-2577

GLOSSARY

- In cases where several variants of a term are known, the Sanskrit version is listed first, followed by a commonly used version or versions.

- Words that appear in **bold** type within the definitions are separately defined in the Glossary.

abhisheka, abhishekam - "Bathing, ablution," derived from Sanskrit root meaning "to sprinkle," to which is added the prefix *abhi*, "all around." Ritual bathing of the image of a deity with water, yogurt, milk, honey, ghee, rosewater, and other substances. For a *Kumbhabhisheka*, a golden pot (*kalasa* or *kumbha*) is used for holding the water and other substances used in the ritual.

Agama - "Tradition; that which has come down." Traditional principles governing worship, construction, and festivals in temples. *Agama Shastras* are the scriptures outlining those traditional principles. Like the Vedas, they are revered as revealed scripture (*shruti*).

agnihotra - Fire sacrifice.

ahimsa - Nonviolence.

antarala - Intermediate vestibule in a temple.

aradhana - Worship, devotional service.

arati, arotika - "Light." The circling of a lamp (oil, ghee, or camphor) in front of a deity in a temple or in front of a holy person.

archana - Devotional worship, *puja*, conducted by a priest, to invoke guidance and blessings for a devotee. Also refers to chanting the names of the deity, a central part of every *puja*.

ardhamandapa - A porch or a small room leading up to the *mandapa*; entrance portico.

Ashtabhandhana - Installation of a deity in the sanctum sanctorum. *Ashta* (eight) refers to the eight different materials used to fix the idol to the base during installation.

asura - Demon, evil spirit.

avatara, avatar - "Descent." God born in human form.

Azhwar, Alwar - One of the Vaishnavite saints whose hymns in praise of Vishnu constitute the Tamil canon, considered to be on par with the Vedas.

balipitha, bali peetham - "Offering place." A pedestal of offerings in the shape of a lotus bloom, situated near the temple flagpole (*dhvajastambha*). As they enter the temple, devotees are to leave their negative thoughts at this place of offering.

bhajana, bhajan - Group singing of divine songs.

bhakta - Devotee of God; one who follows the path of *bhakti yoga*, the path of devotion.

bhakti yoga - The path of devotion.

Bodhisattva - In Mahayana Buddhism, a highly evolved soul who postpones his full enlightenment to help humankind.

Bhumi Puja - Ground-breaking ceremony.

Brahma - God of in the aspect of Creator. One of the Hindu Trinity, the other two being **Shiva** and **Vishnu**.

Brahman - The Supreme Reality that pervades all of life, as well as transcends it.

Brahmasthana, Brahmasthanam - The central energy field of the *vastu-purusha-mandala*, the energy grid of a building layout from where waves of energy spread out to various parts of the layout. In a temple, the main deity is located in this central energy space. Also referred to as *mulasthana*.

chaitya - A shrine, especially a Buddhist prayer-hall with a votive *stupa* at one end.

chamukh - Four-faced temple at Jain religious sites.

chhatri (cenotaph) - "Umbrella," referring to the shape of a dome. Dome or domes supported by pillars, usually standing on a raised platform.

darshana, darshan - Beholding a deity, holy person, or holy place

devasthana, devasthanam - A body administering the affairs of a temple. See also **Tirumala Tirupati Devasthanams.**

deva - Deity, angelic being.

devi - Goddess.

dharma - From *dhri*, "to sustain or hold." Righteousness, duty. The inherent quality of anything, as the heat in fire and the sweetness in sugar.

dharmachakra - In Buddhism, a pattern that represents "Wheel of the Law"; the most important symbol of Buddhism.

dhvajastambha - Flagpole, usually a pillar fixed outside the main shrine in line with the sanctum sanctorum.

Divali, Diwali, Deewali, Dipavali - "Row of lights." A festival in October-November that is celebrated by lighting lamps to celebrate the victory of good over evil.

dvarapalaka - Statue of a doorkeeper or guard at the entrance to a shrine in a temple.

Ganesha Chaturthi - Birthday of Lord Ganesha, a ten-day festival in August-September.

Garbhadhana - A ritual that invites the soul of the temple to enter within the building's confines. As part of this ritual, the priest places a golden box in the earth during the ground-breaking ceremony.

garbhagriha, garbhagriham - "Womb house." The small area within the *vimana* that constitutes the innermost chamber, or sanctum sanctorum, of a Hindu temple.

garbhagudi - Main shrine.

garbha koshta - Niche.

gopi - Milkmaid devotee of Lord Krishna.

gopura, gopuram - Entrance; temple tower crowning an entrance; the foremost of these towers crowning the main entrance is the *rajagopura*.

Guru Granth Sahib - The holy book of the Sikh faith, a compilation of spiritual/mystical hymns with a common philosophy but written by different spiritual masters, prominent saints, and spiritual poets from the Indian subcontinent.

Guru Purnima - A full-moon day dedicated to honoring the guru.

havana, havan - A fire pit for sacred offerings and oblations.

homa, homam - "Fire offering." Sacrificial ritual conducted with an altar of fire, as a part of daily worship, festivals, and special occasions.

Ishta Devata - The deity chosen for one's personal worship.

japa - Chanting the name of God, usually with the help of prayer beads.

Jeeyar, Jeer - A spiritual head of Vaishnavites.

jyotirlinga, jyotirlingam - "*Linga* of light." It is believed that twelve such *lingas* exist. Shiva is supposed to have first manifested himself as a *jyotirlinga*. It is believed that a spiritually evolved person sees these *lingas* as columns of fire piercing through the Earth. SEE **Shivalinga.**

kailasa - "Heavenly abode." Golden spire crowning the *vimana*.

kalasha, kalasham Water vessel, pot, jar. Ornamental top cover (finial) for the temple tower. In a temple structure, which is a representation of the human form, the *kalasha* represents a tuft of hair on the head (the temple tower).

Kaliyuga - "Dark age." The fourth period (comprising some 432,000 years) in a repetitive cycle of phases of time through which the world passes. It is a time when the forces of ignorance predominate.

kalyana mandapa - A special **mandapa** (hall), also called *vasanta mandapa* and *alankara mandapa*, dedicated to the celebration of the marriage of the deity with his consort. The metal icons of the main deity, accompanied by his consort, are placed here, decorated, and taken out in procession from this location.

karnakuta, karnakutam - The corner architectural member in the composition of a *vimana* or *gopura*. In modern English, known as a turret.

kalyana, kalyanam - Wedding.

kirtana, kirtan - "Praising." Devotional singing and dancing.

kumbha - Water vessel, pot, jar.

Kumbhabhisheka, Kumbhabhishekam - Purification rites carried out after construction or renovation of a temple or holy image by pouring water, milk, curd, ghee, etc. over the idol from a *kumbha*, vessel.

langar - In a *guruduwara*, a free community kitchen for pilgrims, travelers, and others. The institution of *langar* came into being almost with the inception of the faith.

lila, leela - Divine play, divine pastimes.

mahamandapa - Large hall in the temple.

mahanasi - Fanlike motif.

Maha Pranapratishtha Mahotsav - Consecration of a deity, establishing the life force (*prana*) in an idol, *linga*, or other sacred symbol. SEE ALSO **Prana-pratishtha.**

mahatma - "Great soul." A saint or highly evolved human being, spiritual leader.

Mahavira, Mahavir - The last of the great Jaina teachers, who lived in the sixth century B.C. SEE ALSO **Tirthankara.**

mandapa, mandapam - Pillared hall in a temple where devotees congregate for prayers.

mandira, mandir - Temple.

Maya Danava, Mayan - The earliest known master of **Vastu Shastra**, treatise on the sacred architecture of India.

moksha - Liberation from the constraints of the material world.

mukhamandapa - Entrance hall in a temple.

mulasthana, mulasthanam - SEE **Brahmasthana.**

mulavigraha, mulavigraham - Presiding deity.

murti - An image or icon of a deity

Mushika - Ganesha's *vahana*, divine mount, which is a mouse, traditionally associated with abundance.

nakshatra - One of 32 small squares in the *vastu-purusha-mandala* that represent the lunar mansions through which the moon passes in one month.

namakarana - Name-giving ceremony, performed 11 to 41 days after birth.

Nandi - Bull, the ceremonial mount of Shiva. An image of Nandi usually faces Shiva's sanctum.

naqqash - Decorations consisting of floral patterns interspersed with animal motifs. Some of these decorations may contain 300 different patterns on a wall, which, from a distance, look like hung Persian carpets.

Navagrahas - Nine planet deities, the heavenly bodies that Hindus believe have considerable influence on the life of mankind: the planets, Sun, Moon, Mars, Mercury, Jupitor, Venus, Saturn, and two other celestial features known as Raghu and Kethu.

nirguna Brahman - **Brahman** without form or attributes, the formless aspect of the Supreme Reality. SEE ALSO ***saguna Brahman***.

Omkara - The sacred syllable *Om*.

padmasana - "Lotus posture." Cross-legged meditation posture.

panchaloha - An alloy of five metals used for ***utsavamurtis***.

Paramatman - Supreme Self.

parampara - Lineage.

Parivara, Parivar - Deity image portrayed in a family group, for example, Rama with Sita, brother Lakshmana, and devoted servant Hanuman—known as Rama Parivar.

pradakshina - "Moving to the right." Circumambulation of a temple.

pradakshina patha - Passage used for circumambulating the temple.

pradhana devata - Primary deity.

prakara - Series of courtyards enclosing a temple, providing paths for circumambulating the temple. Passage around the sanctum. Also, a wall of the temple.

pramanasutra - The end-to-end measurement of the side wall of the main sanctum. Also called *manasutra*, and in Tamil, *kalpuravai*.

Pranapratishthana, Pranapratishthapana - Series of ritualistic processes by means of which the presiding deity and other deities are made to "come alive" (by invoking the life force, *prana*) in a sacred setting such as a temple. Same as **Pratishtha** and **Pratishthana**.

Pranava - The syllable *Om*, representing the Absolute.

prasada, prasad, prasadam - Sacred offering.

prastara - Flat ceiling that covers the hall in the temple and the sanctum.

pratima - Statue.

Pratishtha, Pratishthana - Installation of a deity; inauguration ritual for a temple. SEE ALSO ***Pranapratishthana***.

puja - Worship; ceremonial worship offered to a deity or consecrated object.

pujari - Priest; one who performs rituals, chants prayers, and worships the deity representative of the devotee.

purnima - "Full." The full moon. *Purnima* is generally used to designate a full moon day.

rajagopura, rajagopuram - Main tower (*gopura*), usually the highest of all temple towers, crowning the main entrance to the temple.

saguna Brahman - **Brahman** with attributes; God or the Lord. SEE ALSO **nirguna Brahman**.

sampradaya - Traditional doctrine transmitted verbally from generation to generation.

samprokshana - Initiation.

samsara - The cycle of birth, death, and rebirth that we are subjected to before illumination.

sannidhi - Sanctum sanctorum.

sannyasa - Renunciation; the vow of *sannyasa* involves leaving the worldly life of a householder to devote oneself fully to spiritual pursuits.

satsanga, satsang - "Good company. "A gathering for devotional purposes.

Shankushthapana - Installation of the first brick of a temple structure.

shastra - Scripture, sacred text.

shikhara - Pinnacle, tower; the upper and outer pyramidal and tapering roof of the *vimana*, the sanctuary. SEE ALSO ***vimana***.

Shilpa Shastra - *Shilpas* or *Shilpa Shastras* are treatises codifying the rules for art, sculpture, and architecture. The *Shilpas* were committed to memory and passed down through the generations by learning them by heart. SEE ALSO **Vastu Shastra**.

shilanyasam - Laying of the foundation stone.

shakti - "Power, energy." The active, manifest aspect of Shiva. Also one of the names of Shiva's consort, also known as Parvati, Uma, Durga, and others.

shilpi - Traditional stone cutter, carver, sculptor, or wood worker employed in construction of temples; he works under the guidance of a master architect, ***sthapati***.

Shiva - God in the aspect of Destroyer. One of Hindu Trinity, the other two being **Vishnu** and **Brahma**.

Shivalinga, Shivalingam - "The body of Shiva" or "sign of Shiva." An elliptical stone image representing the simplest and most ancient symbol of Shiva. It signifies the Divine beyond all forms.

srivimana - Sanctum tower. SEE ALSO ***vimana***.

sthambha - Carved pillar.

Sthapana - Consecration ceremony of a deity. SEE ***Pranapratishtha***.

sthapati - Master architect of *Agamic* temples; master of sacred iconography. SEE ALSO ***Agama***.

svayambhu - "Self-existent"; that which comes of its own accord; that which is untouched by a tool. *Svayambhu* **linga** is a **Shivalinga** that occurs in nature, not carved by human hands. A number of ***Shivalingas*** in temples are believed to be naturally created forms, held sacred for centuries.

tattva - "Thatness." The essence or principle of something.

Tirthankara, Tirthankar - "Crosser of the Ford". In Jainism, one who has attained perfect knowledge; there have been 24 such beings in the current Jain time-cycle, Mahavira being the most recent.

Tirumala Tirupati Devasthanams - In 1933, the Madras legislature passed an act that empowered the Tirumala Tirupati Devasthanams (TTD) Committee to control and administer a group of temples in the Tirumala-Tirupati area. TTD oversees the renowned Sri Venkateswara Temple as well as many cultural and educational projects, including a Sculpture Training Centre for temple artisans.

torana - Gateway to a Buddhist *stupa*.

Tripitaka - The Buddhist Canon, which is traditionally divided into different parts, as expressed in the word *Tripitaka*, which means "three baskets", i.e., the *sutras*, **shastras**, and the *vinaya*.

utsava - Religious celebration or holy day, observed either at home or in a temple.

utsavamurti, utsavavigraha - An idol, often fashioned out of a metal alloy or bronze, that is taken in procession and worshiped on festival days; traditionally made from a metal alloy called **panchaloha**.

vahana, vahanam - Divine mount, an animal or bird on which a deity rides; for example, **Shiva** rides on a bull, **Nandi**, symbol of strength.

vastu-purusha-mandala - Square-shaped plan, a mystical diagram, that forms the basis of a temple's architectural drawings.

Vastu Shastra - A Sanskrit treatise on the sacred architecture of India. The science of the *Vastu Shastra* is traceable to at least 3,000 B.C. The earliest known master of the *Vastu Shastra* was **Maya Danava**.

vedika - Pillared platform in the temple.

vel - "Spear." Symbol of Lord Karttikeya's (Shanmukha's) divine authority.

vighraha - Image of a deity.

vihara - Monastery.

vimana, vimanam - The towered roof of a sanctum sanctorum; also, the sanctum as a whole. Types of *vimanas* are the *gajaprishta*, *ashtanga*, and *sabha*. SEE ALSO **shikhara**.

vina - Stringed musical instrument.

Vishnu - God of in the aspect of Maintainer. One of the Hindu Trinity, the other two being **Brahma** and **Shiva**.

yagashala, yajnashala - The place in which sacrificial ceremonies, such as **havanas**, are observed.

yajna - "Worship, sacrifice." A form of ritualistic worship in which oblations are offered into the fire.

yajna kund, yagna kund - The fire pit for fire rituals, **yajnas**.

yaksha/yakshi - A male or female nature spirit; deity of wealth and guardian of treasure, especially associated with trees, pools, and vegetation.

yantra - Mystic diagram.

yoga nidra - The sleeping form of Lord **Vishnu**.

Sarve bhavantu sukhinaḥ	May all of mankind be happy;
Sarve santu nirāmayāḥ	May all of mankind be healthy;
Sarve bhadrāṇi paśyantu	May all of mankind experience prosperity;
Ma kaścid duhkḥa-bhāg-bhavet	May none [in the world] suffer.